D1605811

Entrepreneurship and Economic Growth

Entrepreneurship and Economic Growth

David B. Audretsch
Max C. Keilbach
Erik E. Lehmann

Max Planck Institute of Economics

UNIVERSITY PRESS

2006

OXFORD
UNIVERSITY PRESS

Oxford University Press, Inc., publishes works that further
Oxford University's objective of excellence
in research, scholarship, and education.

Oxford   New York
Auckland   Cape Town   Dar es Salaam   Hong Kong   Karachi
Kuala Lumpur   Madrid   Melbourne   Mexico City   Nairobi
New Delhi   Shanghai   Taipei   Toronto

With offices in
Argentina   Austria   Brazil   Chile   Czech Republic   France   Greece
Guatemala   Hungary   Italy   Japan   Poland   Portugal   Singapore
South Korea   Switzerland   Thailand   Turkey   Ukraine   Vietnam

Copyright © 2006 by Oxford University Press, Inc.

Published by Oxford University Press, Inc.
198 Madison Avenue, New York, New York 10016

www.oup.com

Oxford is a registered trademark of Oxford University Press

Library of Congress Cataloging-in-Publication Data
Audretsch, David B.
Entrepreneurship and economic growth / David B. Audretsch,
Max C. Keilbach, Erik E. Lehmann.
p. cm.
Includes bibliographical references and index.
ISBN-13 978-0-19-518351-1
ISBN 0-19-518351-7
1. Entrepreneurship.   2. Creative ability in business.   3. Small business—
Technological innovations.   4. Technological innovations—Economic
aspects.   5. Diffusion of innovations—Economic aspects.
6. Economic development.   I. Keilbach, Max C., 1962–
II. Lehmann, Erik.   III. Title.

HB615.A935 2006
338'.04—dc22   2005050893

9 8 7 6 5 4 3 2 1

Printed in the United States of America
on acid-free paper

Acknowledgments

The origins of this book began when Erik Lehmann served as an Ameritech Research Scholar at the Institute for Development Strategies at Indiana University in 2000 and David Audretsch served as a Research Professor at the Zentrum für Europäische Wirtschaftsforschung (ZEW) in Mannheim in 2002, where he began to work closely with Max Keilbach. We are grateful to the University of Konstanz and the Institute for Development Strategies for supporting Erik Lehmann's research leave at Indiana University, and the ZEW Mannheim and the German Science Foundation (DFG) for supporting the joint research project of Max Keilbach and David Audretsch. We are also grateful for a generous grant to David Audretsch from the Ewing Marion Kauffman Foundation.

The book crystallized when all three authors came together at the Entrepreneurship, Growth and Public Policy Research Unit of the Max Planck Institute of Economics in Jena, Germany. We are grateful to the Max Planck Society for supporting our research and making a significant commitment to economic research on entrepreneurship. We are also grateful to a research team at the Max Planck Institute of Economics including Taylor Aldridge, Iris Beckmann, Adam Lederer, Kerstin Schück, and Madeleine Schmidt for their capable and commendable research assistance. Our team of research assistants, Katrin Halm, Anja Klaukien, Mathias Langner, Katerina Malandina, and Stephan Schütze gave great support putting together the data and editing the references.

We are especially grateful to Betty Fiscus of Indiana University for her assistance.

Portions of chapters 3–5 have been published in Audretsch and Keilbach's (2004a, b, c). Portions of chapters 6–9 are based on material published in Audretsch and Lehmann (2004a, b; 2005b, c). We thank the publishers for permission to publish material from "Entrepreneurship Capital and Economic Performance" by David B. Audretsch and Max C. Keilbach, in *Regional Studies* (2004), 28, 949–959 (http://www.tandf.co.uk); "Entrepreneurship and Regional Growth: An Evolutionary Interpretation," by David B. Audretsch and Max C. Keilbach, in *Journal of*

Evolutionary Economics (2004), 14, 605–616, with kind permission of Springer Science and Business Media; "Does Entrepreneurship Capital Matter?" by David B. Audretsch and Max C. Keilbach, in *Entrepreneurship Theory and Practice* (2004), Fall, 419–429; "Debt or Equity: The Role of Venture Capital in Financing High-Tech Firms in Germany" by David B. Audretsch and Erik E. Lehmann, in *Schmalenbach Business Review* (2004), 56, 340–357; "Ownership, Knowledge, and Firm Survival" by David B. Audretsch and Erik E. Lehmann, in *Review of Accounting and Finance* (2004), 4(4), 13–33; "Mansfield's Missing Link: The Impact of Knowledge Spillovers on Firm Growth," by David B. Audretsch and Erik E. Lehmann, in *Journal of Technology Transfer* (2005), 30(1/2), 207–210, with kind permission of Springer Science and Business Media; and "Do University Policies Make a Difference?" by David B. Audretsch and Erik E. Lehmann, in *Research Policy* (2005), 34, 343–347.

Terry Vaughn at Oxford University Press shared some of his rich experiences on the craft of writing and producing a book with us, especially in the early stages of the project. We certainly appreciate his generosity and support. Finally, the three authors collectively have a large number of wives, partners, and children. Their patience and understanding of early morning or late night calls across different time zones, lengthy trips, and occasional bouts of distracted attention are greatly appreciated. It is for them that this book is written.

Contents

Entrepreneurship and Economic Growth

Introduction

Following the 1990s, the decade of Europe's worst economic performance since World War II, including record unemployment, it may not have been surprising when a bold new strategy to spur economic growth was unveiled. However, the focus of this new European growth policy would have seemed unimaginable only a few years earlier. With the 2000 Lisbon Proclamation, Romano Prodi, president of the European Commission, committed the European Union (EU) to becoming the world's entrepreneurship leader by 2020 in order to ensure prosperity and a high standard of living throughout the EU.

Romano Prodi and the European Union are not alone in turning to entrepreneurship to provide the engine of economic growth. The entrepreneurial policy mandate mirrored similar efforts throughout the developed world. As Edward Lazear emphasizes, "The entrepreneur is the single most important player in a modern economy" (Lazear, 2002, p. 1). Public policy spanning a broad spectrum of national, regional, and local contexts is turning to entrepreneurship to replace old jobs that have been lost to outsourcing and globalization, while at the same time harnessing the potential that remained largely dormant from significant long-term investments in knowledge, such as universities, education, and research institutions.

Only a few years earlier the policy debate focusing on growth and employment had looked to the macroeconomic instruments of fiscal and monetary policy on the one hand and the size and scale economies yielded by the large corporation on the other. After all, scholars such as Joseph Schumpeter (1942), John Kenneth Galbraith (1962), and Alfred Chandler (1977) had convinced a generation of policy-makers that efficiency and growth lay in the domain of large corporations and that small business would simply fade away under the weight of its own inefficiency.

Linking entrepreneurship to economic growth is certainly not new. In his 1911 classic treatise, *Theorie der wirtschaftlichen Entwicklungen* (Theory of Economic Development), Schumpeter proposed that entrepreneurs starting new businesses provided the engine for economic growth. Even in his 1942 classic, *Capitalism, Socialism, and Democracy*, Schumpeter (p. 13) still argued that entrenched large corporations tend to resist change, forcing entrepreneurs to start new firms in order to pursue innovative activity:

> The function of entrepreneurs is to reform or revolutionize the pattern of production by exploiting an invention, or more generally, an untried technological possibility for producing a new commodity or producing an old one in a new way.... To undertake such new things is difficult and constitutes a distinct economic function, first because they lie outside of the routine tasks which everybody understands, and secondly, because the environment resists in many ways.

While the intellectual contribution of Schumpeter remains enormous and virtually unrivaled, his impact on public policy debate seemed limited at best. Certainly in the decades following his work, very little policy attention focused on new and small firms as engines of economic growth.

The purpose of this book is to explain why this changed and how entrepreneurship became more important, particularly in the arena of public policy to foster growth and create jobs. In particular, this book provides an explicit link between entrepreneurship and economic growth by asking, "Why does entrepreneurship matter?" along with "How does entrepreneurship matter?"

Chapter 2 explains how the role of entrepreneurship evolved over time. The role of small and new firms, at least as analyzed by the prevailing literature during the second half of the previous century, generally focused on productive efficiency. Just as the Solow model directed the public policy focus on capital as the driving factor of economic growth, the structure most conducive to the efficient organization of that capital, at both the industry and firm levels, did not seem particularly receptive to small business. When it came to productive efficiency, small firms were clearly at a competitive disadvantage.

Of course, as William Baumol (2002, p. 1) recently pointed out, innovative activity may be more important than productive efficiency, particularly in terms of generating economic growth: "Under capitalism, innovative activity—which in other types of economy is fortuitous and optional—becomes mandatory, a life-and-death matter for the firm." Certainly the intellectual revolution triggered by the introduction of the endogenous growth models (Romer, 1984; Lucas, 1993) placed knowledge and innovation at the center of economic growth. A more recent literature has focused on the innovative capabilities of small and new enterprises. Though some studies found that small and new firms were surprisingly innovative, they provided less compelling insights about why and how entrepreneurial firms were able to contribute to innovative activity. After all, as the Griliches (1979) model of the knowledge production function made clear, knowledge inputs are a prerequisite for innovative output, and the limited size and resources of small and new firms seemingly restrict their capacity to generate new knowledge, at least in absolute terms.

Thus, in order to understand the link between entrepreneurship and economic growth, the *Knowledge Spillover Theory of Entrepreneurship* is introduced in chapter 3. Like any theory of entrepreneurship, the Knowledge Spillover Theory of Entrepreneurship is based on the cognitive processes of individuals involving recognition and exploitation of (entrepreneurial) opportunities. However, unlike the traditional theories of entrepreneurship, in this theory these opportunities are not taken to be exogenous, or given. Rather, they are endogenously created as the result of targeted and systematic efforts to produce knowledge and new ideas by private firms, universities, and research institutes.

Thus, in this view entrepreneurial opportunities are created not by the entrepreneurial firms themselves but rather as a by-product of efforts by incumbent firms and other organizations to generate new knowledge without, however, the ability to fully and exhaustively appropriate the returns from their own knowledge investments. Chapter 3 develops the *Endogenous Entrepreneurship Hypothesis*, which posits that entrepreneurial opportunities will be systematically greater in contexts that are rich in knowledge investments but more restricted in contexts with impoverished knowledge.

Models of endogenous growth (Romer, 1984, 1990; Lucas, 1988) recognized not only that knowledge should be endogenously included in the production function as an explicit factor generating economic growth but also that, as result of the propensity for knowledge to spill over for use by third-party firms, it is particularly potent in generating growth. Chapter 3 contests the assumption that knowledge automatically spills over for use and commercialization by third-party firms. Rather, evoking the properties of knowledge and new ideas identified by Arrow (1962), we suggest the existence of a knowledge filter that impedes the commercialization and spillover of knowledge. The mere fact that firms and universities invest in the creation of new knowledge by itself does not guarantee the commercialization of that knowledge. Thus, entrepreneurship makes an important contribution to economic growth by providing a conduit for the spillover of knowledge that might otherwise have remained uncommercialized.

Of course, the existence of entrepreneurial opportunities alone does not result in the recognition and implementation through the creation of new firms and other organizations. Rather, barriers to entrepreneurship may impede or even preempt the entrepreneurial response to perceived opportunities. This suggests that the capacity to generate entrepreneurial activity, or the endowment of entrepreneurship capital, is specific to each context. The *Growth Hypothesis* posits that by serving as a mechanism for knowledge spillovers, entrepreneurship should have a positive impact on economic performance in general and on growth in particular.

Endogenous entrepreneurship serving as a conduit of knowledge spillovers and ensuring positive impact on economic growth emanates from commercializing knowledge and new ideas that might otherwise not have been pursued. An important insight from the new economic geography is that knowledge spillovers tend to be geographically bounded. Thus, the *Localization Hypothesis* posits that entrepreneurial firms derived from knowledge spillovers also tend to cluster within close geographic proximity to knowledge sources. That geographic proximity to a knowledge source bestows competitive advantage to entrepreneurial firms is posited by the *Performance Hypothesis*.

The existence of external knowledge may not guarantee that entrepreneurial firms can access and absorb knowledge spillovers. Just as Cohen and Levinthal (1989) suggested that large corporations invest in research and development (R&D) to generate the requisite absorptive capacity for accessing external knowledge, new and small knowledge-based firms may also need to access and absorb external knowledge. However, the strategies deployed by their larger and more established counterparts, such as investing in large R&D laboratories, may be preempted by the inherently small size of new startups. Thus, the *Entrepreneurial Access Hypothesis* suggests that entrepreneurial firms will develop and deploy strategies to facilitate the access and absorption of external knowledge. Similarly, the *Entrepreneurial Finance Hypothesis* posits that entrepreneurial firms are more likely be financed by nontraditional sources of finance, such as venture capital.

These main hypotheses, introduced in chapter 3, suggest why and how entrepreneurship will affect economic growth. In the subsequent seven chapters, they are subjected to systematic econometric scrutiny to shed light on their plausibility and possible validity.

All of these chapters center on measurement, but they also evoke a number of conceptual issues common across all chapters. One of these involving both conceptual and measurement issues is the idea of entrepreneurship. Although entrepreneurship is widely acknowledged as a vital force in the economies of developed countries, there is little consensus about what actually constitutes entrepreneurial activity. Scholars have proposed a broad array of definitions, which, when operationalized, have generated a number of different measures (Hébert and Link, 1989).

Hébert and Link (1989) have identified three distinct intellectual traditions in the development of the entrepreneurship literature: the German tradition, based on von Thuenen and Schumpeter; the Chicago tradition, based on Knight and Schultz; and the Austrian tradition, based on von Mises, Kirzner, and Shackle. The Schumpeterian tradition has had the greatest impact on the contemporary entrepreneurship literature. The distinguishing feature of the Schumpeterian view is that entrepreneurship is a disequilibrating phenomenon rather than an equilibrating one.

Despite the Schumpeterian emphasis on the process of starting a new enterprise as the defining feature of entrepreneurial activity, there is no generally accepted definition of entrepreneurship for developed countries (Organization for Economic Cooperation and Development [OECD], 1998). The lack of a single definition of entrepreneurship reflects the fact that it is a multidimensional concept. The actual definition used to study or classify entrepreneurial activities reflects a particular perspective or emphasis. Usually, definitions of entrepreneurship vary most between the economic and management perspectives.

From the economic perspective, Hébert and Link (1989) distinguish between the supply of financial capital, innovation, allocation of resources among alternative uses, and decision making. Thus, the entrepreneurial function encompasses the entire spectrum of these functions: "The entrepreneur is someone who specializes in taking responsibility for and making judgmental decisions that affect the location, form, and the use of goods, resources or institutions" (Hébert and Link, 1989, p. 213).

By contrast, from the management perspective, Sahlman and Stevenson (1991, p. 1) differentiate between entrepreneurs and managers in that "entrepreneurship is a way of managing that involves pursuing opportunity without regard to the resources currently controlled. Entrepreneurs identify opportunities, assemble required resources, implement a practical action plan, and harvest the reward in a timely, flexible way."

The most prevalent and compelling views of entrepreneurship focus on the perception of new economic opportunities and the subsequent introduction of new ideas in the market. As Audretsch (1995) argues, entrepreneurship is about change, just as entrepreneurs are agents of change; entrepreneurship is thus about the process of change. This corresponds to the definition of entrepreneurship proposed by the OECD: "Entrepreneurs are agents of change and growth in a market economy and they can act to accelerate the generation, dissemination and application of innovative ideas.... Entrepreneurs not only seek out and identify potentially profitable economic opportunities but are also willing to take risks to see if their hunches are right" (OECD, 1998, p. 11).

Although the simplicity of defining entrepreneurship as activities fostering innovative change is attractive, such simplicity also masks considerable ambiguity. The notion of entrepreneurship is a complex one for at least two reasons. First, entrepreneurship crosses multiple organizational forms. Does entrepreneurship refer to the change-inducing activities of individuals; groups of individuals such as networks, projects, lines of business, firms, and even entire industries; or even geographic units of observation, such as agglomerations, clusters, and regions? Part of the complexity involved with entrepreneurship is that it involves all of these types of organizational forms. No single organizational form can claim a monopoly on entrepreneurship.

The second reason for entrepreneurial complexity is that the concept of change is relative to some benchmark. What may be perceived as change to an individual or enterprise may not involve any new practice for the industry. Or it may represent change for the domestic industry but not for the global industry. Thus, the concept of entrepreneurship is embedded in the local context. At the same time, the value of entrepreneurship is likely to be shaped by the relevant benchmark. Entrepreneurial activity that is new to the individual but not the firm or industry may be of limited value. Entrepreneurial activity new to the region or country may be significant but ultimately limited. By contrast, entrepreneurial activity new across all organizational forms, all the way to the global scale, carries the greatest potential value.

Thus, one of the most striking features of entrepreneurship is that it crosses a number of key units of analysis. At one level, entrepreneurship involves the decisions and actions of individuals acting alone or within the context of a group. At another level, entrepreneurship involves analyses of firms and industries as well as cities, regions, and countries.

Operationalizing entrepreneurship for empirical measurement is difficult (Storey, 1991). The degree of difficulty involved increases exponentially for cross-country comparisons. Studies focusing on a single country, either in a cross-sectional or time series context, have deployed a variety of proxy measures spanning self-employment rates, business ownership rates, and new-firm startups (births), as well as other measures of industry demography, such as turbulence (turnover) or the extent of simultaneous births and exits and net entry. An ideal measure of entrepreneurship would incorporate all aspects of these. However, systematic measurement conducive to cross-country comparisons is limited.

The different contexts and organizational forms involving entrepreneurship account for the paucity of measures used to reflect entrepreneurial activity.

Measures of self-employment reflect change that is occurring for individuals starting a new business. Because very little of this change is projected onto the larger industry, nation, or global economy, self-employment as a measure of entrepreneurial activity has been criticized. What is new and different for the individual may not be so different for the industry or global market. Even for a developed country such as the United States, only a very small fraction of new startups are, in fact, innovative. Still, measures of self-employment are widely used to reflect the degree of entrepreneurial activity, largely because they are measured in most countries, and measured in comprehensive facilitating comparisons across countries and over time (Parker, 2004; Parker, Belghitar, and Barmby, 2005).

Audretsch et al. (2002) and Carree et al. (2001) use a measure of business ownership rates to reflect degree of entrepreneurial activity. This measure is defined as the number of business owners (in all sectors excluding agriculture) divided by the total labor force. A number of important qualifications for this measure should be emphasized. First, it lumps together all types of a very heterogeneous activity across a broad spectrum of sectors and contexts. This measure treats all businesses as the same, both high-tech and low-tech. Second, it is not weighted for magnitude or impact. Again, all businesses are measured identically, even though some clearly have a greater impact. Third, this variable measures the stock of businesses and not the startup of new ones. Still, this measure has two significant advantages. First, while not a direct measure of entrepreneurship, it is a useful proxy for entrepreneurial activity (Storey, 1991). And it is measured and can be compared across countries and over time.

Other measures of entrepreneurship focus more on change that corresponds to innovative activity for an industry. Such measures include indicators of R&D activity, the numbers of patented inventions, and new product innovations introduced into the market (Acs and Audretsch, 1988, 1990). These measures have the advantage of including only firms that actually generate change at the industry level, that is, beyond the firm itself. However, such measures must always be qualified by their failure to incorporate significant types of innovative activity and change (Griliches, 1990).

Similarly, other measures of entrepreneurial activity focus solely on the criterion of growth. Firms exhibiting exceptionally high growth over a prolonged duration are classified as *gazelles*. For example, Birch (1999) measures the number of gazelles to reflect entrepreneurship. Such measures of entrepreneurship must also be qualified for their narrow focus not only on a single unit of observation— enterprises—but also on a single measure of change: growth.

Lundström and Stevenson (2001, 2005) followed the precedent of the Global Entrepreneurship Monitor (GEM) study (Reynolds et al., 2000) by defining and measuring entrepreneurship as "mainly people in the pre-startup, startup and early phases of business" (2001, p. 19). This definition has a tilt toward nascent entrepreneurs and startups because "these are the targets for entrepreneurship policy measures." An obvious limitation of this approach is that it restricts entrepreneurial activity to the process of starting a new firm, which no doubt reflects individual change and innovation but not the contribution of incumbent enterprises of all sizes, or what is sometimes referred to as intrapreneurship. Lundström and

Stevenson (2001, p. 19) justify their emphasis on prestartup and startup as well as the incipient and early stages of business ownership because "these are the targets for entrepreneurship policy measures and we propose that entrepreneurship policy measures are taken to stimulate individuals to behave more entrepreneurially. It is our position that this can be done by influencing motivation, opportunity and skill factors. Therefore, our aim is to see what types of policy actions are taken towards individuals in the pre- and early stages of idea and business development."

Although entrepreneurship is a heterogeneous activity encompassing a broad spectrum of disparate organizations and types of activities, many of the conventional definitions and measures are, in fact, remarkable for reflecting entrepreneurship as a homogeneous activity. Because of the focus of entrepreneurship as a conduit for knowledge spillovers, this study restricts the focus, both in concept and in measurement, to new-firm startups.

In the empirical analyses, the book focuses on a single national context: Germany. Restricting the study to a single country provides an implicit control for a number of crucial factors that can introduce bias into cross-country studies, such as institutions, culture, history, laws, and regulations. We selected Germany as the particular national context for several reasons. First and foremost, it provides a national context where entrepreneurship has not seemingly played an important role, at least in recent decades. Many scholars and policy-makers remain skeptical about whether entrepreneurship is compatible with German institutions, historical traditions, and culture and social capital. We wish to neither support nor contest this proposition. But against such a skeptical background, if the main hypotheses derived from the Knowledge Spillover Theory of Entrepreneurship can be confirmed in the context of Germany, they would certainly have more credibility. While Frank Sinatra's lyric, "If you can make it there, you'll make it anywhere," might not apply exactly, Germany certainly presents a sterner test than other nations more readily associated with and already well under way toward creating an entrepreneurial economy.

Furthermore, we chose Germany as the *Gegenstand* or subject for this analysis because the country confronts substantial job displacements and outsourcing due to globalization, while at the same time having one of the world's most prominent and enviable levels of investment in knowledge and human capital.

Chapters 4 and 5 examine if and why entrepreneurship affects economic growth. In testing the Endogenous Entrepreneurship and Growth Hypotheses, spatially aggregated units of observation are required. It is the premise underlying not just the New Economic Geography but also the Localization Hypothesis that knowledge spillovers are spatially localized. This suggests using a spatially aggregated but geographically bounded unit of observation. We met this requirement by choosing a dataset on German counties (or *Kreise*) for our empirical analysis. The important variables in these chapters include measures of regional growth and startup rates. Such spatial variation within a single national context controls for country-specific factors such as laws and other national institutions but allows for variation across local contexts. Thus, both the national and local contexts matter, but in this case the national context is held constant while variations across the local context are probed for their influence on the relevant dependent variable.

Chapters 6 through 9 test the main hypotheses focusing on how entrepreneurship affects economic growth and use the firm as the unit of observation. These chapters all employ the same database, which is derived from German firms making an Initial Public Offering (IPO). These firms are generally knowledge-based startups, many of which involve high technology. Such a database is, of course, highly biased. While the IPO database is anything but representative of German firms, let alone other firms around the world, it does include firms in which new knowledge and ideas play an important role. Thus, this firm-level database provides a useful window through which to observe and analyze the behavior of entrepreneurs responding to opportunities generated by knowledge and ideas.

The two main databases used in this book provide a useful contrast. Whereas one is at the spatially aggregated level, the other facilitates analysis at the firm level. Both perspectives are essential for making inferences about the relationship between entrepreneurship and economic growth. These two databases are the basis for subjecting each hypothesis to systematic econometric scrutiny. The empirical results emerging from chapters 4 through 9 are generally consistent with the posited hypotheses, albeit considerably more nuanced in some cases.

Based on this general empirical validation, we use the framework provided by the Knowledge Spillover Theory of Entrepreneurship to interpret the emergence of entrepreneurship policy in chapter 10. We discuss what constitutes entrepreneurship policy, the mandate for entrepreneurship policy, the rationale for entrepreneurship policy, as well as why it is diffusing across a broad spectrum of national, regional, and local contexts. It is not only beyond the scope of this book but also beyond the purpose to identify which specific policy instruments are more effective at promoting entrepreneurship. Rather, the goal of chapter 10 is to explain why entrepreneurship policy has emerged as a bona fide approach to promoting economic growth.

Finally, we present in the last chapter a summary and conclusions from the entire book. Both the theoretical framework and the ensuing empirical evidence dispel any conventional wisdom suggesting that entrepreneurship is peripheral to economic growth. Rather, the results of this study provide compelling systematic evidence pointing to the central role that entrepreneurship plays in generating economic growth. The broad public policy goal to create an entrepreneurial economy can be explained by the vital contribution that entrepreneurship makes as a conduit of knowledge spillovers. Entrepreneurship has emerged as the missing link in the process of economic growth.

The book concludes by suggesting that the Schumpeterian view of entrepreneurship as an agent triggering creative destruction may be less appropriate for the young century. Schumpeterian creative destruction has the newly created entrepreneurial firms displacing the old incumbent firms. Our view is that such displacement, at least in terms of employment, is triggered by opportunities created by globalization and foreign outsourcing. By contrast, endogenous entrepreneurship is a response to opportunities created by knowledge investments from incumbent organizations. Thus, knowledge-spillover entrepreneurship is not so much an agent of creative destruction but of *creative construction*—of new opportunities that might otherwise not have been pursued, at least at the particular

Standort. Entrepreneurship may be less of a threat to the status quo organizations and more of a solution to accruing a desperately needed social return on public investments in education, human capital, and research.

Hence, entrepreneurship may be less of an adversarial force than is implied in the Schumpeterian concept of creative destruction. Instead, it may embody a greater element of a social or public good. Perhaps the role of entrepreneurship as creative construction may explain the widespread public policy mandate to create an entrepreneurial economy. How and why such an entrepreneurial economy has emerged, at least in some contexts, and why creating one has become a desirable goal of public policy, is the topic of the following chapters.

The Emergence of the Entrepreneurial Economy

2.1 Small Has Become Beautiful Again

The role of entrepreneurship in the economy has changed drastically over the last half century. During the post–World War II era, the importance of entrepreneurship and small business seemed to fade. While some noted that small business needed to be preserved and protected for social and political reasons, few made the case on the grounds of economic efficiency. This thinking has changed in recent years. Entrepreneurship has come to be perceived as the engine of economic and social development throughout the world. For example, Romano Prodi, who at the time served as president of the European Commission, proclaimed that the promotion of entrepreneurship was a central cornerstone of European economic growth policy: "Our lacunae in the field of entrepreneurship need to be taken seriously because there is mounting evidence that the key to economic growth and productivity improvements lies in the entrepreneurial capacity of an economy" (2002, p. 1).

From the other side of the Atlantic, Mowery (2005, p. 1) observes,

> During the 1990s, the era of the "New Economy," numerous observers (including some who less than 10 years earlier had written off the U.S. economy as doomed to economic decline in the face of competition from such economic powerhouses as Japan) hailed the resurgent economy in the United States as an illustration of the power of high-technology entrepreneurship. The new firms that a decade earlier had been criticized by authorities such as the MIT Commission on Industrial Productivity (Dertouzes et al., 1989) for their failure to sustain competition against large non-U.S. firms, were now seen as important sources of economic dynamism and employment growth. Indeed, the transformation in U.S. economic performance between the 1980s and 1990s is only slightly less remarkable than the failure of most experts in academia, government, and industry, to predict it.

The purpose of this chapter is to explain how and why the economic role of entrepreneurship has changed so dramatically in the past half century. The changing role of entrepreneurship reflects three views of the economy, which correspond to three historical periods: the first can be referred to as the Capital (or Solow) Economy, which corresponds very roughly to the early postwar era; the second can be referred to as the Knowledge (Romer) Economy, which roughly corresponds to the later postwar era (the 1980s); and the third can be referred to as the Entrepreneurial Economy, which may have its roots in the mid-1970s, but really took off in the 1990s.

The next section explains how the economic role of new startups and small business in the capital or Solow economy was generally viewed as imposing inefficiency on the economy. The third section explains how this marginal or negative role of new and small firms in the knowledge economy was actually reinforced. In section 4 we explain why only with the emergence of the entrepreneurial economy has the contribution of entrepreneurship to economic growth become widely recognized. Finally, in the last section, we provide a summary and conclusion. In particular, we propose a view in which the entrepreneurial economy can be defined as an economy where entrepreneurship plays a key role in generating economic growth.

2.2 The Capital (Solow) Economy

Economic growth has been a major preoccupation of economists, dating back at least to Adam Smith. William Stanley Jevons, for example, posited a growth theory based on the activity of sunspots. Robert Solow took a less exotic approach to explaining economic growth. Writing in the postwar era, Solow was awarded the Nobel Prize for his model of economic growth based on the neoclassical production function. In the Solow model two key factors of production—physical capital and (unskilled) labor—were econometrically linked to explain economic growth.

Solow, of course, acknowledged that technical change contributed to economic growth, but in terms of his formal model, it was considered an unexplained residual, which falls like manna from heaven. As Nelson (1981, p. 1030) points out, "Robert Solow's 1956 theoretical article was largely addressed to the pessimism about full employment growth built into the Harrod-Domar model.... In that model he admitted the possibility of technological advance."

Solow's pathbreaking research inspired a subsequent generation of economists to rely on the model of the production function as a basis for explaining the determinants of economic growth. This approach generally consisted of relating measures representing these two fundamental factors of production, physical capital and unskilled labor, in trying to explain variations in growth rates typically over time in a single country or across countries in a cross-sectional context. The unexplained residual, which typically accounted for a large share of the (unexplained) variance in growth rates, was attributed to technological change. As Nelson concluded in his important review article in the *Journal of Economic Literature*, "Since the mid-1950s, considerable research has proceeded closely guided by the neoclassical formulation. Some of this work has been theoretical. Various forms of the production function have been invented. Models have been developed which assume that technological advance must be embodied in new capital.... Much of the work has been empirical and guided by the growth accounting framework implicit in the neoclassical model" (p. 1032). In this growth accounting framework implicit in the neoclassical model, two factors, physical capital and labor, were econometrically linked to growth rates.

Growth policy, or economic policy for growth, if not shaped by the Solow theoretical growth model, certainly corresponded to the view that inducing investments in physical capital in particular was the key to generating economic growth and advances in worker productivity. Both the economics literature and the corresponding public policy discourse were decidedly focused on which instruments, such as monetary policy versus fiscal policy or interest rates versus capital depreciation allowances, were best suited to induce investment in physical capital and ultimately to promote growth. While these debates may never have been satisfactorily resolved, the tenacity of this view reflects the deep-seated belief about the primacy of capital investment as the fundamental source of economic growth.

Though economic growth policy seemingly fell squarely within the domain of macroeconomics, the primacy of capital as a factor of production had implications at the microeconomic level for the organization of the enterprise, the industry, and the market. Both theoretical arguments and empirical verification suggest that the organization of economic activity to efficiently use the factor of physical capital might not, in fact, be consistent with the assumptions needed for perfect competition and, therefore, economic welfare. In particular, capital seemed to be deployed most efficiently in large organizations capable of exhausting significant economies of scale, resulting in a concentrated industry or market, consisting of just a few main producers. The emergence and ascendancy of the applied field of industrial organization in economics reflected the importance of this concern.

During the postwar period a generation of scholars galvanized the field of industrial organization by developing a research agenda dedicated to identifying the issues involving this perceived trade-off between economic efficiency on the one hand and political and economic decentralization on the other (Scherer, 1970). Scholarship in the field of industrial organization generated a massive literature focusing on essentially three issues: (1) What are the gains to size and large-scale production? (2) What are the economic welfare implications of having an oligopolistic or concentrated market structure; that is, is economic performance promoted or reduced in an industry with just a handful of large-scale firms? (3) Given the overwhelming evidence that large-scale production resulting in economic concentration is associated with increased efficiency, what are the public policy implications?

A generation of scholars had arduously and systematically documented empirical evidence that supported the conclusion of Joseph A. Schumpeter (1942, p. 106): "What we have got to accept is that the large-scale establishment or unit of control has come to be the most powerful engine of progress and in particular of the long-run expansion of output." John Kenneth Galbraith (1956, p. 86) provided a postwar interpretation: "There is no more pleasant fiction than that technological change is the product of the matchless ingenuity of the small man forced by competition to employ his wits to better his neighbor."

The pervasive fear of the Soviet Union that emerged during the Cold War went beyond concerns about military competition and the space race. Many in the West worried that Sputnik's launch demonstrated the superior organization of Soviet industry. Facilitated by centralized planning, the Soviet economy apparently generated rates of growth greater than those of the West, threatening, ultimately, to "bury," as Soviet Premier Nikita Khrushchev famously put it, the free market competition. After all, the nations of Eastern Europe, and the Soviet Union in particular, had a "luxury" inherent in their systems of centralized planning—a concentration of economic assets on a scale beyond anything imaginable in the West, where the commitment to democracy seemingly imposed a concomitant commitment to economic decentralization.

Western economists and policy-makers of the day were nearly unanimous in their acclaim for large-scale enterprises. It is no doubt an irony of history that this consensus mirrored a remarkably similar gigantism embedded in Soviet doctrine, fueled by the writings of Marx and ultimately implemented by Stalin's iron fist. This was the era of mass production when economies of scale seemed to be the decisive factor in determining efficiency. This was the world so colorfully described by John Kenneth Galbraith (1956) in his theory of countervailing power, in which big business was held in check by big labor and by big government. This was the era of the man in the gray flannel suit (Riesman, Denney, and Glazer, 1950) and the organization man (Whyte, 1960), when virtually every major social and economic institution acted to reinforce the stability and predictability needed for mass production (Chandler, 1977; Piore and Sabel, 1984).

With a decided focus on the role of large corporations, oligopoly, and economic concentration, the literature on industrial organization yielded a number of key insights concerning the efficiency and impact on economic performance associated with new and small firms:

1. *Small firms were generally less efficient than their larger counterparts.* Studies from the United States in the 1960s and 1970s revealed that small firms produced at lower levels of efficiency, leading Weiss (1976, p. 259) to conclude that "on the average, about half of total shipments in the industries covered are from suboptimal plants. The majority of plants in most industries are suboptimal in scale, and a very large percentage of output is from suboptional plants." Pratten (1971) found similar evidence for the United Kingdom, where suboptimal scale establishments accounted for 47.9 percent of industry shipments.

2. *Small firms provided lower levels of employee compensation.* Empirical evidence from both North America and Europe found a systematic and positive relationship between employee compensation and firm size (Brown and Medoff, 1989; Brown, Hamilton, and Medoff, 1990).

3. *Small firms were only marginally involved in innovative activity.* Based on R&D measures, small- and medium-size firms (SMEs) accounted for only a small amount of innovative activity (Scherer, 1970).

4. *The relative importance of small firms was declining over time in both North America and Europe.* A clear trend was identified toward an

increased share of economic activity accounted for by the largest corporations whereas small firms were losing importance in the economy
(Scherer, 1970).

Thus, in the postwar era, small firms and entrepreneurship were viewed as
a luxury, perhaps needed by the West to ensure a decentralization of decision
making, but in any case obtained only at a cost to efficiency. Certainly, the systematic empirical evidence gathered from the United States documented a sharp
trend toward a decreased role of small firms during the postwar period.

Even advocates of small business agreed that small firms were less efficient
than big companies. Just as passage of the Robinson-Patman Act protected small
business against predatory pricing by larger competitors, who presumably enjoyed
lower costs resulting from scale economies, an entire federal agency, the United
States Small Business Administration, was created to protect and preserve the
interests of small business. Thus, in the traditional capital economy corresponding
to the Solow Model of the postwar era, small firms and entrepreneurship were
viewed as a luxury, perhaps needed by the West to ensure that decision making
remained decentralized, but obtained only at a cost to efficiency.

Despite the preservationist policy, however, the role of small business continued to diminish after World War II. The employment share of small firms in all
industries in the United States declined from 55.1 percent in 1958 to 52.5 percent in
1977. Declines in the small business employment share reached double digits for
minerals, retail, and wholesale, and single digits for construction, manufacturing,
and services.

2.3 The Knowledge (Romer) Economy

It would be a mistake to think that knowledge was not considered as a factor
influencing economic growth prior to the "new endogenous growth theory." As we
previously said, one of the main conclusions of the Solow model was that the
traditional factors of capital and labor were inadequate in accounting for variations
in growth performance. Indeed, it was the residual, attributed to reflect technological change, that typically accounted for most of the variations in economic
growth. As Nelson (1981, p. 1033) concludes, the research "provided evidence that
neoclassical variables do not account for all of the differences among firms in
productivity." Still, most econometric studies restricted their specification of factors explaining economic growth to measures of physical capital and labor. For
example, in an important article comparing U.S. and Japanese economic growth,
Jorgenson and Nishimizu (1978) include measures of physical capital and labor in
their country-specific regressions explaining growth.

The focus on labor and capital as the primary explicit factors of production,
and the general exclusion or trivialization of the role of knowledge, was not limited
to the sphere of macroeconomics. The most compelling theories of international
trade were based on factors of capital and labor as well as land, on occasion. For
example, the fundamental theorem for international trade, the Heckscher-Ohlin
theory, later extended to the Heckscher-Samuelson-Ohlin model, focused on the

factors of land, labor, and capital. According to the Heckscher-Ohlin theory, the proportion of production factors determines the trade structure. If there is an abundance of physical capital relative to labor, a country will tend toward the export of capital-intensive goods; an abundance of labor relative to physical capital leads to the export of labor-intensive goods.

In fact, what became known as the Leontief Paradox was based on the statistical evidence refuting, or at least not consistent with, the Heckscher-Samuelson-Ohlin model. In particular, the Leontief Paradox pointed out that the actual patterns of U.S. trade did not correspond to the predictions of the model (Bowen, Leamer, and Sveikauskas, 1987). Rather than the import of labor-intensive goods and export of capital-intensive goods, systematic empirical evidence found exactly the opposite for the United States, which suggested that the comparative advantage for the postwar United States was based on (unskilled) labor rather than on capital.

As economists struggled to resolve the Leontief Paradox, they began shifting the perspective of the model from an exclusive focus on the factors of inputs of capital and labor to probing inclusion of various aspects of knowledge. Early extensions included human capital and skilled labor and technology. The neo-technology theories focused on the role of R&D and the creation of new economic knowledge in shaping the comparative advantage and flows of foreign direct investment. Gruber, Mehta, and Vernon (1967) suggested that R&D expenditures reflect a temporary comparative advantage resulting from products and production techniques that have not yet been adapted by foreign competitors. Thus, industries with a relatively high R&D component are considered to be conducive to the comparative advantage of firms from the most developed nations.

The human skills hypothesis extended the Heckscher-Ohlin theory by including human capital as a third factor (Keesing, 1966, 1967). In the presence of a relative abundance of a labor force with a high level of human capital, countries were found to export human capital-intensive goods. Similarly, the abundance of skilled labor tended to promote the export of skill-intensive goods.

Even as international trade theory began to incorporate factors reflecting knowledge, technology, skills, R&D, and human capital into more realistic models, growth theory also began to probe including various representations of knowledge as an explicit or even endogenous factor generating economic growth. As Nelson pointed out in 1981, "It is worth noting that, during the early post-war era, the microeconomic conceptions underlying empirical analyses of productivity growth seem closer to the older theoretical tradition than to the newer one" (p. 1030). Nelson considered the work by Abramovitz (1952 and 1956), Schmookler (1952), Schultz (1953), and Kendrick (1956) as "remarkable in foreshadowing the central conclusion of studies done somewhat later within the neoclassical framework—that the growth of output experienced in the United States has been significantly greater than reasonably can be ascribed to input growth. Technological advance, changing composition of the work force, investments in human capital, reallocation of resources from lower to higher productivity activities, economies of scale, all were recognized as parts of the explanation. But no attempt was made to divide up the credit" (p. 1030).

The introduction of knowledge into macroeconomic growth models was formalized by Romer (1986) and Lucas (1988). Romer's critique of the Solow approach was not with the basic model of the neoclassical production function, but rather what he perceived to be omitted from that model: knowledge. Romer, Lucas, and others argued that knowledge was an important factor of production, along with the traditional factors of labor and capital and that, because it was endogenously determined as a result of externalities and spillovers, it was particularly crucial.

That entrepreneurship could play an important role in a knowledge-based economy seems to be contrary to many of the conventional theories of innovation. The starting point for most theories of innovation is the firm. In such theories the firms are exogenous and their performance in generating technological change is endogenous. For example, in the most prevalent model found in the literature of technological change, the model of the knowledge production function, formalized by Griliches (1979), firms exist exogenously and then engage in the pursuit of new economic knowledge as an input into the process of generating innovative activity. The most decisive input in the knowledge production function is new economic knowledge.

Subsequent to Griliches's seminal article, a number of studies empirically testing the knowledge production function emerged. Numerous measurement issues confronted this research agenda. Innovative output had to be measured and knowledge inputs had to be operationalized. Though the economic concept of innovative activity does not lend itself to exact measurement (Griliches, 1990), scholars developed measures such as the number of patented inventions, new product introductions, the share of sales accounted for by new products, productivity growth and export performance as proxies for innovative output.

Developing measures that reflected investments in knowledge inputs by the firm proved equally challenging. Still, a plethora of studies (Griliches, 1984; Cohen and Klepper, 1992a, 1992b) developed proxies of firm-specific investments in new economic knowledge in the form of R&D expenditures and human capital as key inputs that yield a high innovative output.

The ensuing literature that empirically tested the knowledge production function model generated a series of econometrically robust results substantiating Griliches's view that firm investments in knowledge inputs were required to produce innovative output. Cohen and Levinthal (1989) provided an even more compelling interpretation of the empirical link between firm-specific investments in knowledge and innovative output. According to Cohen and Levinthal, by developing the capacity to adapt new technology and ideas developed in other firms, firm-specific investments in knowledge such as R&D provided the capacity to absorb external knowledge. This key insight implied that by investing in R&D, firms could develop the absorptive capacity to appropriate at least some of the returns accruing to investments in new knowledge made external to the firm. This insight only strengthened the conclusion that the empirical evidence linking firm-specific investments in new knowledge to innovative output verified the assumptions underlying the model of the knowledge production function.

Considerable empirical evidence supports the knowledge production function model. This empirical link between knowledge inputs and innovative output apparently becomes stronger as the unit of observation becomes increasingly aggregated. For example, at the unit of observation of countries, the relationship between R&D and patents is very strong. The most innovative countries, such as the United States, Japan, and Germany, also tend to undertake high investments in R&D. By contrast, little patent activity is associated with developing countries, which have little R&D expenditure. Similarly, the link between R&D and innovative output, measured in terms of either patents or new product innovations, is also very strong when the unit of observation is the industry. The most innovative industries, such as computers, instruments, and pharmaceuticals, also tend to be the most R&D intensive. Acs and Audretsch (1990) find a simple correlation coefficient of 0.74 between R&D inputs and innovative output at the level of four-digit standard industrial classification (SIC) industries.

Thus, certainly both theoretical models and corroborative empirical evidence support the view that in a knowledge economy, small firms would be at least as disadvantaged as in the Solow economy. Just as small and new firms confronted size-inherent scale disadvantages in the Solow economy, their inability to generate large investments in knowledge, at least in absolute terms, seemed to preclude them from developing a competitive advantage in the knowledge-based Romer economy.

Thus, there were compelling theoretical reasons supported by empirical evidence that entrepreneurship, at least in the form of new-firm startups, was not compatible with a knowledge-based economy. Equally striking, in the 1990s a plethora of empirical evidence mounted indicating that the economic factor of knowledge was rapidly gaining in importance, especially in relation to the two traditional factors, physical capital and (unskilled) labor. Thus, as the factor of knowledge gained importance, most predictions suggested that new and small firms would play only a marginal role in contributing to innovation and growth.

Globalization combined with technological change, and in particular the information and communication technology breakthroughs had rendered the comparative advantage in low-technology and even traditional moderate-technology industries incompatible with high wage levels. At the same time, the emerging comparative advantage that is compatible with high wage levels is based on innovative activity. Many indicators reflect the shift in the comparative advantage of the high-wage countries toward an increased importance of innovative activity. For example, the sector of information and communication technology (ICT) in the United States experienced an increase in the annual growth rate from 5 percent in 1991 to nearly 20 percent by 1998. By contrast, the rest of the economy experienced fairly steady growth at around 3 percent over this period. Kortum and Lerner (1997, p. 1) document an unprecedented jump in patenting in the United States, as evidenced by the explosion in applications for patents by American inventors since 1985. Throughout this century, patent applications fluctuated within a band between 40,000 and 80,000 per year. In contrast, there were over 120,000 patent applications in 1995. Similarly, Berman, Bound, and Machin (1997) showed that the demand for less skilled workers has decreased dramatically throughout the OECD, while at the same time the demand for skilled workers exploded.

Inclusion of the additional factor—knowledge—in growth models did not trigger a shift in the public policy focus but certainly corresponded to the emergence of a new set of public policy instruments to promote economic growth. Just as Lucas (1988) and Romer (1990) conclude, the role of investments in new economic knowledge became the focus of economic policy to generate employment, and international competitiveness, even as the earlier preoccupation with investments in capital faded, or at least were no longer the focus in public policy debates. A fundamental implication emerging from the models of endogenous growth was that higher rates of economic growth could be attained through knowledge investments. Such a policy conclusion certainly was consistent with the ascendancy of university research, technology investments, and focus on human capital in the 1990s.

2.4 The Spatial Context

Globalization and the telecommunications revolution have brought two developments that were largely unanticipated. The first involves economic geography. Regions and geographic proximity have (re)emerged as important spatial units of economic activity. The second is organizational. Entrepreneurship has (re)emerged as a significant organizational form generating innovation and economic growth.

That innovative activity has become more important over time is not surprising. As we showed in the previous section, a plethora of economic indicators reflected an explosion in both knowledge inputs and in the ensuing output, or innovative activity.

What was less anticipated is that much of the innovative activity is less associated with footloose transnational corporations and more associated with high-tech entrepreneurship located in innovative regional clusters, such as Silicon Valley, Research Triangle Park, Boston's Route 128, and Austin, Texas. Only a few years ago the conventional wisdom predicted that globalization would render the demise of the region as a meaningful unit of economic analysis and the small firm as archaic. According to *The Economist* (1995b), "The death of distance as a determinant of the cost of communications will probably be the single most important economic force shaping society in the first half of the next century." Yet the obsession of policymakers around the globe to "create the next Silicon Valley" reveals the increased importance of geographic proximity and regional agglomeration.

Thus, one of the apparent paradoxes of globalization is the (re)emergence of location as a spatial platform for the efficient organization of economic activity. That globalization is one of the defining changes at the turn of the century is clear from a reading of the popular press. Like all grand concepts, a definition for globalization is elusive and elicits criticism. That domestic economies are globalizing is a cliché makes it no less true. In fact, the shift in economic activity from a local or national sphere to an international or global orientation ranks among the most significant changes shaping the current economic landscape.

Globalization would not have occurred to the degree that it has if the fundamental changes were restricted to the advent of the microprocessor and telecommunications. It took a political revolution in significant parts of the world to reap the benefits from these technological changes. The political counterpart of the technological revolution was the increase in democracy and concomitant stability in areas of the world that had previously been inaccessible. The Cold War combined with internal political instability rendered potential investments in Eastern Europe and much of the developing world too risky and impractical. During the postwar era most trade and economic investment was generally confined to Europe and North America, and later a few of the Asian countries, principally Japan and the Asian Tigers. Trade with countries behind the Iron Curtain was restricted and in some cases prohibited. Even trade with Japan and other Asian countries was highly regulated and restricted. Similarly, investments in politically unstable countries in South America and the Mideast resulted in episodes of nationalization and confiscation where the foreign investors lost their entire investments. Such political instability rendered foreign direct investment outside of Europe and North America particularly risky.

The fall of the Berlin Wall and subsequent changes in governments in Eastern Europe and the former Soviet Union were a catalyst for change and accessibility to parts of the world that had previously been inaccessible for decades. As Thurow (2002, pp. 25–26) points out, "Much of the world is throwing away its communist or socialist inheritance and moving towards capitalism. Communism has been abandoned as unworkable (China), imploded (the USSR), or has been overthrown (Eastern Europe)." Within a few years it became possible not just to trade with but also to invest in countries such as Hungary, the Czech Republic, Poland, Slovenia, as well as China, Vietnam, and Indonesia. For example, India became accessible as a trading and investment partner after opening its economy in the early 1990s. Trade and investment with the developed countries quickly blossomed. Trade and investment with the United States tripled between 1996 and 1997, reflecting the rapid change in two dimensions. First, India confronted sudden changes in trade and investment, not to mention a paradigmatic shift in ways of doing business. Second, to the foreign partner, in this case the United States, taking advantage of opportunities in India also meant downward pressure on wages and even plant closings in the originating country. As Thurow (2002, pp. 38–39) concludes, "As long as communism was believed to be a viable economic system, there were limits to global capitalism whatever the technological imperatives. Capitalism could not go completely global because much of the globe was beyond its reach. Forty percent of humanity lived under communism."

With the opening of some of these areas and participating in the world economy for the first time in decades, the postwar equilibrium came to a sudden end. Opportunities associated with the gaping disequilibria were abruptly created. Consider the large differentials in labor costs. As long as the Berlin Wall stood, and countries such as China and Vietnam remained closed, large discrepancies in wage rates could be maintained without eliciting responses in trade and foreign direct investment. The low wage rates in China or parts of the former USSR neither encouraged foreign companies to build plants nor resulted in large-scale trade with the West based on access to low production costs. Investment by foreign companies was either prohibited by local governments or deemed to be too risky by the companies. Similarly, trade and other restrictions limited the capabilities of firms in those countries to produce and trade with the West.

Thus, the gaping wage differentials existing while the Iron Curtain stood and much of the communist world was cut off from the West were suddenly exposed in the early 1990s. There were not only unprecedented labor cost differentials but also massive and willing populations craving to join the high levels of consumption that had become the norm in Western Europe and North America.

Of course, the productivity of labor is vastly greater in the West, which compensates to a significant degree for such large wage differentials. Still, given the magnitude of these numbers, both trade and investment have responded to the opportunities made possible by the events of 1989.

While the most salient feature of globalization involves interaction and interfaces among individuals across national boundaries, the more traditional measures of transnational activity reflect an upward trend of global activities. These traditional measures include trade (exports and imports), foreign direct investment (inward and outward), international capital flows, and intercountry labor mobility. The overall trend for all of these measures has been strongly positive.

Location has (re)emerged as an important spatial unit of observation in a rapidly globalizing economy because of the shift in comparative advantage of high-wage countries to knowledge. Despite the claim of "The Death of Distance" (as *The Economist* put it) to access knowledge, and in particular knowledge spillovers, local proximity to the knowledge source(s) bestows competitive advantage.

As we discussed in the previous section, the spillover of knowledge is a key mechanism in the models of endogenous growth. However, the spatial dimension has been less clear. For example, in disputing the role of knowledge externalities in explaining the geographic concentration of economic activity, Krugman (1991a, b) and others do not question the existence or importance of such knowledge spillovers. In fact, they argue that such knowledge externalities are so important and forceful that there is no compelling reason for a geographic boundary to limit the spatial extent of the spillover. According to this line of thinking, the concern is not that knowledge does not spill over but that it should stop spilling over just because it hits a geographic border, such as a city limit, state line, national boundary, or intercontinental ocean.

Thus, it took more than theories of knowledge spillover, or knowledge externalities, to explain the (re)emergence of location as a platform for harnessing knowledge and generating innovative activity. The second theoretical leg involves explanations or theories of localization, which explain why the economic value of knowledge tends to decline as it is transmitted across geographic space. As Audretsch and Feldman (1996) explain, the theory of the localization of knowledge spillovers lies in a distinction between knowledge and information. *Information* has a singular meaning and interpretation. It can be codified at low cost and the transaction cost is trivial. In contrast, *knowledge* is vague, difficult to codify, and often only serendipitously recognized. Even though the marginal cost of transmitting information across geographic space has been rendered trivial by the telecommunications revolution, the marginal cost of transmitting knowledge, and especially tacit knowledge, rises significantly with distance.

Why is geographic proximity so important for the transmission of knowledge, and especially tacit knowledge? Localization theories suggest that face-to-face interaction and nonverbal communication facilitate the transmission of ideas and intuition that cannot be communicated through codified instructions. While information is often context-free, tacit knowledge is often derived from specific contexts. Thus, in order to access knowledge and participate in the generation of new ideas, local proximity is significantly more cost-effective than trying to attain the same knowledge across distance. Perhaps it was this insight that led Glaeser et al. (1992, p. 1126) to conclude that "intellectual breakthroughs must cross hallways and streets more easily than oceans and continents."

The importance of local proximity for the transmission of knowledge spillovers has been observed in many different contexts. It has been pointed out that "business is a social activity, you have to be where important work is taking place" (*Fortune*, 1993, citing a survey carried out by Moran, Stahl, & Boyer of New York City). The survey of nearly one thousand executives located in America's 60 largest metropolitan areas ranked Raleigh/Durham as the best metropolitan area for knowledge workers and for innovative activity.

> A lot of brainy types who made their way to Raleigh/Durham were drawn by three top research universities.... U.S. businesses, especially those whose success depends on staying at the top of new technologies and processes, increasingly want to be where hot new ideas are percolating. A presence in brainpower centers like Raleigh/Durham pays off in new products and new ways of doing business. Dozens of small biotechnology and software operations are starting up each year and growing like kudzu in the fertile climate.

The findings from the literature on the new economic geography provide compelling evidence that the spatial context matters. Geography matters for the generation of knowledge spillovers and for the capacity of firms and economic agents to access those knowledge spillovers. However, a more subtle and less well-known finding emerged in the literature, suggesting that it is not just the magnitude of factors that matters in generating localized spillovers but also the organization of that economic activity within the black box of the localized spatial unit of analysis (Feldman and Audretsch, 1999). This is what leads to the second main implication emanating from investment in economic knowledge: the organization of economic activity matters in such a way as to lead to an increased role for entrepreneurship.

Thus, when Thurow (2002, p. 25) observed, "The world is moving from an industrial era based upon natural resources into a knowledge-based era based upon skills, education, and research and development," the ascendence of knowledge as the factor generating comparative advantage in globally linked markets also had implications not only for the geography of innovation but also for the organization of economic activity within the relevant geographic unit of a localized knowledge cluster. As we will show in the next section, the ascendance of knowledge as an important factor of competitiveness and economic growth ushered in a new economic role for an old organizational form—entrepreneurship.

2.5 The Entrepreneurial Economy

Increased globalization of economic activity seemingly condemned entrepreneurship, in the form of new-firm startups and small firms, to the path to extinction, or at least to an even more diminished role than it had ever played in the Solow Economy. Conventional wisdom would predict that increased globalization would present an even more hostile environment to small business (Vernon, 1970). Caves (1982, p. 71) argued that the additional costs of globalization that would be incurred by small business "constitute an important reason for expecting that foreign investment will be mainly an activity of large firms." Certainly, the empirical evidence by Horst (1972) showed that even after controlling for industry effects, the only factor significantly influencing the propensity to engage in foreign direct investment was firm size. As Chandler (1990, p. 130) concluded, "to compete globally you have to be big." Gomes-Casseres (1997, p. 33) further observed that "students of international business have traditionally believed that success in foreign markets required large size. Small firms were thought to be at a disadvantage compared to larger firms, because of the fixed costs of learning about foreign environments, communicating at long distances, and negotiating with national governments."

Thus, it was particularly startling and a seeming paradox, when scholars first began to document that what had seemed like the inevitable demise of entrepreneurship actually began to reverse itself starting in the 1970s.

Loveman and Sengenberger (1991) and Acs and Audretsch (1993) carried out systematic international studies examining the reemergence of small firms and entrepreneurship in North America and Europe. Two major findings emerged from these studies. First, the relative role of small firms varies systematically across countries. Second, in most European countries and in North America, small firms began increasing their relative importance starting in the mid-1970s. In the United States the average real GDP per firm increased by nearly two thirds from $150,000 to $245,000 between 1947 and 1980, reflecting a trend toward larger enterprises and a decreasing importance of small firms. However, within the subsequent seven years, by 1987, it had fallen by about 14 percent to $210,000, reflecting a sharp reversal of this trend and the reemergence of small firms (Brock and Evans, 1989). Similarly, small firms accounted for a fifth of manufacturing sales in the United States in 1976, but by 1986 the small-firm share of sales had risen to over a quarter (Acs and Audretsch, 1990).

The recent emergence of entrepreneurship was first identified in job generation. In 1981, David Birch revealed the startling findings from his long-term study of U.S. job generation. Despite the conventional wisdom prevailing at the time, Birch (1981, p. 8) found that "whatever else they are doing, large firms are no longer the major providers of new jobs for Americans." Instead, he discovered that most new jobs emanated from small firms. While his exact methodology and application of the underlying data have been a source of considerable controversy, as have the exact quantitative estimates, his qualitative conclusion that the bulk of new jobs has emanated from small enterprises in the United States has been largely substantiated.

More recently, Davis, Haltiwanger, and Schuh (1996a, 1996b) corrected for the regression to the mean fallacy they claim is inherent in Birch's results in estimating employment generation for the United States between 1972 and 1988. While their quantitative results differ from Birch's, their study still indicates that small firms account for more than their share of new employment. In particular, in their study large firms created 53 percent of the new jobs, but their employment share is 65 percent. At the same time, large firms destroyed 56 percent of the jobs, which is greater than their share of new jobs created. Their measure was static and gave no indication whether this share has been increasing or decreasing over time.

Methodologies similar to Birch's were also used in the European context. In some of the first studies, Gallagher and Stewart (1986) and Storey and Johnson (1987) found similar results for the United Kingdom, that small enterprises create most of the new jobs. Similarly, Konings (1995) linked gross job flows in the United Kingdom to establishment size. He finds that the gross job creation rate is the highest in small establishments and the lowest in large establishments. By contrast, the gross job destruction rate is the lowest in small establishments and the highest in large establishments.

Evidence from Sweden (Heshmati, 2001) based on data from the 1990s also suggests that employment creation is negatively related to firm size. Similarly, Hohti (2000) finds that gross employment creation and destruction are negatively related to firm size in Finland. Using data from Finnish manufacturing between 1980 and 1994, Hohti finds that the annual job flow rates, in terms of births and deaths, is similar to that identified by Broesma and Gautier (1997, p. 216) for Dutch manufacturing firms and by Klette and Mathiassen (1996) for Norwegian manufacturing firms. In particular, new establishments have the greatest job creation rates as well as the greatest rates of job destruction. Thus, the evidence from Finland, as well as from Sweden and the Netherlands, suggests entrepreneurial dynamics similar to that found in the United States.

Thus, the weight of the empirical evidence on employment generation is remarkably robust and indicates that the role of entrepreneurship in employment generation in Europe is not inconsistent with the findings for the United States. Small and new enterprises serve an engine of employment creation on both sides of the Atlantic. However, an important qualification of the "Job Generation" literature is that it links employment changes of the firm to the size and, in some cases, the age of the firm. So the performance criterion is not focused on employment changes in general, but only employment changes occurring at the unit of the firm. This assumes that there is no externality or spillover from one enterprise to other firms. This also holds for the analyses of employment change by small firms reported by the European Observatory for SMEs (EIM, 2002a).

The reversal of the trend from large enterprises toward the reemergence of small firms was not limited to the United States. In fact, a similar trend was found in Europe as well. For example, in the Netherlands the business ownership rate fell during the postwar period, until it reached a trough of 0.085 in 1982. But this downward trend was subsequently reversed, rising to a business ownership rate of 0.10 by 1998 (Audretsch et al., 2002). Similarly, the small-firm employment share in manufacturing in the Netherlands increased from 68.3 percent in 1978 to 71.8 percent in 1986; in the United Kingdom from 30.1 percent in 1979 to 39.9 percent by 1986; in West Germany from 54.8 percent in 1970 to 57.9 percent by 1987; in Portugal from 68.3 percent in 1982 to 71.8 percent in 1986; in Northern Italy from 44.3 percent in 1981 to 55.2 percent by 1987; and in Southern Italy from 61.4 percent in 1981 to 68.4 percent by 1987 (Acs and Audretsch, 1993). Another EIM study documents how the relative importance of

SMEs in Europe (19 countries), measured in terms of employment shares has continued to increase between 1988 and 2001 (EIM, 2002b).

As the empirical evidence mounted documenting the reemergence of entrepreneurship as a vital factor, scholars began to look for explanations and to develop a theoretical basis. The early explanations (Brock and Evans, 1989) revolved around six hypotheses:

1. Technological change had reduced the extent of scale economies in manufacturing;
2. Increased globalization had rendered markets more volatile as a result of competition from a greater number of foreign rivals;
3. The changing composition of the labor force, toward a greater participation of women, immigrants, and young and old workers, may be more conducive to smaller rather than larger enterprises, due to the greater premium placed on work flexibility;
4. A proliferation of consumer tastes away from standardized mass-produced goods toward stylized and personalized products facilitates small niche producers;
5. Deregulation and privatization facilitate the entry of new and small firms into markets that were previously protected and inaccessible; and
6. The increased importance of innovation in high-wage countries has reduced the relative importance of large-scale production and instead fostered the importance of entrepreneurial activity.

According to Audretsch and Thurik (2001), entrepreneurship in the form of new and small firms did not become obsolete as a result of globalization, but their role changed as the comparative advantage has shifted toward knowledge-based economic activity. This has occurred for two reasons. First, large enterprises in traditional manufacturing industries had lost their competitiveness in producing in the high-cost domestic countries. Second, small entrepreneurial enterprises had taken on a new importance and value in a knowledge-based economy.

The loss of competitiveness by large-scale producers in high-cost locations is manifested by the fact that, confronted with lower cost competition in foreign locations, producers in the high-cost countries have four options apart from doing nothing and losing global market share: (1) reduce wages and other production costs sufficiently to compete with the low-cost foreign producers, (2) substitute equipment and technology for labor to increase productivity, (3) shift production out of the high-cost location and into the low-cost location, and (4) outsource the production of inputs to third-party firms, typically located in lower-cost locations.

Pressed to maintain competitiveness in traditional low- and moderate-technology industries, where economic activity can be easily transferred across geographic space to access lower production costs, large corporations throughout the OECD countries deployed two strategic responses. The first was to offset greater wage differentials between Europe and low-cost locations by increasing productivity through the substitution of technology and capital for labor. The second was to locate new plants and establishments in a lower-cost location, either through outward foreign direct investment, or outsourcing, or both. As Thurow (2002, p. 11) observes,

A seismic shift in technology has either seduced or forced, depending upon your views, national business firms into becoming global business firms. With the new computer-telecommunications technologies, a profit-maximizing company must make its products wherever in the world they are the cheapest to make and it must sell its products wherever in the world the greatest profits are to be earned. If the firm does not find the cheapest places to produce its products and the most profitable places to sell its products, others will. The firm that doesn't go global will be driven out of business by those that do.... From the point of view of business, improvements in communications have made global sales and out-sourcing possible, highly profitable, and necessary, all at the same time.

What these strategic responses have in common is that the flagship companies have been downsizing the amount of employment in their domestic economy. This has been at least as true in Europe as in the United States. For example, between 1991 and 1995, manufacturing employment in German plants decreased by 1,307,000 while it increased in foreign subsidiaries by 189,000 (BMWi, 1999). In the chemical sector, the decrease of domestic employment was 80,000, while 14,000 jobs were added by German chemical companies in plants located outside of Germany. Electrical engineering employment in German plants decreased by 198,000. In automobiles, employment in Germany decreased by 161,000, while 30,000 jobs were added outside of Germany. As table 2.1 shows, between 1991 and 1995 manufacturing employment in German plants decreased by 1,307,000 while it increased in foreign subsidiaries by 189,000 (BMWi, 2000).

Globalization has adversely impacted domestic employment not just at the firm and industry levels. Figure 2.1 shows how globalization has affected a particular *Standort*, Stuttgart, which is not just the capital of Baden-Württemberg, one of the manufacturing stalwarts of Germany, Europe, and the world, but also the capital of the automobile industry. Employment in manufacturing increased throughout the postwar period before peaking at the end of the 1980s. But manufacturing employment suffered a sharp loss, which has never recovered. Thus, globalization has adversely affected employment at the levels of the firm, the industry, and the Standort.

Much of the policy debate responding to the displaced employment resulting from globalization has revolved around a perceived trade-off between maintaining higher wages but suffering greater unemployment versus higher levels of employ-ment but at the cost of lower wage rates. There is, however, an alternative. It does

TABLE 2.1 Change in Employment Figures in Germany and at Foreign Subsidiaries (1991–1995, in Thousands)

Employment sector	Manufacturing	Chemicals	Electrical engineering	Automotive	Mechanical engineering	Textiles	Banking and insurance
Foreign	189	14	−17	30	16	−6	21
Domestic	−1,307	−80	−198	−161	−217	−68	28

Source: Bundesministerium fuer Wirtschafts und Technologie (German Federal Ministry of Economics and Technology, 2000).

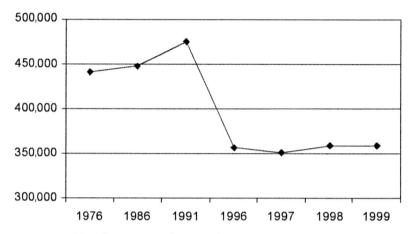

FIGURE 2.1. Manufacturing employees in Stuttgart, 1976–1999

not require sacrificing wages to create new jobs, nor does it require fewer jobs to maintain wage levels and the social safety net. This alternative involves shifting economic activity out of the traditional industries where the high-cost countries of Europe and North America have lost the comparative advantage and into those industries where the comparative advantage is compatible with both high wages and high levels of employment—knowledge-based economic activity. Globalization has rendered the comparative advantage in traditional moderate technology industries incompatible with high wage levels. At the same time, the emerging comparative advantage that is compatible with high wage levels is based on innovative activity.

Thus, the regional response to globalization has been the emergence of a new policy for the strategic management of places. As long as corporations were inextricably linked to their regional location by substantial sunk costs, such as capital investment, the competitiveness of a region was identical to the competitiveness of the corporations located in that region. A quarter century ago, while the proclamation, "What is good for General Motors is good for America" may have been controversial, few would have disagreed that "What is good for General Motors is good for Detroit." And so it was with U.S. Steel in Pittsburgh and Volkswagen in Wolfsburg. As long as the corporation thrived, so did the region.

As globalization has not only reduced the degree to which the traditional economic factors of capital and labor are sunk but also shifted the comparative advantage in the high-wage countries of North America and Europe towards knowledge-based economic activity, corporations in traditional industries have been forced to shift production to lower-cost locations. This has led to the delinking of firm competitiveness from regional competitiveness. The advent of the strategic management of regions has been a response to the realization that the strategic management of corporations includes a policy option not available to regions—changing the production location.

At the heart of the strategic management of places has been the development and enhancement of factors of production that cannot be transferred across geographic space at low cost—principally, although not exclusively, knowledge and ideas.

But why should the shift in the comparative advantage of leading industrialized countries toward knowledge involve a more pronounced role for entrepreneurship? This question is particularly exacerbating in view of the model of the knowledge production function, which posited and found compelling evidence suggesting that new economic knowledge, conceptually and econometrically linked to investments in human capital, university research, and private R&D, is an essential ingredient for firm innovation. After all, new startups rarely have investments in human capital and R&D that can even be compared to, let alone match, the multimillion dollar investments in R&D and development of human capital made annually by leading corporations such as Microsoft, Intel, IBM, and General Motors.

One hint into resolving this breakdown of the model of the knowledge production function was provided by the meticulous econometric research linking measures of knowledge investments to innovative output. As we mentioned before, these econometric studies all confirmed the validity of the model of the knowledge production function at both the country level and industry level. However, studies linking knowledge inputs to innovative output were more ambiguous when analyzed at the unit of observation of the firm, especially when the data set included a broad spectrum of firm sizes spanning both small and larger enterprises. These studies found, in some cases, a positive relationship between firm investments in knowledge and innovative output; in other cases, no relationship; and in still other cases, a negative relationship.

Acs and Audretsch (1990) showed that, in fact, the most innovative U.S. firms are large corporations. Further, the most innovative American corporations also tended to have large R&D laboratories and be R&D intensive. At first glance, these findings based on direct measures of innovative activity seem to confirm the conventional wisdom concerning the model of the knowledge production function. However, in the most innovative industries, large firms, defined as enterprises with at least 500 employees, contributed more innovations in some instances, whereas in other industries, small firms produced more innovations. For example, in computers and process control instruments, small firms contributed the bulk of the innovations. By contrast, in the pharmaceutical preparation and aircraft industries the large firms were much more innovative.

Probably the best measure of innovative activity is the total innovation rate, defined as the total number of innovations per thousand employees in each industry. The large-firm innovation rate is defined as the number of innovations made by firms with at least 500 employees, divided by the number of employees (thousands) in large firms. The small-firm innovation rate is analogously defined as the number of innovations contributed by firms with fewer than 500 employees, divided by the number of employees (thousands) in small firms.

The innovation rates, or the number of innovations per thousand employees, have the advantage in that they measure large- and small-firm innovative activity relative to the presence of large and small firms in any given industry. That is, in a direct comparison between large- and small-firm innovative activities, the absolute number of innovations contributed by large firms and small enterprises is somewhat misleading, for these measures are not standardized by the relative presence of large and small firms in each industry. When a direct comparison is made between the innovative activity of large and small firms, the innovation rates are presumably a more reliable measure of innovative intensity because they are weighted by the relative presence of small and large enterprises in any given industry. Thus, while large firms in manufacturing introduced 2,445 innovations and small firms contributed slightly fewer, 1,954, small-firm employment was only half as great as large-firm employment, yielding an average small-firm innovation rate in manufacturing of 0.309, compared to a large-firm innovation rate of 0.202 (Acs and Audretsch, 1988, 1990).

The breakdown of the model of the knowledge production function at the level of the firm raised this question: Where do small innovative firms with little or no R&D get the knowledge inputs? This question becomes particularly relevant for small and new firms that undertake little R&D themselves yet contribute considerable innovative activity in newly emerging industries such as biotechnology and computer software (Audretsch, 1995). One clue supplied by the literature on the new economic geography identifying the local nature of knowledge spillovers is from other, third-party firms or research institutions, such as universities, that may be located within spatial proximity. Economic knowledge may spill over from the firm conducting the R&D or the research laboratory of a university for access by a new and small firm.

How can new and small firms access such knowledge spillovers? And why should new and small firms have a competitive advantage accessing knowledge produce elsewhere vis-à-vis their larger counterparts? That is, what are the mechanisms transmitting the spillover of knowledge from the source producing that knowledge, such as the R&D laboratory of a large corporation or a university, to the small firm actually engaged in commercializing that knowledge. At least two major channels or mechanisms for knowledge spillovers have been identified in the literature. Both of these spillover mechanisms involve the appropriability of new knowledge. Cohen and Levinthal (1989) suggest that firms develop the capacity to adapt new technology and ideas developed in other firms and are therefore able to appropriate some of the returns accruing to investments in new knowledge made externally. An extensive literature focusing on small-firm linkages through networks and strategic alliances has developed in an effort to identify and analyze the mechanisms by which small firms access, internalize, and commercialize knowledge external to the firm. Such an approach is entirely consistent with the knowledge production model view of the firm. The (small) firm exists exogenously. Because it is too constrained by size to make sufficient investments in generating new knowledge, it must engage in strategies to access knowledge essential for innovation by other means, such as resorting to networks, linkages, and other types of spillover conduits.

In contrast, Audretsch (1995) proposed inverting the model of the knowledge production of the function. Rather than assume the firm exists exogenously and then undertakes the necessary investments (if large) or strategic alliances and networks (if small) to endogenously create the knowledge required to innovate, Audretsch (1995) instead inverts the model and assumes that the knowledge is exogenous. New and potentially valuable knowledge does not exist abstractly "in the air" or "in the firm," but rather is embodied in people, either as individuals or in groups and teams of individuals. As Arrow (1962) emphasized, such new knowledge is inherently uncertain, asymmetric, and involves a high cost of transaction. Such knowledge conditions result in significant divergences in both the expected value of a new idea and the variance in the expected outcomes involved in pursuing or commercializing it. Such divergences in the valuation of new ideas by economic agents, such as scientists, engineers, and other knowledge workers, can result in an appropriability problem. Whereas a large literature emerged focusing on the problem confronting firms in accruing the benefits emanating from investments they undertake in the production of new knowledge and ideas, much less research has focused on an analogous problem confronting individual knowledge workers faced with appropriating the returns from their investments and endowments in new knowledge. Because of the fundamental characteristics inherent in new ideas, what one economic agent thinks is a potentially valuable idea may not be valued so highly by the decision-makers of her firm. Such divergences in the valuation of new ideas are even more likely to result if the new knowledge is not compatible with the core of the firm's competence or consistent with the technological trajectory of the firm. A divergence in the valuation of any idea between an individual, or team of knowledge workers, and the decision-making hierarchy of an incumbent organization or firm forces the individual knowledge worker (or team of knowledge workers) to make a fundamental choice: either ignore the idea and redirect activities and work in a direction more compatible with the organization or appropriate the value of that new idea within the organizational context of a new firm.

The industry life-cycle theory introduced by Raymond Vernon (1966) is typically considered to link trade and foreign direct investment to the stage of the life cycle, with no direct implications for the relevance of radical versus incremental innovations, and certainly few implications for entrepreneurship. However, a different interpretation of the framework of the industry life cycle suggests that the relative importance of radical versus incremental innovations is shaped by the industry life cycle.

There have been multiple versions of what actually constitutes the industry life cycle. For example, Oliver Williamson (1975, p. 122) depicted the industry lifecycle as follows:

> Three stages in an industry's development are commonly recognized: an early exploratory stage, an intermediate development stage, and a mature stage. The first or early formative stage involves the supply of a new product of relatively primitive design, manufactured on comparatively unspecialized machinery, and marketed through a variety of exploratory techniques. Volume is typically low. A high degree of uncertainty characterizes business experience at this stage. The second stage is the intermediate development state in which manufacturing techniques are more refined and market definition is sharpened, output grows rapidly in response to newly recognized applications and unsatisfied market demands. A high but somewhat lesser degree of uncertainty characterizes market outcomes at this stage. The third stage is that of a mature industry. Management, manufacturing, and marketing

techniques all reach a relatively advanced degree of refinement. Markets may continue to grow, but do so at a more regular and predictable rate.... [E]stablished connections, with customers and suppliers (including capital market access) all operate to buffer changes and thereby to limit large shifts in market shares. Significant innovations tend to be fewer and are mainly of an improvement variety.

While not explicitly stated by Vernon (1966) or Williamson (1975), the role of R&D is not constant over the industry life cycle. In the early stages of the life cycle, R&D tends to be highly productive so that there are increasing returns to R&D. Indeed, radical innovation tends to initiate new industry. In addition, the costs of radical innovation tend to be relatively high while the costs of incremental innovation and imitation tend to be relatively low. As innovation in newly emerging industries tends to be more radical and less incremental, it is more costly to diffuse it across geographic space for economic application in lower-cost locations.

By contrast, as an industry evolves over the life cycle, the cost of radical innovation tends to increase relative to the cost of incremental innovation and imitation; thus, diminishing returns to radical innovative activity set in. This is not the case for incremental innovation and especially imitation. An implication is that it requires an increasing amount of R&D effort to generate a given amount of innovative activity as an industry matures over its life cycle. At the same time, it requires a decreasing amount of R&D expenditures to transfer new technology to lower-cost locations, because innovation activity tends to become less radical and more incremental (Dosi, 1982, 1988; Nelson, 1990, 1995). So information generated by R&D in mature industries can be transferred to lower-cost locations for economic commercialization. By contrast, the knowledge resulting from R&D in newly emerging industries cannot be easily transferred to lower-cost locations for economic commercialization. Thus, under the managed economy, incremental innovative activity along with diffusion played a more important role. This type of innovative activity, while often requiring large investments of R&D, generated incremental changes in products along the existing technological trajectories.

In the entrepreneurial economy, the comparative advantage of the high-cost location demands innovative activity earlier in the life cycle. Early stage innovative activity consists of radical innovation, which is more involved in creating and developing new technological trajectories rather than following existing technological trajectories.

Globalization has affected economic geography to shift the comparative advantage of leading developed countries away from the factor of capital and toward the factor of knowledge. This would suggest that the comparative advantage in the leading developed countries is increasingly found in economic activity characterized by the early stage of the industry life cycle, where new ideas play a predominant role and little has been standardized in the industry. In such industries, the process of recognizing new opportunities and then commercializing those perceived opportunities by starting a new firm is particularly important. Thus, the entrepreneurial economy that is emerging in North America and Europe has a new role for entrepreneurship. Rather than imposing an efficiency burden on the economy, as seemingly was the case in the Solow economy, entrepreneurship serves as an engine of growth by providing a vital conduit for the spillover and commercialization of knowledge and new ideas.

2.6 Conclusions

The role of entrepreneurship in the economy and, in particular, the impact of entrepreneurship on economic growth and employment has evolved considerably since World War II. In the postwar economy, investments in physical capital were the driver of economic growth. Economic activity based on physical capital was most efficiently organized in large-scale operations. In the physical capital economy, there was little room for entrepreneurship and small business, at least not as an engine of economic growth. At best, small firms were tolerated for social and political values, and the ensuing inefficiency associated with small-scale production was endured as the cost of such noneconomic goals.

As recognition grew, both among scholars and policy-makers that knowledge was also a key factor shaping economic growth, a new set of public policy instruments for generating economic growth became prominent, with a focus on research, intellectual property, and human capital. If anything, the inclusion of knowledge as a factor of production served only to reinforce the view that small firms were anathema to economic growth. Recognition of the model of the knowledge production function seemed to mandate economic organization in large-scale enterprises in the knowledge economy, just as it had in the capital economy.

In fact, small firms and entrepreneurship emerged as essential to economic growth in the 1990s. Part of this recognition came from the empirical or policy experience emanating from investments in new knowledge in the absence of entrepreneurship. Much has been made about the so-called European Paradox, wherein high levels of investment in new knowledge exist from private firms as well as public research institutes and universities. Countries such as Sweden rank among the highest in terms of investment in research, at least as measured by the ratio of R&D to GDP. Similarly, levels of human capital and education in Sweden as well as throughout many parts of Europe rank among the highest in the world. Yet growth rates remained stagnant and employment creation sluggish throughout the 1990s and into the new century.

As we will discuss in chapter 10, a growing consensus has emerged that investment in new economic knowledge alone will not guarantee economic growth and employment creation. Rather, key institutional mechanisms are a prerequisite for such knowledge investments to become transmitted and transformed into economic knowledge, through the process of spillovers and commercialization. Entrepreneurship has emerged as a driving force of economic growth because it is an important conduit of knowledge spillovers and commercialization.

Thus, as knowledge has become more important as a factor of production, knowledge spillovers have also become more important as a source of economic growth. Entrepreneurship takes on new importance in a knowledge economy because it serves as a key mechanism by which knowledge created in one organization becomes commercialized in a new enterprise, thereby contributing to the economic growth, employment, and vitality of the overall economy.

The Knowledge Spillover Theory of Entrepreneurship

3.1 Linking Entrepreneurship and Knowledge

Why do some people start firms? And if they do, what impact will such entrepreneurship have on employment, growth, and prosperity? These questions have been at the heart of considerable research, not just in economics but throughout the social sciences. Hébert and Link (1989) identified three distinct intellectual traditions in the development of the entrepreneurship literature: the German tradition, based on Johann Heinrich von Thünen and Schumpeter; the Chicago tradition, based on Frank Knight and Theodore Schultz; and the Austrian tradition, based on Ludwig von Mises, Israel Kirzner, and George Shackle.

It is a virtual consensus that entrepreneurship revolves around the recognition of opportunities and the pursuit of those opportunities (Venkataraman, 1997). Much of the contemporary thinking about entrepreneurship focuses on the cognitive process by which individuals reach the decision to start a new firm. According to Sarasvathy et al. (2003, p. 142), "An entrepreneurial opportunity consists of a set of ideas, beliefs and actions that enable the creation of future goods and services in the absence of current markets for them." Sarasvathy et al. provide a typology of entrepreneurial opportunities as consisting of opportunity recognition, opportunity discovery, and opportunity creation.

In asking the question of why some do it and others do not, scholars have focused on differences across individuals (Stevenson and Jarillo, 1990). As Krueger (2003, p. 105) observes, "The heart of entrepreneurship is an orientation toward seeing opportunities," which frames the research questions: "What is the nature of entrepreneurial thinking?" and "What cognitive phenomena are associated with seeing and acting on opportunities?"

The traditional approach to entrepreneurship essentially holds the context constant and then asks how the cognitive process inherent in the entrepreneurial decision varies across different individual characteristics and attributes (Carter et al., 2003; McClelland, 1961). Shane and Eckhardt (2003, p. 187) summarize this literature in introducing the individual-opportunity nexus: "We discussed the process of opportunity discovery and explained why some actors are more likely to discover a given opportunity than others." Some of these differences involve the willingness to incur risk, others involve the preference for autonomy and self-direction, still others involve differential access to scarce and expensive resources, such as financial capital, human capital, social capital, and experiential capital. This approach focusing on individual cognition in the entrepreneurial process has generated a number of important and valuable insights, such as the contribution made by social networks, education and training, and familial influence (Acs and Audretsch, 2003). The literature certainly leaves the impression that entrepreneurship is a personal matter largely determined by DNA, familial status, and access to crucial resources.

The purpose of this chapter is to invert the traditional approach to entrepreneurship. Rather than taking the context as given and then asking how variations across individual attributes shape the cognitive process underlying the decision to become an entrepreneur, this chapter instead assumes the individual characteristics to be constant and then analyzes how the cognitive process inducing the entrepreneurial decision is influenced by placing that same individual in different contexts. In particular, we compare high knowledge contexts with impoverished knowledge contexts. This leads to a different view of entrepreneurship. It is not a phenomenon exogenously determined by preconditioned personal attributes and family history, but instead entrepreneurship is an endogenous response to opportunities generated by investments in new knowledge made by incumbent firms and organizations, combined with their inability to fully and completely exhaust the ensuing opportunities to commercialize that knowledge. In this chapter, we show how entrepreneurship can be an endogenous response to investments in new knowledge when commercialization of that knowledge is constrained by a formidable knowledge filter.

Not only does holding the individual attributes constant but varying the knowledge context give rise to the knowledge theory of entrepreneurship, but entrepreneurship as an endogenous response to the incomplete commercialization of new knowledge provides the missing link in recent economic growth models. As a conduit of knowledge spillovers, entrepreneurship serves as an important source of economic growth that otherwise remains unaccounted for. Thus, entrepreneurship is the mechanism by which society more fully appropriates its investments in the creation of new knowledge, such as research and education.

The next section explains how entrepreneurship combines the cognitive process of recognizing opportunities with pursuing those opportunities by starting a new firm. The third section introduces the Knowledge Spillover Theory of Entrepreneurship, which suggests that entrepreneurship is an endogenous response to investments in knowledge that are not fully appropriated by incumbent firms. The fourth section links endogenous entrepreneurship based on knowledge spillovers to economic growth. Finally, a summary and conclusions are provided in the last section. In particular, this chapter proposes a series of main hypotheses at the heart of the knowledge spillover theory of endogenous growth, which will be empirically tested in the following six chapters.

3.2 Entrepreneurship as Opportunity Recognition and Action

The starting point for analyzing the determinants of entrepreneurship has been the individual. These studies cross a broad spectrum of academic disciplines, ranging from psychology to sociology and to economics. The early studies centered on North America, but they now have been duplicated and extended to Europe.

Within the economics literature, the prevalent theoretical framework has been the general model of income choice, which has been at times referred to as the general model of entrepreneurial choice. The model of income or entrepreneurial choice dates back at least to Knight (1921), but was more recently extended and updated by Lucas (1978), Kihlstrom and Laffont (1979), Holmes and Schmitz (1990), and Jovanovic (1994). In its most basic rendition, individuals confront a choice of earning their income either from wages earned through employment in an incumbent enterprise or from profits accrued by starting a new firm (Parker, 2004, 2005). The essence of the income choice is made by comparing the wage an individual expects to earn through employment, W, with the profits expected to accrue from a new-firm startup, π^*. Thus, the probability of starting a new firm, E, can be represented as $\Pr(E) = f(\pi^* - W)$.

The model of income choice has been extended by Kihlstrom and Laffont (1979) to incorporate aversion to risk, and by Lucas (1978) and Jovanovic (1994) to explain why firms of varying size exist, and has served as the basis for empirical studies of the decision to start a new firm by Blau (1987), Evans and Leighton (1989a, 1989b, 1990), Evans and Jovanovic (1989a, 1989b), Blanchflower and Oswald (1990), and Blanchflower and Meyer (1994).

Empirical tests of the model of income or entrepreneurial choice have focused on personal characteristics with respect to labor market conditions. For example, using U.S. data, Evans and Leighton (1989a, 1989b, 1990) link personal characteristics, such as education, experience, age, and employment status, of almost 4,000 white men to the decision to start a new firm. They found unequivocal evidence that, for young white men in the United States, the probability of starting a new firm tends to increase when an individual loses his job. Other studies, such as Bates (1990), also using U.S. data, and Blanchflower and Meyer (1994), emphasize human capital in the income choice. This approach emphasizes the employment status of individuals in making the income choice. Certain ambiguities exist in linking unemployment to the decision to start a new firm (Storey, 1991). In particular, Storey observed that while consistent results tended to emerge from cross-section studies as well as from time series analysis, the results are inconsistent between these two approaches; hence, the discrepancy in results appeared to be along the lines of methodology. Storey (1991, p. 177) concludes:

> The broad consensus is that time series analyses point to unemployment being, ceteris paribus, positively associated with indices of new firm formation, whereas cross-sectional, or pooled cross-sectional studies appear to indicate the reverse. Attempts to reconcile these differences have not been wholly successful. They may reflect possible specification errors in the estimating equations, since none include all the independent variables, which have been shown to be significant in the existing literature. In particular we suggest that more attention is given to the issue of taxation, savings and state benefits than has been the case in the past.

In the European context, Foti and Vivarelli (1994) analyze self-employment data from Italy and find that unemployment has a positive impact on entry into self-employment. Ritsila and Tervo (2002) use panel data models and microlevel data at the level of the individual to link three different levels of unemployment—the country, the region, and the individual—to the decision to start a new firm in Finland between 1987 and 1995. Their results suggest the existence of a positive and nonlinear effect of personal unemployment on the likelihood of an individual to become an entrepreneur. However, at the national level, the relationship is reversed—low unemployment and high levels of macroeconomic growth increase the likelihood of starting a new firm. The evidence linking regional unemployment to the likelihood of starting a new firm is ambiguous.

DeWit and van Winden (1989) analyze panel data of individuals making a decision between employment and self-employment in the Netherlands. Their main findings suggest that the probability of self-employment is positively influenced on the earnings differential, between self-employed and wages from employment, by intelligence, measured through an IQ test at the age of 12, and by self-employment of the father.

A series of studies (Klandt, 1984, 1996; Boegenhold, 1985; Kulicke, 1987) identified fundamental characteristics possessed by the typical German entrepreneur who starts a new firm (*Gründer*). These studies consistently showed that the startup decision was based on these entrepreneurial characteristics. According to these studies, the characteristics of German entrepreneurs vary considerably from those of their fellow countrymen who choose to remain employed by firms or by the government. Among the most prominent entrepreneurial characteristics is independence. Entrepreneurs generally place a higher value on independence in their career than people who do not start new firms. Similarly, responsibility and leadership rank more highly among entrepreneurs than among the general population.

Using data from the United Kingdom, Westhead and Birley (1995) find that owner-manager characteristics at startup, including human capital factors, do not have much influence on the employment growth of the firm.

A study by the ADT (1998) found that the number of spin-offs from research institutes has increased dramatically in Germany, from 30 in 1990 to 167 in 1997. The study classifies scientific workers at the main German scientific research institutes as either "potential entrepreneur" or not. Potential entrepreneurs working at scientific research institutes have considerably different work values than their colleagues who are not classified as entrepreneurial. Potential entrepreneurs place a greater value on being responsible for their own future, having a position of responsibility, having less hierarchical organizations, and having greater independence than those scientific workers with no entrepreneurial interest. On the other hand, they place less importance on a secure income and a secure pension than those with no entrepreneurial potential.

Colombo and Delmastro (2001) examine the characteristics of high-tech entrepreneurs in Italy. In particular, they identify differences in the characteristics found between the Internet sector and other ICT industries. Their findings suggest that entrepreneurs who started firms in Internet-based businesses are younger than their counterparts in other ICT industries.

Klofsten and Jones-Evans (2000) analyze academic entrepreneurship, or the process by which professors and university researchers start and develop technology-based firms, in the European context. They find that personal characteristics such as gender, age, previous entrepreneurial experience, work experience, and the university environment all contribute to academic entrepreneurial activities in Sweden and Ireland. This view of entrepreneurship corresponds to that in a different scholarly tradition— that of management research—provided by Gartner and Carter (2003, p. 195): "Entrepreneurial behavior involves the activities of individuals who are associated with creating new organizations rather than the activities of individuals who are involved with maintaining or changing the operations of on-going established organizations."

The fields of management and psychology provide insights into the decision process leading individuals to establish a new firm. This research trajectory focuses on the emergence and evolution of entrepreneurial cognition. Stevenson and Jarillo (1990) assume that entrepreneurship is an orientation toward opportunity recognition. Central to this research agenda are these questions: How do entrepreneurs perceive opportunities? How does one distinguish between a credible opportunity and an illusion? Kruger (2003) examines the nature of entrepreneurial thinking and the cognitive process associated with opportunity identification and the decision to undertake entrepreneurial action to establish a new firm. Thus, a perceived opportunity and intent to pursue that opportunity are the necessary and sufficient conditions for entrepreneurial activity. The perception of an opportunity is shaped by a sense of the anticipated rewards accruing from and the costs of becoming an entrepreneur. Some of the research focuses on the role of personal attitudes and characteristics, such as self-efficacy (an individual's sense of competence), collective efficacy, and social norms. Shane (2000) identified how prior experience and the ability to apply specific skills influence the perception of future opportunities. The concept of an entrepreneurial decision resulting from the cognitive processes of opportunity recognition and ensuing action is introduced by Shane and Venkataraman (2001) and Shane and Eckhardt (2003). They suggest that an equilibrium view of entrepreneurship stems from the assumption of perfect information. In contrast, imperfect information implies divergent perception of opportunities across people. The sources of heterogeneity across individuals include different access to information, different cognitive abilities, psychological differences, and differences in access to financial and social capital.

One of the best data sources available to analyze the cognitive process triggering the entrepreneurial decision is provided by the Panel Study of Entrepreneurial Dynamics (PSED), a longitudinal survey study of 830 individuals identified while they were in the process of starting a new business. The unique feature of the database is that it provides information on how the entrepreneurial opportunity and action were conceived and operationalized (Gartner and Carter, 2003). Kim, Aldrich, and Keister (2003) use the PSED to test the theory that access to resources, in the form of financial resources such as household income and wealth, and human capital, in the form of education, prior work experience, entrepreneurial experience, and influence from family and friends, affect the decision to become an entrepreneur.

Kim et al. (2003) found that the external environment has a strong influence on the entrepreneurial decision. The greatest focus of research has been on the influence of networks on the cognitive process involving entrepreneurship. Thornton and Flynn (2003) argue that geographic proximity leads to networking, which creates opportunities and hones the capacity to recognize and act on those opportunities. They suggest that networks in which trust is fostered facilitate the transmission of tacit knowledge.

Research has considered the formation and the impact of networks on entrepreneurship. In comparing Route 128 around Boston with Silicon Valley, Saxenian (1994) documented how entrepreneurial advantages are based on differences in network structures and social capital. Hoang and Antoncic (2003) characterize research as systematically focusing on network content, governance, and structure. Thus, considerable evidence and theory suggest that external linkages and influences will shape an individual's entrepreneurial decision.

Accordingly, there is a solid research tradition focusing on the decision confronting individuals to start a firm. Theory and empirical evidence provide compelling reasons to conclude that characteristics specific to the individual help shape the cognitive processes guiding the entrepreneurial decision, which is characterized by the model of income or entrepreneurial choice (Parker, 2004).

3.3 Knowledge Spillovers as Entrepreneurial Opportunities

While much has been made about the key role played by the recognition of opportunities in the cognitive process underlying the decision to become an entrepreneur, relatively little has been written about the actual source of such entrepreneurial opportunities. The Knowledge Spillover Theory of Entrepreneurship identifies one source of entrepreneurial opportunities: new knowledge and ideas. In particular, this theory posits that new knowledge and ideas created in one context, such as a research laboratory in a large corporation or a university, but left uncommercialized or not vigorously pursued by the source, generates entrepreneurial opportunities. Thus, in this view, one mechanism for recognizing new opportunities and actually implementing them by starting a new firm involves knowledge spillovers. This implies that the source of knowledge and ideas, and the organization actually making (at least some of) the investments to produce these, is not the same as the organization actually attempting to commercialize and appropriate the value of that knowledge—the new firm. If the use of that knowledge by the entrepreneur does not involve full payment to the firm making the investment that originally produced that knowledge, such as a license or royalty, then the entrepreneurial act of starting a new firm serves as a mechanism for knowledge spillovers.

While entrepreneurship theory revolves around opportunities, in fact such entrepreneurial opportunities are assumed as exogenous to the individual. In contrast, a very different literature suggests that opportunities are endogenous. In the model of the knowledge production function, introduced by Griliches (1979), innovation is the result of purposeful firm-specific investments in knowledge inputs. The unit of analysis in this literature is the firm. Innovative opportunities are generated through investing resources in R&D and other types of knowledge, such as human capital.

Thus, the firm is exogenous while the opportunity is created endogenously. An important implication is that the opportunity recognition and exploitation take place within the same organizational unit creating those opportunities—the firm. Just as the firm serves as the organizational unit generating the opportunities, that same firm appropriates the returns to those purposeful knowledge investments through innovative activity.

The evidence from systematic empirical testing of the model of the knowledge production function contradicted the assumption of singularity between the organization creating the opportunities and the organization exploiting the opportunities. In particular, the empirical evidence pointed to a much more vigorous contribution to small and new-firm innovative activity than would have been warranted from their rather limited investments in new knowledge, as measured by R&D and human capital (Acs and Audretsch, 1988, 1990).

The discrepancy in organizational context between the organization creating opportunities and those exploiting the opportunities that seemingly contradicted Griliches's model of the firm knowledge production function was resolved by Audretsch (1995), who introduced the Knowledge Spillover Theory of Entrepreneurship. Audretsch (1995, pp. 179–180) affirmed the following:

> The findings challenge an assumption implicit to the knowledge production function—that firms exist exogenously and then endogenously seek out and apply knowledge inputs to generate innovative output.... It is the knowledge in the possession of economic agents that is exogenous, and in an effort to appropriate the returns from that knowledge, the spillover of knowledge from its producing entity involves endogenously creating a new firm.

The Knowledge Spillover Theory of Entrepreneurship suggests that knowledge spillovers serve as the source of knowledge creating the entrepreneurial opportunities for small and new firms: "How are these small and frequently new firms able to generate innovative output when undertaking a generally negligible amount of investment into knowledge-generating inputs, such as R&D? One answer is apparently through exploiting knowledge created by expenditures on research in universities and on R&D in large corporations" (p. 179).

The empirical evidence supporting the Knowledge Spillover Theory of Entrepreneurship is provided from analyzing variations in startup rates across different industries reflecting different underlying knowledge contexts. In particular, those industries with a greater investment in new knowledge exhibited higher startup rates, whereas those industries with less investment in new knowledge exhibited lower startup rates. These results have been interpreted as evidence in favor of startups as a conduit of knowledge spillovers (Audretsch, 1995; Caves, 1998).

Thus, compelling evidence was provided suggesting that entrepreneurship is an endogenous response to opportunities created but not exploited by the incumbent firms. This implies an organizational dimension involving the mechanism transmitting knowledge spillovers—the startup of a new firm. In addition, Jaffe (1989), Audretsch and Feldman (1996), and Audretsch and Stephan (1996) provide evidence concerning the spatial dimension of knowledge spillovers. Their findings suggest that knowledge spillovers are geographically bounded and localized within spatial proximity to the knowledge source. However, none of these studies identified the actual mechanisms transmitting knowledge spillovers; rather, the spillovers were implicitly assumed to automatically exist but only within a geographically bounded spatial area.

Why should entrepreneurship play an important role in the spillover of new knowledge and ideas? And why should new knowledge play an important role in creating entrepreneurial opportunities? In the Romer model of endogenous growth, new technological knowledge is assumed to automatically spill over; that is, investment in new technological knowledge is automatically accessed by third-party firms and economic agents. The assumption that knowledge automatically spills over is, of course, consistent with the important insight by Arrow (1962) that knowledge differs from the traditional factors of production—physical capital and (unskilled) labor—in that it is nonexcludable, nonrivalrous, or nonexhaustible. When the firm or economic agent uses the knowledge, it is neither exhausted nor can it be, in the absence of legal protection, precluded from being used by third-party firms or other economic agents. Thus, in the spirit of the Romer model, drawing on the earlier insights about knowledge from Arrow, a large and vigorous literature has emerged obsessed with the links between intellectual property protection and the incentives for firms to invest in the creation of new knowledge through R&D and investments in human capital.

However, the preoccupation with the nonexcludability and nonexhaustibility of knowledge, first identified by Arrow and later carried forward and assumed in the Romer model, neglects another key insight from the original Arrow (1962) article. Arrow identified another dimension by which knowledge differs from the traditional factors of production. This other dimension involves the greater degree of uncertainty, higher extent of asymmetries, and greater cost of transacting new ideas. The expected value of any new idea is highly uncertain and, as Arrow pointed out, has a much greater variance than is associated with the deployment of traditional factors of production. After all, there is relative certainty about what a standard piece of capital equipment can do, or what an (unskilled) worker can contribute to a mass-production assembly line. In contrast, Arrow emphasized that, in innovation, there is uncertainty about whether the new product can be produced, how it will be produced, and whether sufficient demand for that new product will actually materialize.

In addition, new ideas are typically associated with considerable asymmetries. In order to evaluate a proposed new idea concerning, for example, a new biotechnology product, a decision maker might need not only a doctorate in biotechnology but also a specialization in the specific scientific area. Such divergences in education, background, and experience can result in a divergence in expectations about the expected value or the variance of the outcomes so that the recognition and evaluation and therefore the motivation of pursuing these opportunities differ across economic agents and decision-making hierarchies. Such divergences in the valuation of new ideas will increase if the new idea is not consistent with the core competence and technological trajectory of the incumbent firm.

Thus, because of the conditions inherent in knowledge—high uncertainty, asymmetries, and transactions costs—decision-making hierarchies can decide not to pursue and not to commercialize new ideas that individual economic agents, or groups or teams of economic agents, think are potentially valuable. The basic conditions characterizing new knowledge, combined with a broad spectrum of institutions, rules, and regulations, impose what Acs et al. (2004) call the *knowledge filter*, or the gap between new knowledge and what Arrow (1962) referred to as economic knowledge or commercialized knowledge. The greater the knowledge filter, the more pronounced the gap between new knowledge and newly commercialized knowledge.

The knowledge filter is a consequence of the basic conditions inherent in new knowledge, but it is also what creates the opportunity for entrepreneurship in the Knowledge Spillover Theory of Entrepreneurship. According to this theory, opportunities for entrepreneurship are generated by the knowledge filter. The less permeable the knowledge filter, the greater the differences in the valuation of new ideas across economic agents and the decision-making hierarchies of incumbent firms. Entrepreneurial opportunities are generated not just by investments in new knowledge and ideas but also in the propensity for only a distinct subset of those opportunities to be pursued by incumbent firms.

Thus, the Knowledge Spillover Theory of Entrepreneurship shifts the fundamental decision-making unit of observation in the model of the knowledge production function away from exogenously assumed firms to individuals, such as scientists, engineers, or other knowledge workers—agents with endowments of new economic knowledge. When the lens is shifted away from the firm to the individual as the relevant unit of observation, the appropriability issue remains, but the question becomes, How can economic agents with a given endowment of new knowledge best appropriate the returns from that knowledge? If the scientist or engineer can pursue the new idea within the organizational structure of the firm developing the knowledge and appropriate roughly the expected value of that knowledge, he or she has no reason to leave the firm. On the other hand, if they value the ideas more than the decision-making bureaucracy of the incumbent firm does, they may choose to start a new firm to appropriate the value of that knowledge.

In the Knowledge Spillover Theory of Entrepreneurship, the knowledge production function is actually inverted. The knowledge is exogenous and embodied in a worker. The firm is created endogenously through an effort to appropriate the value of one's knowledge through innovative activity. Typically, an employee from an established large corporation, often a scientist or engineer working in a research laboratory, will have an idea for an invention and ultimately for an innovation. Accompanying this potential innovation is an expected net return from the new product. The inventor would expect to be compensated for his or her potential innovation accordingly. If the company has a different, presumably lower, valuation of the potential innovation, managers may decide not to pursue its development or that it merits a lower level of compensation than that expected by the employee.

In either case, the employee will weigh the alternative of starting his or her own firm. If the gap in the expected return accruing from the potential innovation between the inventor and the corporate decision maker is sufficiently large, and if the cost of starting a new firm is sufficiently low, the employee may decide to leave the large corporation and establish a new enterprise. Since the knowledge was generated in the established corporation, the new startup is considered to be a spin-off from the existing firm. Such startups typically do not have direct access to a large R&D laboratory. Rather, the entrepreneurial opportunity emanates from the knowledge and experience accrued from the R&D laboratories where the employees worked. Thus, the Knowledge Spillover Theory of Entrepreneurship is actually a theory of endogenous entrepreneurship, where entrepreneurship is an endogenous response to opportunities created by investments in new knowledge that are not commercialized because of the knowledge filter.

3.4 Endogenous Entrepreneurship

3.4.1 Entrepreneurship as an Endogenous Response to Knowledge Spillover Opportunities

The Knowledge Spillover Theory of Entrepreneurship challenges two of the fundamental assumptions implicitly driving the results of the endogenous growth models. The first is that knowledge is automatically equated with economic knowledge. In fact, as Arrow (1962) emphasized, knowledge is inherently different from the traditional factors of production, resulting in a gap between knowledge and what he called economic knowledge, or commercialized knowledge.

The second involves the assumed spillover of knowledge. The existence of the factor of knowledge is equated with its automatic spillover, yielding endogenous growth. In the Knowledge Spillover Theory of Entrepreneurship, the knowledge filter imposes a gap between new knowledge and new economic knowledge and results in a lower level of knowledge spillovers.

Thus, as a result of the knowledge filter, entrepreneurship becomes central to generating economic growth by serving as a conduit for knowledge spillovers. The process involved in recognizing new opportunities emanating from investments in knowledge and new ideas, and attempting to commercialize those new ideas through the process of starting a new firm, is the mechanism by which some knowledge spillovers occur. In the counterfactual situation, that is, in the absence of such entrepreneurship, the new ideas would not be pursued, and that part of the new knowledge would not be commercialized. Thus, entrepreneurs serve an important mechanism in the process of economic growth. An entrepreneur is an agent of change, who recognizes an opportunity, in this case generated by the creation of knowledge not adequately pursued (in the view of the entrepreneur) by incumbent organizations, and ultimately chooses to act on that opportunity by starting a new firm.

As we argued earlier, recognition of what Arrow (1962) called the nonexcludability of knowledge inherent in spillovers has led to a focus on issues concerning the appropriability of such investments in knowledge and the need for the protection of intellectual property. However, as investments in new knowledge increase, entrepreneurial opportunities will also increase. A vigorous literature has already shown that knowledge spillovers are greater in the presence of knowledge investments. Just as Jaffe (1989) and Audretsch and Feldman (1996) show, those regions with higher knowledge investments experience higher level of knowledge spillovers, and those regions with lower knowledge investments experience a lower level of knowledge spillovers, since there is less knowledge to be spilled over.

The Knowledge Spillover Theory of Entrepreneurship analogously suggests that, *ceteris paribus*, entrepreneurial activity will tend to be greater in contexts where investments in new knowledge are relatively high, since the new firm will be started from knowledge that has spilled over from the source producing that new knowledge. A paucity of new ideas in an impoverished knowledge context will generate only limited entrepreneurial opportunities. In contrast, in a high knowledge context, new ideas will generate entrepreneurial opportunities by exploiting (potential) spillovers of that knowledge. Thus, the knowledge spillover view of entrepreneurship predicts that entrepreneurial activity will result from investments in new knowledge.

3.4.2 A Model

The starting point for models of economic growth in the Solow tradition is that the rate of technical change, the rate with which new technological knowledge is created, is exogenous. This view has been challenged by the endogenous growth theory (Romer, 1986, 1990; Lucas, 1988). Consider the Romer (1990) growth model. The production function is expressed as

$$Y = K^{\alpha}(AL_Y)^{(1-\alpha)}, \tag{3.1}$$

where Y represents economic output, K is the stock of capital, L_Y is the labor force in the production of Y, and A is the stock of knowledge capital. The capital accumulation function is standard from the Solow (1956) model:

$$\dot{K} = s_K Y - \Delta K, \tag{3.2}$$

where s_K is the saving rate and Δ is the depreciation rate of capital. The R&D sector is modeled as

$$\dot{A} = \bar{\delta} L_A, \tag{3.3}$$

where $\bar{\delta}$ is the *discovery rate* of new innovations with

$$\bar{\delta} = \delta L_A^{1-\lambda} A^{\phi}. \tag{3.4}$$

L_A denotes the amount of labor active in the generation of new knowledge (such as R&D personnel), λ denotes returns to scale in R&D, and ϕ is a parameter that expresses the intensity of *knowledge spillovers*. Inserting (3.4) into (3.3), we obtain the rate of creation of new knowledge (the rate of endogenous technical change):

$$\dot{A} = \delta L_A^{\lambda} A^{\phi}. \tag{3.5}$$

In the Romer, Lucas, and Jones models, knowledge automatically spills over and is commercialized, reflecting the Arrow observation about the nonexcludability and nonexhaustive properties of new knowledge. Thus, investments in R&D and human capital automatically affect output in a multiplicative manner because of their external properties, suggesting that new knowledge, A, is tantamount to commercialized economic knowledge A_c, that is, $A = A_c$.

As we discussed earlier, the emphasis on, or rather assumption about, the nonexcludability property is better suited for information than knowledge. Information has, by its definition, a very low level of uncertainty, and its value is not greatly influenced or shaped by asymmetries across economic agents possessing that information. Thus, information can be characterized as being nonexcludable and nonexhaustive. In contrast, as Arrow points out, there is a gap between new knowledge and what actually becomes commercialized, or new economic knowledge, $A - A_c > 0$. In fact, the knowledge filter is defined as the gap existing between investments in knowledge and the commercialization of knowledge, or economic knowledge. We denote the knowledge filter as θ, hence

$$\theta = A_c/A, \quad \text{with} \quad 0 \leq A_c \leq A \quad \text{hence} \quad \theta \in [0, 1], \qquad (3.6)$$

hence θ denotes the *permeability* of the knowledge filter. It is the existence of the knowledge filter, or knowledge not commercialized by incumbent enterprises, that generates the entrepreneurial opportunities for commercializing knowledge spillovers. As long as the incumbent enterprises cannot exhaust all of the commercialization opportunities arising from their investments in new knowledge, opportunities will be generated for potential entrepreneurs to commercialize that knowledge by starting a new firm. Thus, the actual level of new technological knowledge used by incumbent firms is

$$\dot{A}_c = \theta \cdot \delta L_A^\lambda A^\phi. \qquad (3.7)$$

Correspondingly, the remaining "untapped" part $(1 - \theta)$ is opportunities *opp* that can be taken on by new firms. We denote this part *entrepreneurial opportunities*. Thus, we have

$$\dot{A}_{opp} = (1 - \theta)\dot{A} = (1 - \theta) \cdot \delta L_A^\lambda A^\phi. \qquad (3.8)$$

The observation that knowledge conditions dictate the relative advantages in taking advantage of opportunities arising from investments in knowledge of incumbents versus small and large enterprises is not new. Nelson and Winter (1982) distinguished between two knowledge regimes. What they call the routinized technological regime reflects knowledge conditions where the large incumbent firms have the innovative advantage. In contrast, in the entrepreneurial technological regime, the knowledge conditions bestow an innovative advantage on small enterprises (Winter, 1984).

However, there are two important distinctions to emphasize. The first is the view that, in the entrepreneurial regime, the small firms exist and will commercialize the new knowledge or innovate. In the lens provided by the spillover theory of entrepreneurship, the new firm is endogenously created via entrepreneurship, or the recognition of an opportunity and pursuit by an economic agent (or team of economic agents) to appropriate the value of that knowledge. These knowledge-bearing economic agents use the organizational context of new firm creation to attempt to appropriate their endowments of knowledge.

The second distinction is that the knowledge will be commercialized, either by large or small firms. In the lens provided by the Knowledge Spillover Theory of Entrepreneurship, the knowledge filter impedes and preempts at least some of the knowledge spillover and commercialization of knowledge. Only select spillover mechanisms, such as entrepreneurship, can permeate the knowledge filter. But this is not a forgone conclusion; rather, the situation will vary across specific contexts and depends on a broad range of factors, spanning individual characteristics, institutions, culture, and laws, and is characterized by what we call in chapter 4 entrepreneurship capital. Thus, to merely explain entrepreneurship as the residual from $\dot{A}_{opp} = \dot{A} - \dot{A}_c$ assumes that all opportunities left uncommercialized will automatically result in the commercialized spillover of knowledge via entrepreneurship.

This was clearly not the case in the former Soviet Union and its Eastern European allies, just as, according to Annalee Saxenian, in *Regional Advantage* (1994), it was not the case for Silicon Valley or Route 128. That is, the capacity of each context, or Standort, to commercialize the residual investments in knowledge created by the knowledge filter through entrepreneurship is not identical. Rather, it depends on the capacity of that Standort to generate an entrepreneurial response that permeates the knowledge filter and creates a conduit for transmitting knowledge spillovers.

Both the West and the former Soviet Union invested in the creation of new knowledge. Both the West and the former Soviet Union innovated in what Nelson and Winter characterized as the routinized regime. The divergence in growth and economic performance emanated from differences in the knowledge filter and the ability to overcome that knowledge filter. Just as the West proved to have the institutional context to generate entrepreneurial spillovers and commercialize a far greater level of knowledge investments, so, too, as Saxenian documents, the organizational structure and social capital of Silicon Valley provided a more fertile context than Route 128 did for knowledge spillovers through entrepreneurship. Both Silicon Valley and Route 128 had the requisite knowledge inputs to generate innovative output. Saxenian's main conclusion is that the differences between the two Standorts that resulted in a greater degree of knowledge spillovers and commercialization in Silicon Valley than in Route 128 were institutional. Thus, just as the knowledge filter should not be assumed to be impermeable, the capacity of a Standort to generate knowledge spillovers via entrepreneurship to permeate the knowledge filter should also not be assumed to be automatic. Rather, entrepreneurship, whether it emanates from opportunities from knowledge spillovers or from other sources, is the result of a cognitive process made by an individual within the institutional context of a particular Standort.

This cognitive process of recognizing and acting on perceived opportunities, emanating from knowledge spillovers as well as other sources, E, is characterized by the model of occupational (or entrepreneurial) choice, where E reflects the decision to become an entrepreneur, π^* is the profit expected from starting a new firm, and w is the anticipated wage that would be earned from employment in an incumbent enterprise.

$$E = f(\pi^* - w). \tag{3.9}$$

But what exactly are the sources of these entrepreneurial opportunities based on expected profits accruing from entrepreneurship? As we said, most of the theoretical and empirical focus has been on characteristics of the individual, such as attitudes towards risk and access to financial capital and social capital. Thus, the entrepreneurial opportunities are created by variation in individual characteristics within a context held constant. Entrepreneurial opportunities are generated because individuals are heterogeneous, leading to variation in the ability of individuals to recognize opportunities and their willingness to act upon those opportunities. Thus, the focus on entrepreneurship, and why it varies across contexts, or Standorts, seemingly leads to the conclusion that individuals must differ across the different contexts.

In the view presented here, we invert this analysis. Instead of holding the context constant and asking how individuals endowed with different characteristics will behave differently, we take all of the characteristics of the individual, all of his or her various propensities, proclivities, and peculiarities, as given. We will let the context, or Standort, in which he or she finds herself vary and then ask, Holding the (characteristics of the) individual constant, how will behavior change as the context changes?

Of course, guided by the Knowledge Spillover Theory of Entrepreneurship, we know that the contextual variation of interest is knowledge. We want to know whether and how, in principle, the same individual(s) with the same attributes, characteristics, and proclivities will be influenced in terms of the cognitive process of making the entrepreneurial choice, as the knowledge context differs. In particular, some contexts are rich in knowledge, while others are impoverished in knowledge. Does the knowledge context alter the cognitive process weighing the entrepreneurial choice?

According to the Knowledge Spillover Theory of Entrepreneurship, it will. We certainly do not claim that knowledge spillovers account for all entrepreneurial opportunities, or that any of the existing explanations of entrepreneurship are any less valid. The major contextual variable that has been previously considered is growth, especially unanticipated growth. Hence, we can rewrite equation (3.9) as

$$E = f(\pi^*[g_Y, \dot{A}_{opp}, \theta] - w), \tag{3.10}$$

which states that the expected profits are based on opportunities that accrue from general economic growth, g_Y, on one hand and from potential knowledge spillovers, $\dot{A}_{opp}$, on the other. Therefore, the total amount of entrepreneurship can be decomposed into knowledge spillover entrepreneurship, which is denoted as E^*, and entrepreneurship from rather traditional sources, that is nonknowledge sources, such as growth $\bar{E}$, that is,

$$E = \bar{E} + E^*. \tag{3.11}$$

Economic growth that is anticipated by incumbent firms will be met by those firms as they invest to expand their capacity to meet expected growth opportunities. If, however, there is any type of constraint in expanding the capacity of incumbent enterprises to meet (unexpected) demand, then growth of GDP, g_Y, will generate entrepreneurial opportunities that have nothing to do with new knowledge, or

$$\bar{E} = f(\pi^*[g_Y] - w). \tag{3.12}$$

Let us distinguish this type of traditional entrepreneurship from the one based on opportunities from knowledge spillovers. As we claimed, investments in new knowledge in a given context will generate entrepreneurial opportunities. The extent of such entrepreneurial opportunities is shaped by two sources. The first is the amount of new knowledge being produced. The second is the permeability of the knowledge filter, which limits the commercialization of that new knowledge by the incumbent firms. If there were neither new knowledge nor ideas being generated, then there would be no spillover opportunities for potential entrepreneurs to consider. There might be entrepreneurship triggered by other factors, but not by knowledge opportunities. Similarly, in the absence of a knowledge filter, all opportunities for appropriating the value of that knowledge would be pursued and commercialized by incumbent firms. In this case, knowledge spillovers would be considerable, just not from entrepreneurship.

Thus, two factors shape the relative importance of knowledge spillover entrepreneurship: the amount of investment in creating new knowledge, $\dot{A}$, and the magnitude of the knowledge filter, θ. Thus, knowledge spillover entrepreneurship, E^*, is the attempt to appropriate profit opportunities accruing from the commercialization of knowledge not commercialized by the incumbent firms, or $1 - \theta$,

$$E^* = f(\pi^*[\dot{A}_{opp}, \theta] - w). \tag{3.13}$$

Equation (3.13) implicitly suggests that the only contextual influence on entrepreneurship emanating from knowledge spillovers is the extent of knowledge investments and permeability of the knowledge filter. Such a simple assumption neglects the basic conclusion from Saxenian (1994) that some contexts, such as Boston's Route 128, have institutional and social barriers to entrepreneurship, while other contexts, such as Silicon Valley, have institutions and social networks that promote entrepreneurship. The exact nature of such impediments to entrepreneurship spans a broad spectrum of financial, institutional, and individual characteristics (Acs and Audretsch, 2003). Incorporating such impediments or barriers to entrepreneurship, β, yields

$$E^* = \frac{1}{\beta} f(\pi^*[\dot{A}_{opp}, \theta] - w), \tag{3.14}$$

where β represents those institutional and individual barriers to entrepreneurship, spanning factors such as financing constraints, risk aversion, legal restrictions, bureaucratic and red tape constraints, labor market rigidities, lack of social acceptance, and so on (Lundström and Stevenson, 2005). Although we do not explicitly specify these individual entrepreneurial barriers, we duly note that they reflect a wide range of institutional and individual characteristics, which, taken together, constitute barriers to entrepreneurship. The existence of such barriers, or a greater value of β, explains why economic agents choose not to become entrepreneurs, even when endowed with knowledge that would otherwise generate a potentially profitable opportunity through entrepreneurship.

Since $E > E^*$, the total amount of entrepreneurial activity exceeds that generated by knowledge spillovers. Thus, we also restate equation (3.10):

$$E = \frac{1}{\beta} f(\pi^*[g_Y, \dot{A}_{opp}, \theta] - w). \tag{3.15}$$

Equation (3.15) and the corresponding discussion lead to the following propositions:

Entrepreneurial Opportunities Proposition: Entrepreneurship will be greater in regions with a greater amount of nonknowledge entrepreneurial opportunities, such as growth.

Barriers to Entrepreneurship Proposition: Entrepreneurship will be lower in regions burdened with barriers to entrepreneurship.

3.4.3 The Hypotheses

On the basis of the arguments given in the previous sections, we can derive a number of hypotheses concerning the determinants of entrepreneurship and its impact on economic performance. The first hypothesis to emerge from the Knowledge Spillover Theory of Entrepreneurship is the following:

Endogenous Entrepreneurship Hypothesis: Entrepreneurship will be greater in the presence of higher investments in new knowledge, ceteris paribus. Entrepreneurial activity is an endogenous response to higher investments in new knowledge, reflecting greater entrepreneurial opportunities generated by knowledge investments.

This hypothesis is consistent with the growth model. Equation (3.8) describes the generation of new opportunities. Investments in new knowledge are denoted L_A within the model. Deriving (3.8) with respect to L_A, we obtain

$$\frac{d\dot{A}_{opp}}{dL_A} = (1 - \theta) \cdot \delta \lambda L_A^{\lambda-1} A^\phi, \tag{3.16}$$

which is positive for all L_A and A^ϕ. Hence, opportunities increase with investment in new knowledge. Again, these hypotheses are consistent with the formal model given, Deriving (3.8) with respect to A^ϕ we obtain

$$\frac{d\dot{A}_{opp}}{dA^\phi} = (1 - \theta) \cdot \delta L_A^\lambda, \tag{3.17}$$

which is positive for all L_A. Hence, opportunities increase with spillovers and therefore firms will locate near the source of spillovers ceteris paribus, which suggests this hypothesis:

Economic Performance Hypothesis: Entrepreneurial activity will increase the level of economic output since entrepreneurship serves as a mechanism facilitating the spillover and commercialization of knowledge.

On the basis of the arguments given, we state production function (3.1) as

$$Y = K^\alpha (\theta_r A)^{(1-\alpha)} L_Y^{(1-\alpha)}, \tag{3.18}$$

where θ_r denotes the *realized permeability* of the knowledge filter, that is, that level that includes the part of $(1 - \theta)$ that has been taken on by startup firms. Thus, we have $\theta_r \in [0, 1-\theta]$ or $\theta \leq \theta_r \leq 1$. An increase in entrepreneurial activity increases θ_r and therefore the distance between θ and θ_r. Deriving

$$\frac{dY}{d\theta_r} = (1 - \alpha)\theta_r^{-\alpha}K^{\alpha}A^{(1-\alpha)}L_Y^{(1-\alpha)} = \frac{1 - \alpha}{\theta_r}Y, \qquad (3.19)$$

which is greater than 0 for all Y, thus, economic output, or GDP, increases with entrepreneurial activity.

The third hypothesis emerging from the Knowledge Spillover Theory of Entrepreneurship concerns the location of the entrepreneurial activity. Access to knowledge spillovers requires spatial proximity. Though Jaffe (1989) and Audretsch and Feldman (1996) showed that spatial proximity is a prerequisite to accessing such knowledge spillovers, they provided no insight about the actual mechanism transmitting such knowledge spillovers. As for the Romer, Lucas, and Jones models, the Jaffe (1989) and Audretsch and Feldman (1999) studies assume that investment in new knowledge automatically generates knowledge spillovers. The only additional insight involves the spatial dimension—knowledge spills over but these spillovers are spatially bounded. Since we have identified just one such mechanism by which knowledge spillovers are transmitted—the startup of a new firm—it follows that knowledge spillover entrepreneurship is also spatially bounded in that local access is required to access the knowledge facilitating the entrepreneurial startup:

> *Localization Hypothesis*: Knowledge spillover entrepreneurship will tend to be spatially located within close geographic proximity to the source of knowledge actually producing that knowledge.

One of the important findings of Glaeser et al. (1992) and Feldman and Audretsch (1999) is that economic performance is improved by knowledge spillovers. However, their findings, as well as corroborative results from a plethora of studies, focused on a spatial unit of observation, such as cities, regions, and states. For example, Glaeser et al. (1992) found compelling empirical evidence suggesting that a greater degree of knowledge spillover leads to greater economic growth rates of cities. If higher knowledge spillovers bestow higher growth rates for cities, this relationship should also hold for the unit of observation of the knowledge firm. The performance of entrepreneurial firms accessing knowledge spillovers should exhibit a superior performance:

> *Entrepreneurial Performance Hypothesis*: Opportunities for knowledge-based entrepreneurship, and therefore performance of knowledge-based startups, is superior when they are able to access knowledge spillovers through geographic proximity to knowledge sources, such as universities, when compared to their counterparts without a close geographic proximity to a knowledge source.

Knowledge spillovers may be necessary but not sufficient for firms to access and absorb external knowledge. As Cohen and Levinthal (1989) pointed out, firms may also need to invest in absorptive capacity. Since entrepreneurial startups are usually constrained by size, such absorptive capacity, at least measured in absolute terms, is limited. Thus,

Entrepreneurial Access Hypothesis: Knowledge-based entrepreneurial firms will strategically adjust the composition of their boards and managers toward higher levels of knowledge and human capital so that they can contribute to the access and absorption of external knowledge spillovers.

Entrepreneurial firms may be able to access and even absorb external knowledge spillovers, but they will still typically need an external source of finance as well. Thus,

Entrepreneurial Finance Hypothesis: Knowledge-based entrepreneurial firms will tend to be financed from equity-based sources, such as venture capital, and less typically from traditional debt-based sources, such as banks.

3.5 Linking Endogenous Entrepreneurship to Growth

The Knowledge Spillover Theory of Entrepreneurship, which focuses on how new knowledge can influence the cognitive decision-making process inherent in the entrepreneurial decision and thus links entrepreneurship and economic growth, is consistent with theories of industry evolution (Jovanovic, 1982; Lambson, 1991; Hopenhayn, 1992; Audretsch, 1995; Ericson and Pakes, 1995; Klepper, 1996). Whereas traditional theories suggest that small firms will slow economic growth by imposing a drag on productive efficiency, these evolutionary theories suggest exactly the opposite—that entrepreneurship will stimulate and generate growth. The reason for these theoretical discrepancies lies in the context of the underlying theory. In the traditional theory, new knowledge does not have a role; rather, static efficiency, determined largely by the ability to exhaust scale economies, dictates growth. In contrast, the evolutionary models are dynamic and emphasize the role that knowledge plays. Because knowledge is inherently uncertain, asymmetric, and associated with high costs of transactions, divergences emerge concerning the expected value of new ideas. Economic agents therefore have an incentive to leave an incumbent firm and start a new firm in an attempt to commercialize the perceived value of their knowledge. Entrepreneurship is the vehicle by which (the most radical) ideas are sometimes implemented and commercialized.

A distinguishing feature of these evolutionary theories is the focus on change as a central phenomenon. Innovative activity, one of the central manifestations of change, is at the heart of much of this work. Entry, growth, survival, and the way firms and entire industries change over time are linked to innovation. The dynamic performance of regions and even entire economies, or the Standort, is linked to the efficacy of transforming investments in new knowledge into innovative activity.

Why are new firms started? The traditional, equilibrium-based view is that new firms in an industry, whether they are startups or firms diversifying from other industries, enter when incumbent firms in the industry earn supranormal profits. By expanding industry supply, entry depresses price and restores profits to their long-run equilibrium level. Thus, in equilibrium-based theories, entry serves as a mechanism to discipline incumbent firms. In contrast, the new theories of industry evolution develop and evaluate alternative characterizations of entrepreneurship based on innovation and costs of firm growth. These new evolutionary theories correspond to the disequilibrating theory of entrepreneurship proposed by Shane and Eckhardt (2003).

For example, Audretsch (1995) analyzes the factors that influence the rate of new firm startups. He finds that such startups are more likely in industries where small firms account for a greater percentage of the industry's innovations. This suggests that firms are created to capitalize on distinctive knowledge about innovation that originates from sources outside of industry leaders. This initial condition of uncertainty, even greater uncertainty vis-à-vis incumbent enterprises in the industry, is captured in the theory of firm selection and industry evolution proposed by Jovanovic (1982). Jovanovic presents a model in which the new firms, or *entrepreneurs*, face costs that are not only random but also different across firms. A central feature of the model is that a new firm does not know what its cost function is, that is, its relative efficiency, but rather discovers it through the process of learning from its actual postentry performance. In particular, Jovanovic assumes that entrepreneurs are unsure about their ability to manage a new-firm startup and therefore about their prospects for success. Although entrepreneurs may launch a new firm based on a vague sense of expected postentry performance, they only discover their true ability—in terms of managerial competence and of having based the firm on an idea that is viable on the market—once their business is established. Those entrepreneurs who discover that their ability exceeds their expectations expand the scale of their business, whereas those discovering that their postentry performance is less than commensurate with their expectations will contact the scale of output and possibly exit from the industry. Thus, Jovanovic's model is a theory of *noisy selection*, where efficient firms grow and survive and inefficient firms decline and fail. The links between entrepreneurship on the one hand and growth and survival on the other have been found across a number of social science disciplines, including economics, sociology, and regional studies.

Survey articles by Geroski (1995), Sutton (1997), and Caves (1998) summarize the findings from a plethora of empirical studies examining the relationship between firm size and growth within North America. The early studies were undertaken using data from the United States. These studies (Mansfield, 1962; Hall, 1987; Dunne, Roberts, and Samuelson, 1989; Audretsch, 1991) established that the likelihood of a new entrant surviving is quite low and also that the likelihood of survival is positively related to firm size and age. A stylized result emerging from this literature is that, when a broad spectrum of firm sizes is included in samples of U.S. enterprises, smaller firms exhibit systematically higher growth rates than their larger counterparts (Geroski, 1995). The growth advantage of small and new firms vis-à-vis large enterprises has been shown to be even greater in high-technology industries (Audretsch, 1995).

These stylized results between firm size and age on the one hand and growth and survival on the other hand were subsequently confirmed for a number of European countries. A wave of studies has confirmed these findings for different European countries, including Portugal (Mata, 1994; Mata, Portugal, and Guimaraes, 1995), Germany (Wagner, 1994; Tveteras and Eide, (2000), Norway (Klette and Mathiassen, 1996), and Italy (Audretsch, Santarelli, and Vivarelli, 1999).

However, the links between firm size and growth as well as firm age and growth are somewhat more ambiguous within the European context. Whereas some studies have found no systematic relationship between firm size and growth (Wagner, 1992), some studies have found a positive relationship (Bürgel et al., 1999). Still, most studies have found results in the European context that are strikingly similar to those in the United States (Harhoff, Stahl, and Woywode, 1998; Almus and Nerlinger, 2000). From the evidence in a large, comprehensive panel data set from the ZEW Startup Panel for Western Germany, Gibrat's Law is rejected for the group of young firms belonging to technology-intensive branches as well as those operating in nontechnology-intensive branches (Almus and Nerlinger, 2000), indicating that smaller enterprises grow faster than their larger counterparts.

Heshmati (2001) examined the relationship between size, age, and growth for a large sample of small firms in Sweden documented from 1993 through 1998. The results indicate that, in Sweden, firm size and age are negatively related to employment growth, which is consistent with the findings for the United States. However, in terms of sales growth, a positive relationship emerges, suggesting that, at least for this period, larger firms generated more growth in sales than in employment.

Harhoff and Stahl (1995) use a database of 11,000 firms in manufacturing, construction, trade, finance, and services to examine how the postentry performance of German firms varies across different sectors, in terms of the likelihood of survival and growth. They found evidence that the likelihood of survival is positively related to firm size. In addition, firm growth is negatively related to firm size. Also, the likelihood of survival and growth rates differed systematically across different sectors of the economy. The results of Harhoff and Stahl are not consistent with those found in earlier studies, according to the survey by Wagner (1992). After reviewing the most important studies, Wagner concludes that studies using German data tend to show that firm size and firm growth are uncorrelated.

Wagner (1995 and 2001) analyzed the performance of small and large firms prior to exit. He used a longitudinal database identifying the performance of cohorts of firms exiting in 1990, 1991, and 1992. One striking result was that more than half of the exiting firms (between 53 percent and 61 percent) were founded prior to 1979, making them over 11 years old. He also found that young firms, classified as younger than five years old, accounted for about a quarter of all exits, and three quarters of exiting businesses were from middle-aged firms. At the same time, he found that the likelihood of survival increases with firm size.

Almus and Nerlinger (2000) use the ZEW Startup Panel to examine how the postentry performance of new firms varies across sectors. In particular, they find that new-firm growth tends to be greater in very high-tech industries than in high-tech industries and other manufacturing industries. This mirrors the results found in North America. Using the same database, Almus and Nerlinger (1998) study why entrepreneurial growth varies between new technology-based firms (NTBFs) and noninnovative startups. They perform multivariate analyses on the impact of characteristics specific to the entrepreneur, as well as the industry, on subsequent firm growth. The authors find that the growth of new-firm startups is shaped by characteristics specific to the founder, the firm, and the industry environment. For example, large and mature firms have lower growth rates than do small and young firms, both innovative and noninnovative. The greater the degree of human capital of the founder, the greater the growth rate, especially in innovative industries.

Using firm-level data from Italy, Audretsch, Santarelli, and Vivarelli (1999) find that growth rates are negatively related to firm size. In addition, they find that the likelihood of survival is greater in the startup year than in the second year but subsequently increases. Similarly, Tveteras and Eide (2000) provide evidence for Norwegian manufacturing using the estimation technique of a semi-proportional Cox Model showing that the probability of survival is lower for smaller and younger establishments. Brüderl and Preisendörfer (1998) examine a database consisting of 1,700 new-firm startups in Germany and find that the subsequent performance, measured in terms of likelihood of survival and growth, is greater for those entrepreneurs that (1) participate in a network with other entrepreneurs, (2) receive active help from their spouse, and (3) receive emotional support from their spouse. In addition, they find that entrepreneurial success is positively influenced by the entrepreneur's ethnicity, educational background, type of work experience, and entrepreneurial experience. Their most striking finding is that entrepreneurial success is highest within the context of a network with other entrepreneurs.

Scarpetta et al. (2002) provide evidence, based on a panel data set of firm-level observations, for a lower degree of firm turbulence, or "churning," in Europe than in the United States. European SMEs have larger startup size, a higher level of labor productivity, and a lower level of employment growth subsequent to entry.

Thus, while there is somewhat more ambiguity in the studies linking growth and survival to firm size and growth, the results for Europe generally mirror the stylized results within North America:

1. Growth rates are higher for smaller enterprises;
2. Growth rates are higher for younger enterprises;
3. Growth rates are even higher for small and young enterprises in knowledge-intensive industries;
4. The likelihood of survival is lower for smaller enterprises;
5. The likelihood of survival is lower for younger enterprises; and
6. The likelihood of survival is even lower for small and young enterprises in knowledge-intensive industries.

What emerges from the new evolutionary theories and corroborative empirical evidence on the role of small entrepreneurial firms is that firm demography is a turbulent process, with new firms entering the industry while existing firms exit the industry. The evolutionary view of entrepreneurship is that new firms typically start at a very small scale of output. They are motivated by the desire to appropriate the expected value of new economic knowledge, but, depending on the extent of scale economies in the industry, the firm may not be able to remain viable indefinitely at its startup size. Rather, if scale economies are anything other than negligible, the new firm must grow to survive. The temporary survival of new firms is presumably supported through the deployment of a strategy of compensating factor differentials that enables the firm to discover whether it has a viable product (Audretsch et al., 2002).

The empirical evidence described supports such an evolutionary view of the role of new firms in manufacturing, because the postentry growth of firms that survive tends to be spurred by the extent to which there is a gap between the minimum efficient scale (MES) level of output and the size of the firm. However, the likelihood of any particular new firm surviving tends to decrease as this gap increases. Such new suboptimal scale firms are apparently engaged in the selection process. Only those firms offering a viable product that can be produced efficiently will grow and ultimately approach or attain the MES level of output. The remainder will stagnate, and, depending on the severity of the other selection mechanism—the extent of scale economies—may ultimately be forced to exit out of the industry. By serving as agents of change, entrepreneurial firms provide an essential source of new ideas and experimentation that otherwise would remain untapped in the economy. The impact of entrepreneurship is therefore manifested by growth at the levels of the firm, the region, and even the nation.

But is this dynamic horizontal, in that the bulk of firms exiting had entered relatively recently, or vertical, in that a significant share of the exiting firms had been established incumbents displaced by younger firms? In trying to answer this question, Audretsch (1995) proposed two different models of the evolutionary process. Some contexts can be characterized best within the model of the conical revolving door, wherein new businesses are started but with a high propensity to subsequently exit the market. Other contexts may be better characterized with the metaphor of the forest, wherein incumbent establishments are displaced by new entrants. Which view is more applicable apparently depends on three major factors: the underlying technological conditions, scale economies, and demand. Where scale economies play an important role, the model of the revolving door seems more applicable. Although the startup and entry of new businesses is apparently not deterred by the presence of high-scale economies, a process of firm selection analogous to a revolving door ensures that only those establishments successful enough to grow will survive beyond a few years. Thus, the bulk of new startups that are not so successful ultimately exit within a few years. By serving as agents of change, new firms provide an essential conduit of knowledge spillovers commercializing new ideas through experimentation that otherwise would remain untapped in the economy.

The Knowledge Spillover Theory of Entrepreneurship is depicted in figure 3.1. The production of new knowledge and ideas in the context of an incumbent organization, such as the research and development lab of a large corporation or the research laboratory at a university, creates knowledge embodied in an individual worker, or team of workers. If divergences in the expected value or outcome from this new knowledge lead to the decision by the incumbent firms not to commercialize the new knowledge, the economic agent could remain employed by an incumbent firm and expect to earn incremental additions to her income over time, as depicted by the positive, linear incumbent earnings profile.

Alternatively, as a result of her endowment of ideas and knowledge not appropriated or rewarded within the context of the incumbent organization, the knowledge agent could reach the decision to start a new firm, which is represented by point A. Why would a rational economic agent choose to settle for a lower

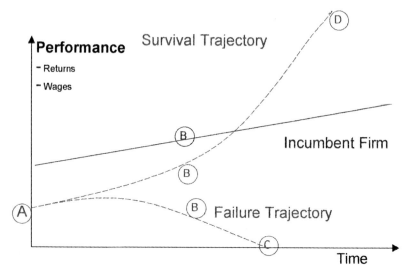

FIGURE 3.1. Entrepreneurship and growth

return at point A than could be earned from a wage paid by an incumbent firm? The answer is that there is some likelihood that the ideas on which the firm is started will prove valuable, resulting in growth of the firm and associated returns along the survival trajectory. As the evolutionary theories and systematic empirical evidence show, the likelihood of a new startup surviving is low. It is even lower for a knowledge-based startup. However, as we said, the same literature has provided theoretical insights and compelling empirical evidence showing that those knowledge-based startups that do survive will experience higher growth rates.

The likelihood that the new idea spawning the entrepreneurial startup is not compatible with market viability and sustainability is high. Thus, the evolutionary interpretation linking knowledge to entrepreneurship and ultimately economic growth suggests that the entrepreneurial act is to learn from the market about the viability and compatibility of a new idea that was rejected or undervalued by incumbent organizations. The new startup serves as a conduit for knowledge spillovers from the source producing that knowledge to commercialization in a new firm.

One could claim that the high failure rates for entrepreneurship more than negate the greater growth rates. At least two important externalities associated with entrepreneurial firms hold just as strongly for failed as for successful entrepreneurial firms. The first is that the entrepreneurial experience can spawn subsequent entrepreneurial startups. For example, the catalyst for Silicon Valley was the founding in 1957 of Fairchild Semiconductor, credited as the pioneering semiconductor firm. Although Fairchild faded, it spawned an impressive number of spin-offs, including Intel, started by Bob Noyce. Noyce and other Fairchild employees clearly gained knowledge from their experiences at Fairchild. Although

Fairchild Semiconductor had "possibly the most potent management and technical team ever assembled" (Gilder, 1989, p. 89),

> Noyce couldn't get Fairchild's eastern owners to accept the idea that stock options should be part of compensation for all employees, not just for management. He wanted to tie everyone, from janitors to bosses, into the overall success of the company.... This management style still sets the standard for every computer, software, and semiconductor company in the Valley today.... Every CEO still wants to think that the place is being run the way Bob Noyce would have run it. (Cringley, 1993, p. 39)

The second important externality is that new knowledge is generated in entrepreneurial failures. This knowledge can be valuable for other firms, including both startups and large incumbent enterprises. Even if that knowledge is restricted to learning about new ideas that are not viable, this can have a positive value.

These externalities may contribute to an impact on economic growth actually greater outside of the boundaries of the entrepreneurial firms than that contributed by the direct growth measured within the boundaries of entrepreneurial startups. Thus, figure 3.1 should not be interpreted as attributing the entire impact of entrepreneurship on growth to be restricted to the growth of entrepreneurial firms themselves. Such an extreme assumption of no external impacts is implicit in the analyses of new and small enterprises found in the path-breaking Birch (1979) study, as well as in the more recent Davis et al. (1996a, 1996b) updates. The Birch and Davis et al. approaches to measuring the impact of small firms on economic performance differ methodologically, but both implicitly agree in an absence of external impact. Thus, in a type of statistical apartheid or segregation, in the Birch and Davis et al. studies, the impact of small and new firms is measured only within that set of firms. In contrast, here we emphasize that the impact of entrepreneurship on economic performance generally, or growth more specifically, is not constrained to manifest itself solely in those entrepreneurial firms, but rather has a far greater external significance. As the Growth Hypothesis suggests, ceteris paribus, a Standort endowed with a higher degree of entrepreneurship capital will facilitate knowledge spillovers and the commercialization of knowledge, thereby generating greater economic growth.

> *Economic Growth Hypothesis*: Given a level of knowledge investment and severity of the knowledge filter, higher levels of economic growth should result from greater entrepreneurial activity, since entrepreneurship serves as a mechanism facilitating the spillover and commercialization of knowledge.

This hypothesis is consistent with the growth model already given. Deriving (3.1) with respect to t, inserting (3.2) and (3.6) and then dividing by (3.1), we obtain

$$g_Y = \alpha g_K + \theta^r(1 - \alpha)g_A + (1 - \alpha)g_L, \qquad (3.20)$$

where g_x denotes the growth rate of x. We denote θ^r as the *realized level* of the knowledge filter, or that level that includes the part of $(1 - \theta)$ that has been taken on by startup firms. Hence, we have $\theta \leq \theta^r$. An increase in entrepreneurial activity increases θ^r and therefore the distance between θ and θ^r. Deriving this growth equation we obtain

$$\frac{dg_Y}{d\theta^r} = (1 - \alpha)g_A, \tag{3.21}$$

which is positive for all g_A; hence, the model shows that GDP growth increases with increasing "permeability" of the knowledge filter, thus with increasing entrepreneurial activity.

The impact of entrepreneurship capital on economic performance leads to a modification of equation (3.1), with the recognition that an additional factor, *entrepreneurship capital*, E, can, along with the traditional factors, also make an important contribution to economic performance:

$$Y = K^\alpha L_Y^\beta A^\gamma E^\delta. \tag{3.1b}$$

The exact nature of the impact of entrepreneurship capital, if in fact any, is the focus of the following chapter.

3.6 Conclusions

Something of a schizophrenic approach has permeated the two disparate strands of literature focusing on opportunities. On the one hand, the entrepreneurship literature has focused mainly on the question of how individuals respond to opportunities taken to be exogenous or outside of the model. Just as firms are price takers in the neoclassical model of perfect competition, individuals are perceived to be opportunity takers in the literature on entrepreneurship. Rather, the focus is on how characteristics, experiences, and proclivities specific to the individual result in a different ability to perceive and actually respond to such exogenous opportunities.

By contrast, the literature focusing on innovation and firm strategy has considered opportunities as anything but exogenous, but as the result of purposeful, targeted investments in the creation of new economic knowledge through investments in R&D and human capital to generate innovative output. Thus, the opportunities are endogenously created by exogenously given firms undertaking strategic investments in R&D and other knowledge-creating activities.

This chapter has attempted to reconcile these two disparate literatures by linking the strategic context of the firm to that of the individual. Whereas in the entrepreneurship literature the opportunities are taken as exogenous and the firm is endogenously created, in the strategy and innovation literatures the firm is taken as exogenous and the opportunities as endogenously created. What links the entrepreneurial opportunity confronting the individual with the incumbent firm is new economic knowledge. Though incumbent organizations may be the source(s) of new ideas, the greater degree of uncertainty, asymmetries, and costs of transacting assessments both within and across organizations and individuals can ultimately generate opportunities for entrepreneurship.

Thus, in this chapter the assumption inherent in the model of the knowledge production function—that firms exogenously exist and endogenously create knowledge—is actually inverted. According to the Knowledge Spillover Theory of Entrepreneurship, the startup of a new firm is an endogenous response to knowledge and ideas that might otherwise not be fully and exhaustively commercialized by incumbent organizations.

Thus, the Knowledge Spillover Theory of Entrepreneurship suggests that entrepreneurial opportunities may not, in fact, be exogenous but are rather systematically created as the result of investments in knowledge. The commercialization of such opportunities through entrepreneurial activity will result in higher rates of economic growth.

By endogenously facilitating the spillover of knowledge created in a different organization and perhaps for a different application, entrepreneurship may provide what Acs et al. (2004) call the missing link to economic growth. Confronted with a formidable knowledge filter, public policy instruments emerging from the new growth theory, such as investments in human capital, R&D, and university research, may not result in satisfactory economic growth. One interpretation of the European Paradox, wherein such investments in new knowledge have certainly been vigorous and sustained, is that such an imposing knowledge filter chokes off the commercialization of those new investments, resulting in diminished innovative activity and ultimately stagnant growth.

By serving as a conduit for knowledge spillovers, entrepreneurship is the missing link between investments in new knowledge and economic growth. Thus, the Knowledge Spillover Theory of Entrepreneurship provides an explanation not just of why entrepreneurship has become more prevalent as knowledge has emerged as a crucial source for comparative advantage but also of why entrepreneurship plays a vital role in generating economic growth. Entrepreneurship is an important mechanism permeating the knowledge filter to facilitate the spillover of knowledge and ultimately generate economic growth.

Entrepreneurship Capital and Economic Performance

4.1 Linking the Entrepreneur to Economic Performance

Why does one Standort, or location, experience stronger economic performance than another? One answer was provided by neoclassical economics. The classical model of the production function suggests that economic performance, measured as economic output, improves as the location's endowment of capital and labor strengthens. Robert Solow (1956), on the other hand, argued that economic growth, another measure of economic performance, is determined explicitly by investment in physical capital. In this growth model, technical change was specified as an exogenous shift factor. More recently, Paul Romer (1986, 1990), Robert Lucas (1988), and others extended the neoclassical model of growth by suggesting that knowledge, because it spills over for use by third-party firms, is actually the most potent factor generating growth. Formally, their analysis implied augmenting the production function with knowledge capital as an additional factor. In this chapter, we certainly do not dispute the importance of the traditional factors, but we suggest an additional factor: the degree of *entrepreneurship capital* specific to a Standort.

By entrepreneurship capital, we mean the capacity for the Standort, the geographically relevant spatial unit of observation, to generate new business startups. As with the traditional framework for economic growth, which assumes the factors of production to be given, we take the endowment of entrepreneurship capital at the Standort as exogenous and then ask, Do variations in the amount of entrepreneurship capital across geographic space help explain spatial variations in economic performance?

The answer to this question is of considerable importance to public policy. If the answer is no, then there is no reason to promote entrepreneurship, at least not for the purpose of generating economic growth. If the answer is yes, then the amount of entrepreneurship capital associated with a Standort contributes to economic growth. However, the production function framework evoked in this chapter, where the factors are taken as exogenous, provides no insights to guide public policy in the selection of instruments that augment a Standort's entrepreneurship capital and ultimately generate a superior economic performance. Chapter 5 addresses this issue.

The results in this chapter provide empirical evidence consistent with the hypothesis that economic performance—output measured as GDP or economic growth—is positively related to the presence of a Standort's entrepreneurship capital. In particular, the empirical evidence based on German regions suggests that the neoclassical two-factor approach does not adequately explain economic performance, at least not in the case of contemporary Germany. Rather, including entrepreneurship provides a better explanation of why some regions exhibit a stronger economic performance than others.

Though the findings from this chapter alone do not enable us to shed any light as to what exactly constitutes entrepreneurship capital or delineate which public policies would best enhance entrepreneurship capital, they do link entrepreneurship and economic performance. Here, we suggest that the degree of entrepreneurial activity, which presumably reflects the underlying stock of entrepreneurship capital associated with a particular Standort, positively affects economic performance.

4.2 Entrepreneurship Capital

Whereas the neoclassical tradition identified investment in *physical capital* as the driving factor of economic performance (Solow, 1956), the endogenous growth theory (Romer, 1986, 1990; Lucas, 1988) emphasizes the accumulation of knowledge, and hence the creation of *knowledge capital*. The concept of *social capital* (Coleman, 1988a, 1988b; Putnam, 1993) adds a social component to those factors shaping economic growth and prosperity. According to Putnam (2000, p. 19),

> Whereas physical capital refers to physical objects and human capital refers to the properties of individuals, social capital refers to connections among individuals—social networks and the norms of reciprocity and trustworthiness that arise from them. In that sense social capital is closely related to what some have called "civic virtue." The difference is that "social capital" calls attention to the fact that civic virtue is most powerful when embedded in a sense network of reciprocal social relations. A society of many virtues but isolated individuals is not necessarily rich in social capital.

Putnam (2000, p. 19) also challenged the standard neoclassical growth model by arguing that social capital is also important in generating economic growth:

> By analogy with notions of physical capital and human capital—tools and training that enhance individual productivity—social capital refers to features of social organization, such as networks, norms, and trust, that facilitate coordination and cooperation for mutual benefits.

An abundant, robust literature has emerged trying to link social capital to entrepreneurship (Aldrich and Martinez, 2003; Thornton and Flynn, 2003).

According to this literature, entrepreneurial activity should be enhanced where investments in social capital are greater (Amin, 2000; Simmie, 2003; Smith, 2003). However, Putnam, though, clearly linking social capital and economic welfare, did not directly include entrepreneurship. Putnam emphasized associational membership and public trust, which, though essential for social and economic well-being, did not involve entrepreneurship, per se.

Social capital and entrepreneurship capital are distinctive concepts. We suggest that what has been called social capital in the entrepreneurship literature may actually be a more specific subcomponent, which we introduce as *entrepreneurship capital*. Entrepreneurship has typically been defined as an action, process, or activity that involves the startup and growth of a new enterprise. By entrepreneurship capital of an economy or a society, that is, a Standort, we mean a milieu of agents and institutions conducive to the creation of new firms. This involves a number of aspects, such as social acceptance of entrepreneurial behavior, individuals willing to deal with the risk of creating new firms,[1] and the activity of bankers and venture capital agents willing to share risks and benefits. Hence, entrepreneurship capital reflects a number of different legal, institutional, and social factors and forces that create a capacity for entrepreneurial activity (Hofstede et al., 2002). Thus, entrepreneurship capital manifests itself through the creation of new firms.

Entrepreneurship capital, however, should not be confused with social capital. The major distinction, in our view, is that not all social capital is conducive to economic performance, let alone entrepreneurial activity. Some types of social capital are more focused on preserving the status quo and are not necessarily directed at creating challenges to the status quo. In contrast, entrepreneurship capital could be considered as a subset of social capital. Whereas social capital may have an impact on entrepreneurship, depending on the specific orientation, entrepreneurship capital, by definition, will have a positive impact on entrepreneurial activity. In the following sections, we provide evidence on the impact of entrepreneurship capital on economic performance.

4.3 Linking Entrepreneurship Capital with Economic Performance

Several studies have attempted to link entrepreneurship to economic growth. The unit of observation for these studies is at the spatial level, either city, region, state, or country. The most common measure of performance is growth, typically measured in terms of employment growth. These studies have tried to link measures of entrepreneurial activity, typically startup rates, to economic growth. Other measures include the relative share of small- and medium-sized enterprises (SMEs), and self-employment rates.

For example, Holtz-Eakin and Kao (2003) examine the impact of entrepreneurship on growth. Their spatial unit of observation is American states. Their measure of growth is productivity change over time. A vector autoregression analysis shows that variations in the birth rate and the death rate for firms are related to positive changes in productivity. They conclude that entrepreneurship has a positive impact on productivity growth, at least in the United States.

Audretsch and Fritsch (1996) analyzed a database identifying new business startups and exits from the social insurance statistics in Germany to examine whether a greater degree of turbulence leads to greater economic growth, as suggested by Schumpeter in his 1911 treatise. These social insurance statistics are collected for individuals. Each record in the database identifies an establishment in which an individual is employed. Thus, new firm startups are recorded when a new establishment identification appears in the database, which usually indicates the birth of a new enterprise. Though some evidence for the United States links a greater degree of turbulence at the regional level to higher rates of growth for regions (Reynolds, 1999), Audretsch and Fritsch (1996) find that the opposite was true for Germany during the 1980s. In both the manufacturing and the service sectors, a high rate of turbulence in a region tends to lead to a lower rate of growth. They attribute this negative relationship to the fact that the underlying components—the startup and death rates—are both negatively related to subsequent economic growth. Those areas with higher startup rates tend to experience lower growth rates in subsequent years. Most strikingly, the same is also true for death rates. German regions experiencing higher death rates also tend to experience lower growth rates in subsequent years. Fritsch (1997) found similar evidence for Germany.

Audretsch and Fritsch (1996) conjectured that one possible explanation for the disparity in results between the United States and Germany may lie in the role that innovative activity, and therefore the ability of new firms to ultimately displace the incumbent ones, plays in startups. It may be that innovative activity did not play the same role for the German *Mittelstand* as it does for SMEs in the United States. So regional growth may emanate from SMEs only when they serve as agents of change through innovative activity.

The empirical evidence suggested that the German model for growth provided a sharp contrast to that for the United States. While Reynolds (1999) found that the degree of entrepreneurship was positively related to growth in the United States, a series of studies by Audretsch and Fritsch (1996) and Fritsch (1997) could not identify such a relationship for Germany. However, the results by Audretsch and Fritsch were based on data from the 1980s.

Divergent findings from the 1980s about the relationship between the degree of entrepreneurial activity and economic growth in the United States and Germany pose a puzzle. On one hand, these results suggested that the relationship between entrepreneurship and growth was fraught with ambiguities. No confirmation could be found for a general pattern across developed countries. On the other hand, they provided evidence for distinct and different national systems. The empirical evidence clearly suggested that there were multiple ways to achieve growth, at least across different countries. Convergence in growth rates seemed to be attainable despite differences in underlying institutions and structures.

However, in a more recent study, Audretsch and Fritsch (2002) find that different results emerge for the 1990s. Regions with higher startup rates exhibit higher growth rates. This would suggest that Germany is changing over time with the engine of growth shifting toward entrepreneurship. Their results suggest an interpretation that differs from their earlier findings. Because of compelling empirical evidence that the source of growth in Germany has shifted away from established incumbent firms during the 1980s to entrepreneurial firms in the 1990s, one may assume that a process of convergence is taking place between Germany and the United States so that entrepreneurship provides the engine of growth in both countries. Despite remaining institutional differences, the relationship between entrepreneurship and growth is apparently converging in both countries.

The positive relationship between entrepreneurship and growth at the regional level is not limited to Germany in the 1990s. For example, Foelster (2000) examines not just the employment impact within new and small firms but also the overall link between increases in self-employment and total employment in Sweden between 1976 and 1995. Using a Layard-Nickell framework, he provides a link between micro behavior and macroeconomic performance, showing that increases in self-employment shares have had a positive impact on regional employment rates in Sweden.

Hart and Hanvey (1995) link measures of new and small firms to employment generation in the late 1980s for three regions in the United Kingdom. Although they find that employment creation came largely from SMEs, they also show that most of the job losses also came from SMEs.

Callejon and Segarra (1999) use a data set of Spanish manufacturing industries from 1980 to 1992 to link new-firm birth rates and death rates, which, taken together, constitute a measure of turbulence, to total factor productivity growth in industries and regions. They adopt a model based on a vintage capital framework in which new entrants embody the edge technologies available and exiting businesses represent marginal obsolete plants. Using a Hall type of production function, which controls for imperfect competition and the extent of scale economies, they find that both new-firm startup rates and exit rates contribute positively to the growth of total factor productivity in regions as well as industries.

The main contribution of the social capital literature is that endowments with "traditional factors" such as capital, labor, and (recently) knowledge are not adequate to sufficiently explain economic performance. Rather, as Putnam argues, social interaction facilitates the creation of communities, personal commitments, and social fabric. A sense of belonging and the concrete experience of social networks, which involves relationships of trust and tolerance, will ultimately be transmitted into economic performance.

As explained in the previous section, we suggest that the notion of entrepreneurship capital may be more useful. Entrepreneurship capital refers to a specific type of social capital that explicitly generates the startup of new enterprises. Even though the concept of entrepreneurship capital is firm, the exact link between entrepreneurship capital and economic performance is less certain. However, we see at least three arguments why entrepreneurship capital will have a positive impact on economic performance.

One argument is provided by Saxenian (pp. 96–97), who examines Silicon Valley:

> It is not simply the concentration of skilled labor, suppliers and information that distinguish the region. A variety of regional institutions—including Stanford

University, several trade associations and local business organizations, and a myriad of specialized consulting, market research, public relations and venture capital firms—provide technical, financial, and networking services which the region's enterprises often cannot afford individually. These networks defy sectoral barriers: individuals move easily from semiconductor to disk drive firms or from computer to network makers. They move from established firms to startups (or vice versa) and even to market research or consulting firms, and from consulting firms back into startups. And they continue to meet at trade shows, industry conferences, and the scores of seminars, talks, and social activities organized by local business organizations and trade associations. In these forums, relationships are easily formed and maintained, technical and market information is exchanged, business contacts are established, and new enterprises are conceived.... This decentralized and fluid environment also promotes the diffusion of intangible technological capabilities and understandings.

Saxenian claims further (pp. 97–98) that even the language and vocabulary used by technical specialists can be specific to the entrepreneurship capital associated with that region, where "a distinct language has evolved in the region and certain technical terms used by semiconductor production engineers in Silicon Valley would not even be understood by their counterparts in Boston's Route 128."

According to the Knowledge Spillover Theory of Entrepreneurship, introduced in chapter 3, and in particular, the Economic Performance Hypothesis and Growth Hypothesis, entrepreneurial capital should have a positive impact on economic output. Holding the level of investment in new knowledge constant, regions with a high degree of entrepreneurship capital will facilitate the new firm startup based on uncertain and asymmetric ideas. On the other hand, regions with less entrepreneurship capital will impede the ability of individuals to start new firms. Entrepreneurship capital promotes knowledge spillover by facilitating new firms startups. Acs et al. (2004) refer to the gap between knowledge and commercialized knowledge as the knowledge filter. By commercializing ideas that otherwise would not be pursued and commercialized, entrepreneurship serves as one mechanism facilitating knowledge spillovers and thus overcoming the filter. In the metaphor provided by Albert O. Hirschman (1970), if voice proves to be ineffective within incumbent organizations, and loyalty is sufficiently weak, a knowledge worker may exit the firm or university where the knowledge was created in order to establish a new company. In this spillover channel, the knowledge production function is actually reversed. The knowledge is exogenous and embodied in a worker. The firm is created endogenously in the worker's effort to appropriate the value of his knowledge through innovative activity. Thus, as described in chapter 3, entrepreneurship serves as the mechanism by which knowledge spills over from the source, creating a new firm where it is commercialized.

A *second* way that entrepreneurship capital exerts a positive influence on economic output is through increased competition through the increased number of enterprises. Jacobs (1969) and Porter (1990) argue that competition is more conducive to knowledge externalities than local monopoly. By local competition, Jacobs does not mean competition within product markets as has traditionally been envisioned within the industrial organization literature. Rather, Jacobs is referring to the competition for the new ideas embodied in economic agents. Not only does an increase in the number of firms provide greater competition for new ideas; greater competition across firms facilitates the entry of new firms specializing in some particular new product niche. This is because the necessary complementary inputs and services are likely to be available from small specialist niche firms but not necessarily from large, vertically integrated producers.

Both Feldman and Audretsch (1999) and Glaeser et al. (1992) found empirical evidence supporting the hypothesis that an increase in competition, as measured by the number of enterprises, in a city increases the growth performance of that city.

A *third* way that entrepreneurship capital generates economic output is by providing diversity among firms. Not only does entrepreneurship capital generate a greater number of enterprises, it also increases the variety of enterprises in a location. A key assumption made by Hannan and Freeman (1989) in the population ecology literature is that each new organization represents a unique approach.

There has been a series of theoretical arguments suggesting that the amount of diversity in a location will influence the growth potential. The theoretical basis linking diversity to economic performance is provided by Jacobs (1969), who argues that the most important source of knowledge spillovers are external to the industry in which the firm operates and that cities are the source of considerable innovation because the diversity of knowledge sources is greatest in cities. According to Jacobs, it is the exchange of complementary knowledge across diverse firms and economic agents that yields a greater return on new economic knowledge. Hertheory emphasizes that the variety of industries within a geographic region promotes knowledge externalities and ultimately fosters innovative activity and economic growth.

The first important test linking diversity to economic performance, measured in terms of employment growth, was accomplished by Glaeser et al. (1992), who employ a data set on the growth of large industries in 170 cities between 1956 and 1987 in order to identify the relative importance of regional specialization, diversity, and local competition in influencing industry growth rates. The authors find evidence that diversity promotes growth in cities. Feldman and Audretsch (1999) identify the extent to which diversity influences innovative output. They link the innovative output of product categories within a specific city to the extent to which the economic activity of that city is concentrated in that industry, or conversely, diversified in terms of complementary industries sharing a common science base.

According to models of evolutionary economics, the degree of diversity at a Standort plays a key role in shaping economic performance. In fact, evolutionary economics focuses on two central principles shaping economic performance: diversity and selection (Nelson and Winter, 1982). Evolution takes place by a process of selection among diverse entities, which propels an economy into a new direction. An economy with no diversity and no selection cannot evolve. It will remain permanently locked in a long-run equilibrium.

Though Nelson and Winter (1982) made significant progress in identifying the role that diversity and selection play in shaping economic evolution, they were less specific about the sources of diversity. What are the sources of diversity, and why does it pay economic agents to invest in diversity? One answer, provided by Nelson and Winter, is that diversity emanates from investments in R&D. Firms have an incentive to invest in the creation of new economic knowledge. Thus, investments in R&D and human capital are an important source of diversity by generating new economic knowledge.

In the previous chapter, we referred to Arrow (1962) about the gap distinguishing general knowledge from economic knowledge. An implication of Arrow's characterization of this gap is that the valuation of new ideas will be distributed differently across individuals, or economic agents. Economic agents placing a high value on knowledge that is not valued as highly by the hierarchical decision-making organizations in incumbent firms will have an incentive to become entrepreneurs to appropriate the value of that knowledge. When economic agents recognize economic opportunities emerging from knowledge generated but not commercially exploited by incumbent firms, and act on that opportunity, they become entrepreneurs.

Thus, when a new firm is established, its prospects are uncertain. If the new firm is built around a new idea, it is uncertain whether there is sufficient demand for this idea once it is transformed into a product or whether some competitor will have the same idea, or even a superior one. Even if the new firm is an exact replica of a successful incumbent enterprise, it is uncertain whether sufficient demand for a new clone, or even for the existing incumbent, will prevail in the future. Tastes change, and new ideas emerging from other firms will influence those tastes.

Finally, an additional layer of uncertainty pervades a new enterprise. It is not known how competent the new firm really is in terms of management, organization, and workforce. Can the new enterprise produce and market the intended product as well as sell it? Incumbent firms know something about their underlying competencies based on past experience. Thus, the degree of uncertainty of new firms will usually exceed that confronting incumbent ones.

Thus, entrepreneurship is an important source of diversity because it transforms knowledge into economic knowledge that would otherwise have remained uncommercialized. This suggests that regions with a greater amount of entrepreneurial activity are likely to have a greater degree of diversity, which should result in higher rates of growth.

Nelson and Winter (1982) and Winter (1984) suggested that more diversity would be generated under the "entrepreneurial regime" than the "routinized regime." Under the routinized technological regime, innovative activity will tend to be more incremental and thus be less diverse. In contrast, under the entrepreneurial regime, innovative activity tends to be characterized by more diversity. Thus, the likelihood for new firms to be started should be associated with a greater degree of diversity and consequently greater growth.

In summary, entrepreneurship capital can contribute to output and growth by serving as a conduit for knowledge spillovers, increasing competition, and injecting diversity. If this holds, measures of entrepreneurship capital in an empirical framework should relate positively to measures of economic performance such as GDP or economic growth. The following sections address this topic.

4.4 Models and Measurement

To test the hypotheses suggesting that a Standort endowed with a greater degree of entrepreneurship capital, ceteris paribus, will exhibit a superior economic performance in general, and economic growth in particular, we employ the econometric framework of the production function to link several measures reflecting entrepreneurship capital to economic performance. Three rather well-established measures are used to reflect economic performance and growth: regional levels of economic output or GDP, regional levels of labor productivity, and regional growth rates of labor productivity.

4.4.1 Assessing the Impact of Entrepreneurship Capital on Regional GDP

Chapter 3 ended with the deriving of equation (3.1b), which suggests that the production function should be augmented with entrepreneurship capital to test the Economic Performance Hypothesis. We use the specification of the Cobb-Douglas type, where K refers to *physical capital*, L represents *labor*, R represents *knowledge capital*, and E represents *entrepreneurship capital*. The subscript i reflects the localized nature of knowledge spillovers and defines the relevant spatial unit of observation as a region. In this case, German *Kreise*, or counties, will be used to represent the spatial dimension, i.

$$Y_i = \alpha K_i^{\beta_1} L_i^{\beta_2} R_i^{\beta_3} E_i^{\beta_4} e^{\varepsilon_i}, \tag{4.1}$$

where β_j represents output elasticities of the respective variables; that is, an increase of the corresponding variable by one percent correspondingly increases the left-hand side (labor productivity) by β_j percent. ε_i is a stochastic error term; its exponential specification indicates that we estimate equation (4.1) in log form. The variables in equation (4.1) are measured as follows.

Output (Y_i) is measured as gross value added corrected for purchases of goods, services, VAT, and shipping costs. Statistics are published every two years for each Kreis by the Working Group of the Statistical Offices of the German *Länder*, under "*Volkswirtschaftliche Gesamtrechnungen der Länder*."

Physical capital (K_i) refers to the stock of capital used in the manufacturing sector of the Kreise and has been estimated using a perpetual inventory method that computes the stock of capital as a weighted sum of past investments. In the estimates, we used a β-distribution with $p = 9$ and a mean age of $q = 14$. The type of survival function, as well as these parameters, has been provided by the German Federal Statistical Office. Data on investment at the level of German Kreise is published annually by the Federal Statistical Office in the series "E I 6," These figures, however, are limited to firms in the producing sector, excluding the mining industry, with more than 20 employees. The vector of the producing sector as a whole has been estimated by multiplying these values such that the value of the capital stock of Western Germany—as published in the Statistical Yearbook— was attained. Note that this procedure implies that estimates for Kreise with a high proportion of mining might be biased. Note also that for protection purposes, some Kreise did not publish data on investment (such as the city of Wolfsburg, whose producing sector is dominated by Volkswagen). Therefore, five Kreise are treated as missing.

Labor (L_i) is based on labor force data published by the Federal Labor Office, Nürnberg, that reports number of employees liable to social insurance by Kreise. *Knowledge capital* (R_i) is expressed as *number of employees engaged in R&D* in the public (1992) and in the private sector (1991). With this approach, we follow the examples of Griliches (1979), Jaffe (1989), and Audretsch and Feldman (1996). Data has been provided by the *Stifterverband für die Wissenschaft* under obligation of secrecy. This data does not distinguish between R&D employees in the producing and nonproducing sectors. Therefore, regression results will implicitly include spillovers from R&D of the nonproducing sector to the producing sectors. We assume however that this effect is low.

Measuring *entrepreneurship capital* (E_i) is no less complicated than measuring the traditional factors of production. Just as measuring capital, labor, and knowledge invokes numerous assumptions and simplifications, creating a metric for entrepreneurship capital is challenging. Many of the elements that determine entrepreneurship capital in our definition defy quantification. In any case, entrepreneurship capital, like all other types of capital, is multifaceted and heterogeneous. However, entrepreneurship capital manifests itself in a singular way: the startup of new firms. Thus, we propose using new-firm startup rates as an indicator of entrepreneurship capital, the latter being an unobservable (i.e., latent) variable. Ceteris paribus, higher startup rates should reflect higher levels of entrepreneurship capital.

From the background of our definition of entrepreneurship capital, alternative measures are possible. A natural candidate would be a region's stock of young firms. However, this measure would implicitly reflect exit and shakeout dynamics. Hence, a measure along these lines would inevitably be influenced by factors external to entrepreneurship capital, and thus be biased. We therefore consider the number of startups as the most appropriate measure reflecting the underlying stock of entrepreneurship capital.

We compute entrepreneurship capital as the *number of startups in the respective region relative to its population*, which reflects the propensity of inhabitants of a region to start a new firm. The data on startups is taken from the "ZEW foundation panels," a data set developed by the Centre for European Economic Research in Mannheim and based on data provided biannually by *Creditreform*, the largest German credit-rating agency. This data contains virtually all entries—hence startups—in the German Trade Register, particularly for firms with large credit requirements such as high-technology firms.[2] By 1995, there were 1.6 million entries for Western Germany. Since number of startups is subject to a greater level of stochastic disturbance over short time periods, it is prudent to compute the measure of entrepreneurship capital based on startup rates over a longer time period. We therefore used the number of startups between 1989 and 1992.

One might argue that, in the setup of equation (4.1), the use of entrepreneurship capital invokes a simultaneity problem in the sense that not only does entrepreneurship capital drive output but high output also drives startups. The argument implies that entrepreneurs move to locations where economic performance is high. However, a similar argument would hold for all variables used in this approach. If this effect holds for entrepreneurs, it will certainly also apply to labor but probably even more to capital, since capital is a weighted sum of past monetary investments, money migrates more easily across borders, and therefore it moves more quickly to productive regions. Thus, our measure of entrepreneurship capital fits well with the tradition of estimating the model of the production function. The use of lagged values of startup rates avoids some of the degree of simultaneity between output and entrepreneurship. In any case, just as the Knowledge Spillover Theory of Entrepreneurship introduced in chapter 3 suggests, entrepreneurship will be treated as an endogenous variable and estimated within the context of a simultaneous model in chapter 5.

We denote the measure including all startups as the general indicator of entrepreneurship capital. While we argue that entrepreneurship capital should include startup activity in any industry, some scholars have suggested that it should apply only to startups involving innovative activity. Therefore, we compute two modified measures of entrepreneurship. The first one restricts the measure reflecting entrepreneurship capital to include only startup activity in high-technology manufacturing industries (whose share of R&D expenditure relative to sales is above 2.5 percent). The second measure restricts the measure of entrepreneurship capital to include only startup activity in the information and communication (ICT) industries, that is, firms in the hard- and software business. Some of these industries are also classified under high-technology manufacturing; hence, there is an intersection between these two measures. These two measures will emphasize the aspect of risk involved in the definition of entrepreneurship capital, since R&D-intensive activities are more uncertain in outcome and since a larger financial commitment is necessary to engage in R&D intensive industries. Finally, a fourth measure includes all startups other than the high-technology and ICT startups. We denote these "low-tech" startups. Note however that "low-tech" startups include those in knowledge-intensive industries (especially service industries) such as lawyers, medical doctors, or any type of consultants. Hence, low-tech refers to the industry's R&D intensity and not to "low-knowledge."

The spatial distribution of the general measure of entrepreneurship capital based on all industries is shown in figure 4.1. This figure illustrates that entrepreneurship capital is a phenomenon of densely populated regions. For example, Frankfurt, Munich, Hamburg, and Düsseldorf, along with their respective surrounding regions, exhibit the highest startup intensity. This is reflected in the correlation matrix shown in table 4.1, where entrepreneurship capital shows a positive and significant correlation with population density, measured as inhabitants per square kilometer.

Table 4.2 ranks the regions according to their endowment of general entrepreneurship capital. Again, Munich, Düsseldorf, Frankfurt, and Hamburg, along with their surrounding regions, are those with the greatest endowment of entrepreneurship capital. This ranking differs slightly, although not fundamentally, if we use startups in high-tech manufacturing industries, in ICT industries, or in

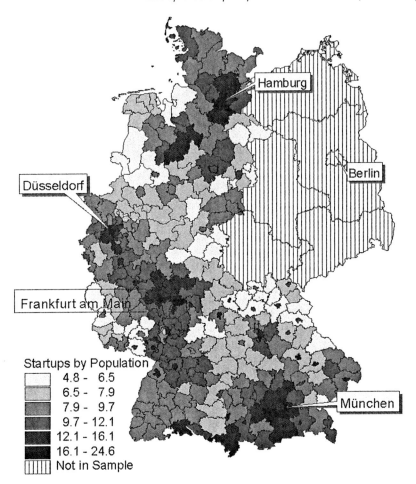

FIGURE 4.1. Spatial distribution of entrepreneurship capital, measured as the number of startups in all industries relative to population in each region

low-tech industries instead of startups in all industries. This is indicated by positive and significant correlations between all four measures of entrepreneurship shown in table 4.3.

Estimation of the production function model of equation (4.1) produces the results displayed in table 4.4. The first equation estimates the traditional Solow model of the production function. As the positive and statistically significant coefficients suggest, both physical capital and labor are important factors of production in determining output in German regions. In the second column, the factor knowledge capital is added. The positive and statistically significant coefficients of all three variables lend support to Romer's argument that knowledge-intensive inputs matter as a factor of production.

The third column shows the results when entrepreneurship capital is included in the production function model (4.1). The positive and statistically significant

TABLE 4.1 Summary Statistics of Variables Used in Regression

	Mean	Standard deviation	Min	Max
GDP (Y) (million DM)	2351.89	2621.77	95.00	22258.00
Capital (K) (million DM)	4248.25	5038.72	211.20	37295.64
Employees (L) (number)	27022.48	24080.32	2562	171938
R&D employees (R) (number)	840.76	2223.75	0	29863
Entrepreneurship capital $(E)^a$	9.406	2.805	4.793	24.635
High-tech E^a	0.755	0.398	0.011	6.004
ICT E^a	0.565	0.310	0.157	2.520
Low-tech E^a	8.086	2.259	4.338	18.650

[a]Entrepreneurship capital is measured as sum of the number of startups in the respective industry in 1989 to 1992 per 1,000 of population. Hence, in average there were 9.4 startups per 1,000 of population in all industries in these years.

coefficient indicates that entrepreneurship is a key factor in explaining variations in output across German regions.

Equation (4.1) also specifies the impact of production factors on output in terms of production elasticities; that is, an increase of a factor *j* by one percent implies an increase of output by β_j percent. Thus, we can deduce from our estimates that an increase of a region's entrepreneurship capital by one percent increases output ceteris paribus by 0.12 percent. On the basis of our adaptation of the production function model approach, we cannot infer what should actually influence a region's entrepreneurship capital. However, our estimates provide evidence suggesting that the impact of entrepreneurship capital is stronger than that of knowledge capital, since the production elasticity of entrepreneurship capital is roughly five times larger than that for knowledge capital. This implies that investments in entrepreneurship capital are more productive than investments in knowledge capital, which in turn suggests a shift in public policy to support the creation of entrepreneurship capital. Of course, this is only first empirical evidence and should be interpreted with caution.

Columns (4) and (5) show the results for equation (4.1) with startup rates in high-tech manufacturing and ICT industries substituted for startup rates of all industries. The results indicate that using these two alternative measures of entrepreneurship capital still generates a positive and statistically significant coefficient, suggesting that entrepreneurship capital is an important addition to the model of the production function. These results provide empirical evidence supporting the Economic Performance Hypothesis posited in the previous chapter.

4.4.2 Assessing the Impact of Entrepreneurship Capital on Regional Labor Productivity

A second specification testing the Growth Hypothesis emerging from the Knowledge Spillover Theory of Entrepreneurship links the measures of entrepreneurship capital to a standard measure of economic performance, labor productivity, which is a region's economic output relative to its labor force. Dividing output by the input of labor corrects for the size of a region and thus increases the relevance of

TABLE 4.2 Regions with Greatest and Least Startup Intensity
(Startups 1989–1992 per 1,000 of population) for all Industries

Rank	Region	Startup intensity
1	München, surrounding area	24.634561
2	Düsseldorf, city	20.241409
3	Hamburg, city	19.669706
4	Offenbach, surrounding area	18.606913
5	Wiesbaden, city	17.671311
6	Starnberg	17.101142
7	München, city	16.081293
8	Frankfurt a. M., city	15.956175
9	Hochtaunuskreis	15.866653
10	Speyer, city	15.395183
11	Passau, city	15.254072
12	Freising	14.850592
13	Memmingen, city	14.805079
14	Landsberg a. Lech	14.792960
15	Offenbach a. M., city	14.620285
16	Segeberg	14.572237
17	Diepholz	14.435722
18	Main-Taunus-Kreis	14.232831
19	Ebersberg	13.811470
20	Dachau	13.779904
. . . .	. . . .	. . . .
308	Wesermarsch	6.006103
309	Wolfsburg, city	6.001654
310	Cham	5.991514
311	Sankt Wendel	5.919445
312	Neckar-Odenwald-Kreis	5.912736
313	Donnersbergkreis	5.896884
314	Schweinfurt	5.896509
315	Emsland	5.774027
316	Uelzen	5.758620
317	Salzgitter, city	5.668607
318	Lichtenfels	5.551670
319	Trier-Saarburg	5.541770
320	Herne, city	5.526887
321	Grafschaft Bentheim	5.428270
322	Höxter	5.287556
323	Bremerhaven, city	5.258049
324	Tirschenreuth	5.198918
325	Coburg	5.193940
326	Cuxhaven	5.168823
327	Kusel	4.793161

this measure. We link this measure of regional economic performance to the traditional factors of *capital, labor,* and *knowledge,* along with our new factor of *entrepreneurship capital,* by dividing output in equation 4.1 by labor to obtain this equation:

$$(Y_i/L_i) = \alpha(K_i/L_i)^{\beta_1} R_i^{\beta_2} E_i^{\beta_3}, \qquad (4.2)$$

TABLE 4.3 Correlation of Variables Based on 327 German Kreise

	Population density	Y	K	L	R	E	High-tech E	ICT E
Y	0.5539							
K	0.5978	0.9172						
L	0.5252	0.9437	0.9244					
R	0.5068	0.7838	0.7250	0.6922				
E	0.3376	0.2671	0.2133	0.2203	0.3036			
High-tech E	0.2668	0.3179	0.2292	0.2756	0.3404	0.8153		
ICT E	0.2870	0.3167	0.2224	0.2579	0.3396	0.8164	0.9138	
"Low-tech" E	0.3326	0.2320	0.1939	0.1895	0.2702	0.9856	0.7104	0.7151

where Y/L is labor productivity, K/L is the capital intensity of the region, R represents *knowledge capital*, and E represents *entrepreneurship capital*. Equation (4.2) represents the classic Cobb-Douglas production function in its intensive form under the assumption that the production elasticities of capital and labor sum to unity. Hence, equation (4.2) is a modification of equation (4.1) with parameter restriction $\beta_1 + \beta_2 = 1$.

Estimation of equation (4.2) produced the results displayed in table 4.5. To test for robustness, we estimated different specifications. In the first column, results are shown for the estimation of regional productivity in Germany using the traditional Cobb-Douglas model (relating output to capital and labor) in its intensive form. The

TABLE 4.4 Results of Estimation of the Production Function Model (4.1) for German Regions

	Dependent variable: GDP (Y) of German counties					
	(1)	(2)	(3)	(4)	(5)	(6)
Constant	−2.755***	−2.380***	−2.696***	−2.280***	−2.278***	−2.639***
	(−10.75)	(−8.13)	(−8.34)	(−7.83)	(−7.85)	(−8.09)
Capital (K)	0.270***	0.261***	0.258***	0.265***	0.267***	0.257***
	(5.31)	(5.18)	(5.15)	(5.33)	(5.37)	(5.12)
Labor (L)	0.805***	0.755***	0.767***	0.753***	0.756***	0.767***
	(13.24)	(11.93)	(12.15)	(12.04)	(12.13)	(12.08)
Knowledge (R)		0.034**	0.026*	0.021	0.019	0.028**
		(2.56)	(1.86)	(1.51)	(1.35)	(2.07)
Entrepreneurship (E)			0.120**			
			(2.24)			
High-tech entrepreneurship (E)				0.096***		
				(3.03)		
ICT entrepreneurship (E)					0.105***	
					(3.31)	
Low-tech entrepreneurship (E)						0.100*
						(1.77)
Adjusted R^2	0.9108	0.9124	0.9134	0.9145	0.9150	0.9129

TABLE 4.5 Results of Estimation of Equation (4.2), Labor Productivity, for German Regions

	(1)	(2)	(3)	(4)	(5)	(6)
Constant	−1.888***	−2.234***	−2.458***	−2.117***	−2.076***	−2.412***
	(−19.23)	(−18.16)	(−15.30)	(−16.61)	(−15.91)	(−14.86)
K/L	0.332***	0.266***	0.266***	0.271***	0.274***	0.265***
	(6.81)	(5.37)	(5.39)	(5.53)	(5.59)	(5.35)
R		0.039***	0.034***	0.027***	0.027***	0.0366***
		(4.46)	(3.75)	(2.78)	(2.76)	(4.03)
Entrepreneurship (E)			0.115**			
			(2.15)			
High-tech E				0.095***		
				(3.02)		
ICT E					0.104***	
					(3.27)	
Low-tech E						0.0936*
						(1.68)
F-test	46.44***	34.50***	24.80***	26.63***	27.26***	24.07***
	(0.000)	(0.000)	(0.000)	(0.000)	(0.000)	(0.000)
Adjusted R^2	0.122	0.170	0.179	0.190	0.195	0.1751

t values in parentheses.
*Statistically significant at the two-tailed test for 90% level of confidence.
**Statistically significant at the two-tailed test for 95% level of confidence.
***Statistically significant at the two-tailed test for 99% level of confidence.

implicitly estimated output elasticities for capital (β_1) and labor ($1 - \beta_1$) are within the usual range.[3] As has been consistently verified in previous studies, those regions with greater capital intensity exhibit greater levels of productivity.

In the second column, knowledge capital is added. The positive and statistically significant coefficient of this variable lends support to the Romer view that knowledge matters as a factor of production and generates higher levels of productivity.

For columns (3) through (6), the four different indicators of entrepreneurship capital are included. All four estimations provide positive and significant results. This supports the hypothesis that entrepreneurship capital is positively linked to economic performance. It is interesting that the estimated output elasticities of the different measures of entrepreneurship capital (β_3) are greater than the output elasticities of knowledge capital (β_2). More precisely, the effect of a one percent increase in the indicator of entrepreneurship capital on regional labor productivity is three to four times larger than a one percent increase of R&D. Again, this is evidence in favor of the Economic Performance Hypothesis, although it is not new evidence since equation (4.2) is a simple parameter restriction of equation (4.1).

4.4.3 Assessing the Impact of Entrepreneurship Capital on Regional Growth of Labor Productivity

To test the Growth Hypothesis suggested in the previous chapter, we linked the growth of labor productivity to the factor inputs. This approach is consistent with the existing literature on the growth of regions and growth convergence (Barro and Sala-i-Martin, 1992, 1995; Mankiw, Romer, and Weil, 1992). To measure the impact of entrepreneurship capital on the growth of labor productivity, we estimate the following simple growth equation:[4]

$$\log(y_{i,t_1}/y_{i,t_0}) = \alpha - (1 - e^{-\beta})\log(y_{i,t_0}) + \mathbf{X}\boldsymbol{\gamma} + u_{i,t_1}, \quad (4.3)$$

where i denotes regions, y_i is GDP in region i divided by the number of employees in a region (hence, labor productivity), t_0 and t_1 are time instances (in our case, 1992 and 2000), and $\mathbf{X}$ is a set of variables that might account for regional differences in the growth rate of labor productivity.

The dependent variable, regional growth of labor productivity, might depend on the structure of the regional economy. That is, regional growth might be more pronounced in regions where a larger proportion of fast-growing industries are located. A priori, a fast-growing industry is also one in which a large number of startups can be observed. If this holds, then both startups and growth depend on a third variable, the industry structure of the region. To avoid the resulting endogeneity bias in the regression process, we control for this industry structure using two steps. First, we include the level of the regional R&D activity in $\mathbf{X}$. This will correct for the fact that knowledge-based industries usually exhibit higher growth rates. Second, we introduce a second equation of the form

$$E_i = f(y_{i,t_0}, H_i), \quad (4.4)$$

which explains *entrepreneurship capital* in region i as a function of the region's *labor productivity* and the region's *human capital* level. Both equations are estimated simultaneously using three-stage least squares regressions. By specifying explicitly both equations as recursive models, we eliminate an endogeneity bias that would occur due to the fact that a startup activity might depend on the growth dynamics of a region (see Intriligator, Bodkin, and Hsiao, 1996, for example).

Table 4.6 reports on the regression results from estimating equations (4.3) and (4.4) simultaneously. First, from the upper part of table 4.6, the coefficient of log (y_{i,t_0}) is negative and within a region that has often been reported within this kind of equation.[5] This finding implies that regions with a higher level of labor productivity exhibit a lower subsequent growth rate for this variable. The estimated impact of regional R&D input is positive and significant for all estimations, implying that R&D activity exerts a positive impact on the region's growth rate of labor productivity.

All our measures of entrepreneurship capital exert a positive influence on the dependent variable. The estimated level is, at first glance, strikingly high. Of course, this is a measurement issue, since these variables are expressed as intensities and, therefore, range between zero and one. Thus, the high coefficients merely reflect the low values of the entrepreneurship measures. It is noteworthy, however, that the impact of our general measure of entrepreneurship is estimated to be smaller and less significant than our more high-tech measures of entrepreneurship capital. Hence, given that we have corrected for R&D input, we find that innovative startups exert a stronger impact on regional productivity growth than do their noninnovative counterparts.

TABLE 4.6 Results of Three Stage Least Squares Regressions of Equations (4.3) and (4.4), Estimating Growth in Labor Productivity

	Dependent variable: Growth rate of labor productivity			
Constant	0.124***	0.134***	0.132***	0.121***
	(5.31)	(5.73)	(5.70)	(5.01)
Log(Y/L) 1992	−0.036***	−0.034***	−0.033***	−0.036***
	(−4.41)	(−4.83)	(−4.82)	(−4.13)
R&D activity	0.002***	0.002**	0.002***	0.002***
	(2.38)	(2.50)	(2.64)	(2.26)
General entrepreneurship	0.003**			
	(2.10)			
High-tech entrepreneurship		0.020**		
		(2.43)		
ICT entrepreneurship			0.023**	
			(2.39)	
Low-tech entrepreneurship				0.004**
				(1.93)
$\chi^2_{(324)}$	32.32***	37.39***	36.88***	29.21***
(p value)	(0.000)	(0.000)	(0.000)	(0.000)

	Dependent variable			
	General E	High-tech E	ICT E	Low-tech E
Constant	−21.209***	−4.273***	−3.635***	−13.072**
	(−2.87)	(−4.18)	(−4.51)	(−2.26)
Growth rate Y/L	77.090**	12.879**	9.890**	54.072*
	(2.05)	(2.46)	(2.40)	(1.79)
Y/L 1992	0.086***	0.012***	0.009**	0.065**
	(2.68)	(2.75)	(2.44)	(2.51)
Human capital	2.068***	0.234***	0.296***	1.438**
	(2.89)	(3.47)	(3.78)	(2.50)
$\chi^2_{(325)}$	58.12***	76.68***	78.15***	45.92***
(p value)	(0.000)	(0.000)	(0.000)	(0.000)

t values in parentheses unless denoted otherwise.
*Statistically significant at the two-tailed test for 90% level of confidence.
**Statistically significant at the two-tailed test for 95% level of confidence.
***Statistically significant at the two-tailed test for 99% level of confidence.
E=entrepreneurship.

The bottom part of table 4.6 shows the results for equation (4.4). This estimation is included to correct for an endogeneity bias from regressing entrepreneurship capital, measured as startups, against productivity growth. We find that startup activity is greater in regions with a higher level of labor productivity as well as in regions with a higher level of human capital.

Overall, the results provide compelling empirical evidence supporting the Growth Hypothesis. The econometric results suggest that entrepreneurship capital fosters economic growth, especially in the high-tech industries, based on the more risk-oriented measures of entrepreneurship capital. We take this as evidence supporting our argument that entrepreneurial activity fosters the selection and transformation of generally available knowledge into economic knowledge. Whereas the Romer growth model assumed that knowledge capital is both necessary and sufficient for knowledge spillovers, in fact, entrepreneurship plays an important role in commercializing knowledge. Knowledge may be important for economic growth, but the capacity for that knowledge to be commercialized is also important. Entrepreneurship is one such mechanism facilitating the spillover of knowledge.

4.5 Conclusions

In this chapter, we have attempted to link entrepreneurship to economic performance. To do so, we introduced the concept of entrepreneurship capital as a subcomponent, or specific aspect, of social capital. Entrepreneurship capital differs from social capital in that it focuses solely on those aspects of social capital that promote entrepreneurial activity. Other aspects of social capital actually may inhibit entrepreneurship. However, this chapter follows the social capital tradition, fueled by the writings of Putnam and Coleman, among others, by arguing that a strong presence of entrepreneurship capital will improve economic performance.

Since the degree of entrepreneurship capital in an economy ultimately manifests itself in the form of newly created businesses, we measured it indirectly, as reflected by the number of business startups in that economy relative to its respective population. Using data from German regions, we find convincing evidence consistent with the hypothesis that entrepreneurship is positively linked to economic performance, as measured by economic output (GDP) and economic growth.

There are two important qualifications in concluding this chapter. First, entrepreneurship capital is not directly measured but rather is inferred by the observable degree of startup activity. Though we are not able to directly measure entrepreneurship capital, we are able to infer something about relative magnitudes across regions based on a manifestation of that entrepreneurship capital—startup activity within that region. Second, the amount of entrepreneurship capital in a region is taken as exogenous. The chapter never considers why entrepreneurship capital varies across regions and which factors actually shape entrepreneurship capital. We leave this for the next chapter.

These two qualifications suggest the sole public policy implication from the chapter. Public policies promoting entrepreneurship capital should be expected to positively affect economic performance. However, which types of public policy instruments are best suited to promote entrepreneurship capital is beyond the scope of this chapter.

Endogenous Entrepreneurship

5.1 Why Do People Start Firms?

The recognition of new opportunities combined with purposeful action in establishing a new firm is at the heart of entrepreneurship. The focus of entrepreneurship literature in general, and entrepreneurship theory in particular, has been on the cognitive process by which individuals recognize entrepreneurial opportunities and then decide to actualize them by starting a new business or organization. As we argued in the previous chapters, this approach typically takes the opportunities as given and focuses instead on differences across individual-specific characteristics, traits, and propensities to explain variations in entrepreneurial behavior. We further establish in chapter 3 that in this book, we consider entrepreneurship to be endogenous, not just to differences in individual characteristics but to differences in the contexts in which a given individual, with an endowment of personal characteristics, propensities, and capabilities, finds themself.

We are not contesting the validity of the pervasive entrepreneurship literature that identifies specific individual characteristics that shape one's decision to become an entrepreneur. What we do propose, however, is that differences in the contexts in which any given individual finds themself, might also influence the entrepreneurial decision.

Rather than taking entrepreneurial opportunity as exogenous, this chapter places it at the center of attention by making it endogenous. Entrepreneurial opportunity is posited to be greater in contexts rich in knowledge but limited in contexts with impoverished knowledge. According to the Endogenous Entrepreneurship Hypothesis, proposed in chapter 3, entrepreneurship is an endogenous response to knowledge investments made by firms and public organizations that do not fully commercialize those new ideas, thus generating opportunities for entrepreneurs. Thus, whereas most literature takes entrepreneurial opportunities to be exogenous, this chapter suggests that they are endogenous and systematically created by investments in knowledge. To suggest that entrepreneurial opportunities are systematically created by contexts with high investments in knowledge sheds little light on what constitutes the analytical unit of observation for comparing such contexts. In the second section of this chapter, we propose such an analytical context: a spatial unit of observation, which constitutes the platform for knowledge spillovers and the generation of entrepreneurial opportunities.

In section 3, we explain the link between investments in new knowledge and the creation of entrepreneurial opportunities. In the fourth section, we test the Endogenous Entrepreneurship Hypothesis. The findings that entrepreneurial opportunities are systematically generated through knowledge investments within spatial contexts challenge the assumption made in chapter 4 that entrepreneurship capital is exogenous. Thus, in section 5, we estimate both entrepreneurship and growth as endogenous variables within the context of three-stage least squares estimation. A summary and conclusions are provided in the final section. In contrast to the prevalent approach in entrepreneurship theory, this chapter concludes that entrepreneurial opportunities are not exogenous but rather systematically generated by investments in ideas and knowledge that cannot be fully appropriated and commercialized by those incumbent firms and organizations creating the new knowledge.

5.2 The Spatial Context

The previous chapters of this book provided both a theoretical argument and supporting evidence suggesting that entrepreneurship matters for economic output, growth, and productivity. Those regions with a greater endowment of entrepreneurship capital tend to exhibit systematically greater levels of economic output as well as labor productivity and economic growth.

However, an important qualification from these findings is that entrepreneurship capital is taken as exogenous. For at least two reasons, the exogeneity assumption for entrepreneurship should not be disturbing. First, in the traditional approach for analyzing economic growth, the factors of production, such as physical capital and labor, have almost always been assumed to be exogenous in determining economic performance, measured as GDP level or GDP growth. The second reason is inherent in the traditional view of entrepreneurship as responding to variations across personal characteristics but holding the external context constant. This traditional view assumes that entrepreneurship is independent of the context.

However, in chapter 3 we challenged the assumption that entrepreneurial opportunities are exogenous by introducing the Endogenous Entrepreneurship Hypothesis, which posits that entrepreneurship is a response to investments in knowledge and ideas by incumbent organizations that are not fully commercialized by those organizations. Thus, contexts that are richer in knowledge will offer more entrepreneurial opportunities and therefore should also endogenously induce more entrepreneurial activity, ceteris paribus. In contrast, contexts that are impoverished in knowledge will offer only limited entrepreneurial opportunities generated by knowledge spillovers and therefore endogenously induce less entrepreneurial activity.

In his 1995 book, Audretsch used the unit of analysis of the industry for analyzing the impact of knowledge spillovers on the startup activity of new firms. In fact, industries where R&D played an important role had previously been considered to pose a high degree of barriers to entry. It was well accepted that industries requiring capital investment posed a barrier to entry by new firms. In order to enter the industry, new firms needed a high level of capital investment, which was thought to impede entry. Similarly, R&D also posed a high barrier to entry. If R&D investments are required to be competitive, new-firm startups would be confronted by an inherent size disadvantage.

However, the empirical evidence provided by Audretsch (1995) found exactly the opposite. In fact, new-firm startups were even more prevalent in highly innovative industries, suggesting that R&D must not pose such a barrier to entry as previously assumed.

How were entrepreneurial startups able to overcome what previously had been viewed as a barrier to entry? The answer provided by Audretsch (1995) was through exploiting knowledge generated externally to the entrepreneurial startup, such as research undertaken at universities and in the laboratories of large corporations. These findings suggested that what had previously been thought to pose a barrier to entry was actually the mechanism generating the opportunity for starting a new firm—new knowledge and ideas. In addition, this suggested an inversion of the model of the knowledge function posited by Griliches. Rather than starting with an exogenously given firm that engages in investments in new knowledge through R&D and augmentation of human capital to endogenously generate innovative output, the Knowledge Spillover Theory of Entrepreneurship started with the exogenous (uncontested) knowledge embodied in knowledge workers that resulted in the endogenous creation of a new firm to pursue an opportunity that otherwise would not have been pursued.

The industry is only one type of knowledge context. A very different platform for organizing both the production of knowledge, as well as harnessing the resulting externalities, or knowledge spillovers, involves geographic space. Geographic space has been identified by Jaffe (1989) and Audretsch and Feldman (1996) as being an important unit of analysis for harnessing knowledge spillovers. However, while these studies provided evidence confirming that knowledge spillovers are geographically bounded and localized within close spatial proximity to the knowledge source, the actual mechanism that actually transmits the spillover of knowledge remained unidentified. Combining these two strands of literature—one focusing on the organizational context and the other on the spatial context—suggests an important mechanism by which knowledge spills over: the creation of a new firm in a localized context.

Thus, Audretsch (1995) found that an explanation for variations in entrepreneurial activity across industries is that the underlying knowledge conditions vary systematically across industries. Some industries are more knowledge intensive than others. By analogy, entrepreneurial opportunities should also vary systematically across spatial contexts. Some regions are more knowledge intensive than are others, and thus generate a greater amount of entrepreneurial opportunities.

That entrepreneurial activity varies across geographic space has long been observed. Efforts to systematically link spatial variations in entrepreneurship with locational specific characteristics showed that such spatial activity is not at all random but shaped by factors associated with particular regions (Reynolds, Storey, and Westhead, 1994). A series of studies, dating back at least to Carlton (1983) and Bartik (1985) and, more recently, Reynolds, Storey, and Westhead (1993), has attempted to identify characteristics specific to particular regions that account for geographic variations in entrepreneurship. The focus of most of these studies has been on relating unemployment to the entrepreneurial decision. Other factors, such as population density, have been included largely as control variables.

Thus, although a large literature links new-firm startup activity to region-specific characteristics and attributes (Carlton, 1983; Bartik, 1985; Audretsch and Fritsch, 1994; Reynolds et al. 1994; Fritsch, 1997), none of these studies provided a theory linking knowledge spillovers to new-firm startup activity, nor did any studies provide a measure of knowledge spillovers.

For example, Audretsch and Fritsch (1994) examined the impact that location plays on entrepreneurial activity in West Germany. Using a database derived from social insurance statistics, which covers about 90 percent of employment, they find that, for the late 1980s, the birth rates of new firms were higher in regions experiencing low unemployment that have a dense population, a high population growth rate, a high share of skilled workers, and a strong presence of small businesses.

Thus, entrepreneurship activity has certainly been observed to vary across geographic space and systematically linked to spatial characteristics specific to the particular Standort. However, virtually no effort has been made to link spatial variations in entrepreneurial activity, either theoretically or empirically, with the knowledge conditions of that Standort. As the link between investments in knowledge and entrepreneurial activity is the driving mechanism inducing endogenous entrepreneurship, we analyze it explicitly in the next section.

5.3 The Role of Knowledge Spillovers in Creating Entrepreneurial Opportunities

In introducing the Knowledge Spillover Theory of Entrepreneurship, chapter 3 posited that entrepreneurial opportunities are not exogenous but rather endogenous. In particular, entrepreneurial opportunities were identified as emanating from investments in new economic knowledge. Such knowledge investments made by incumbent firms and research organizations that are not fully appropriated create potential opportunities for individuals, or teams of individuals, to start new firms. Thus, endogenous entrepreneurship, or knowledge spillover entrepreneurship, refers to the startup of a new firm as an endogenous response to knowledge opportunities emanating from investments in knowledge made by incumbent organizations.

Why do these new opportunities emerge for entrepreneurship, when the investment is made by incumbent firms? As chapter 3 suggests, investments in knowledge create assets that might have a positive expected value but at the same time are characterized by hyperuncertainty, prohibitive asymmetries, and high costs of transacting the potential value of those ideas across economic agents. Thus, investments in new economic knowledge typically have significant divergences in the expected value of pursuing, implementing, and commercializing those new ideas.

A context, or in this case a region, with an absence of investments in new knowledge will limit entrepreneurial activity to a base amount emanating from "normal" entrepreneurship. Such exogenous opportunities are here defined as coming from nonknowledge factors and result in a positive expected return from entrepreneurship, $\pi^* - w > 0$. For example, one important source of such entrepreneurial opportunities is economic growth, g_Y, so that $\pi^*(g_Y) - w > 0$.

However, entrepreneurial opportunities alone do not guarantee the generation of entrepreneurial activity. As chapter 3 suggested, barriers to entrepreneurship, β, can impede the actualization of entrepreneurial opportunities into firm startups. This is consistent with a series of studies (Carlton, 1983; Bartik, 1985; Reynolds et al., 1994; Fritsch, 1997) that identified barriers to entrepreneurship such as prohibitive tax rates, limited (skilled) labor force availability, bureaucratic barriers, and red tape that inhibit the realization of such entrepreneurial opportunities.

The Knowledge Spillover Theory of Entrepreneurship does not dispute the role and influence of such exogenous factors in determining entrepreneurial activity. However, it suggests that an additional factor also influences entrepreneurial activity, the amount of entrepreneurship endogenously induced from investments in knowledge and new ideas. Some of these knowledge investments will be appropriated through commercialization by the incumbent organizations undertaking those investments, which was represented by θ in chapter 3. However, the conditions inherent in new economic knowledge of hyperuncertainty, prohibitive asymmetries across agents, and significant transaction costs will result in a *knowledge filter* of $1 - \theta > 0$. Thus, knowledge spillover entrepreneurship is the endogenous response through the establishment of a new firm to take advantage of knowledge investments not fully commercialized by the incumbent organizations undertaking those investments.

5.4 An Empirical Test

5.4.1 Specification

Do contexts rich in knowledge investment indeed generate more entrepreneurship than knowledge-impoverished contexts as the Endogenous Entrepreneurship Hypothesis predicts? To answer this question, we need to identify and control for factors conducive to, as well as impeding, entrepreneurial activity, or $\dot{A}_{opp}$ and β, in the language of chapter 3.

Considerable progress has been made identifying the factors influencing entrepreneurial opportunities as well as barriers to entrepreneurship. As we said here and in chapter 3, entrepreneurship theory has focused on the existence of opportunities combined with the capacity to pursue them through the creation of new organizations. Generally, empirical studies analyzing the spatial pattern of startup rates have incorporated factors reflecting the sources of entrepreneurial opportunities and factors facilitating or hindering entrepreneurial capabilities.

For example, every country study included in the special issue of *Regional Studies* on "Regional Variations in New Firm Formation," edited by Reynolds et al. (1994), along with the survey by Storey (1991), linked regional startup rates to regional-specific characteristics such as population density, growth, unemployment, skill levels of the labor force, and mean establishment size. These studies suggest that the empirical evidence is generally unambiguous with respect to the findings for population density (a positive impact on startup rates), growth (positive impact), skill levels of the labor force (positive impact), and mean establishment size (negative impact on startup rates). Country studies produced ambiguous and inconsistent results with respect to the relationship between unemployment rates and startup activity.

Even though the specification of these regressions estimates was somewhat ad hoc, one interpretation of their approach and findings is that these variables reflected various elements of entrepreneurial barriers and entrepreneurial opportunities (i.e., β and $\dot{A}_{opp}$). For example, the systematic and positive relationship between population density and startup activity could be interpreted as bestowing entrepreneurial opportunities from the three sources of agglomeration identified by Alfred Marshall (1920): labor market pooling, nonpecuniary economies, and knowledge externalities.

The systematic finding of a positive relationship between startup rates and growth is consistent with the theory of small business flexibility, introduced by Mills and Schumann (1985). They explicitly identified growth as a factor creating opportunities that are not met by incumbent firms, as long as there is a positive cost of adjusting capacity by the incumbent. Thus, economic growth can be interpreted as one source of entrepreneurial opportunity in the Mills and Schumann model, but only because of the existence of capacity constraints and positive costs to capacity adjustment.

The finding of a positive relationship between the level of skills in the labor force and startup rates can be interpreted as indicating that entrepreneurial capabilities are positively related to the level of skilled labor. Similarly, the negative relationship between mean establishment size and startup activity can be interpreted as reflecting both entrepreneurial capabilities and opportunities in regions with a large share of small establishments, where workers have accumulated learning and experiences in small firms and there is a large network of small enterprises with which a new startup can interact.

Unemployment has been linked to entrepreneurship at least since Oxenfeldt (1943), who pointed out that individuals confronted with unemployment and low prospects for wage employment turn to self-employment as a viable alternative. This was an extension of Knight's (1921) view that individuals make a decision among three states: unemployment, self-employment, and employment. The actual decision is shaped by the relative prices of these three activities, but there was a clear prediction that entrepreneurship would be positively related to unemployment. However, as Storey (1991) documents, the empirical evidence linking unemployment to entrepreneurship is fraught with ambiguities. Whereas some studies find that greater unemployment serves as a catalyst for startup activity (Highfield and Smiley, 1987; Hamilton, 1989; Evans and Leighton, 1989a, 1989b, and 1990; Yamawaki, 1990; Reynolds et al., 1994; Reynolds, Miller, and Maki,

1995), still others find that unemployment reduces the amount of entrepreneurial activity (Audretsch and Fritsch, 1994; Audretsch, 1995).

The failure to find an unambiguous relationship between unemployment and startup rates may reflect the two polar impacts of unemployment on entrepreneurship. On one hand, it increases the attractiveness of existing entrepreneurial opportunities; on the other hand, it may also reflect a paucity of entrepreneurial capabilities (Storey, 1991).

In addition to the measures found in the cross-regional country studies compiled by Reynolds et al. (1994), other studies have also uncovered specific location characteristics that might influence barriers and opportunities to entrepreneurship. One such variable creating entrepreneurial opportunities is the demographic composition of the region. People who are "outsiders" or members of marginal social groups may not possess the requisite social capital for their knowledge to be applicable to and compatible with incumbent organizations. This suggests that individuals from marginal groups will have a greater propensity to resort to entrepreneurship to appropriate the expected value of their ideas. In particular, immigrants, as well as young people, have been found to have a greater propensity to start new businesses.

A second demographic characteristic influencing economic growth is the degree of diversity in the workforce. Jacobs (1969) argued that this diversity is an important source of knowledge spillovers. According to Jacobs, the exchange of complementary knowledge across diverse firms and economic agents yields a greater return on new economic knowledge. Her theory emphasizes that the heterogeneity of people within a geographic region promotes knowledge externalities, innovative activity, and, ultimately, economic growth. Thus, entrepreneurial opportunities should be greater in regions with more diverse populations, since more new ideas are generated as a result of social diversity.

Florida (2002) argued that the attractiveness of a Standort facilitates both entrepreneurial capabilities and opportunities by attracting what he terms the creative class. Locations that are more attractive to knowledge workers, or the creative class, should also exhibit higher startup rates, ceteris paribus.

Social diversity has been found to promote the generation of entrepreneurial opportunities by enhancing new ideas and the spillover of knowledge. Florida (2002) argued that social diversity is a proxy for the openness or tolerance of a society to new ideas. Such openness is important in an environment where new ideas are transformed into business ideas and, ultimatively, to new firm startups. Thus, openness is an important asset to the generation of entrepreneurial opportunities.

Glaeser et al. (1992) and Ciccone and Hall (1996) argued that spatial density, including proximity, facilitates knowledge spillovers. Similarly, we expect that in densely populated regions, ideas and knowledge will flow faster, implying that entrepreneurial opportunities will be generated faster and can be appropriated more easily by economic agents. Hence, entrepreneurial opportunities should be greater in agglomerations, or more densely populated regions, than in less agglomerated regions. Both entrepreneurial opportunities and the ability of economic agents to appropriate opportunities through entrepreneurship should be greater in more highly agglomerated regions, where knowledge spillovers are greater and the provision of ancillary services and inputs is greater as well.

The composition of economic activity at the Standort may also influence entrepreneurial opportunities. In the 1990s, there was a debate on how the spatial composition of economic activity facilitated knowledge spillovers. Some studies found that a stronger specialization of economic activity within a single industry at a Standort was more conducive to knowledge spillovers, or the "Marshall-Arrow-Romer" type of externality; other studies argued for (Jacobs, 1969; Porter, 1990) and found evidence (Glaeser et al., 1992; Audretsch and Feldman, 1999) suggesting that, instead, diversity among complementary types of economic activity is more conducive to knowledge spillovers, or "Jacobs" externality.[1] Though the theory and empirical evidence do not specifically identify the link between the composition of economic activity and entrepreneurial opportunities, the focus on knowledge spillovers implicitly suggests that entrepreneurial opportunities should be related to the degree of specialization or diversity of economic activity at the Standort.

Public policy can also influence both entrepreneurial opportunities and the ability of economic agents to take advantage of them. Some public policies affecting entrepreneurship may be obvious, such as taxes, legal barriers, bureaucratic barriers, early stage finance, procurement, or tax credits, as Lundström and Stevenson (2002) point out; public policy affecting entrepreneurship also includes a broad spectrum of instruments. Lundström and Stevenson identify public policies designed to encourage entrepreneurship, ranging from immigration to education. Operationalizing public policy to promote entrepreneurship into a variable that can be measured is a challenging, if not impossible, task.

To these different measures reflecting various aspects of entrepreneurial opportunities and entrepreneurial barriers, we include a measure of investment in new knowledge. According to the Endogenous Entrepreneurship Hypothesis, contexts, or regions, with a greater investment in new knowledge, should generate more entrepreneurial opportunities and therefore exhibit higher rates of observed entrepreneurship. In contrast, contexts, or regions, with little investments in new knowledge, will generate fewer entrepreneurial opportunities and therefore should exhibit lower rates of observed entrepreneurship.

5.4.2 Measurement

The same measure of entrepreneurship from chapter 4 is used: the number of startups in a region relative to the regional population.[2] Since the number of startups is subject to stochastic disturbance over short time periods, it is prudent to compute the measure of entrepreneurial activity based on startup rates over a longer time period. We use the number of startups between 1998 and 2000. Whereas opportunity recognition is probably inherent in most, if not all, of entrepreneurship, the type of endogenous entrepreneurship emanating from knowledge spillovers that is the focus of this chapter suggests a sharper focus on knowledge-based and technology entrepreneurship. Thus, we use and compare four different measures of entrepreneurship in testing the Endogenous Entrepreneurship Hypothesis.

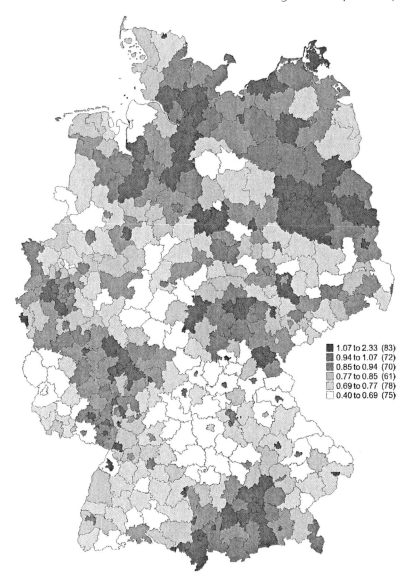

FIGURE 5.1. Startups in all industries, 1998–2000, relative to population in thousands (number of regions within given range listed in parentheses)

The first measure of entrepreneurship is the more general and includes startups in *all* industries. More than 50 percent of these startups are in the retail and gastronomy sectors, that is, shops and restaurants. Figure 5.1 depicts the spatial distribution of this measure.

Two knowledge-based measures of entrepreneurship are considered, the first being startup rates in the high-tech industries, that is, industries with an average R&D intensity of more than 2.5 percent.[3] Start-ups in these industries account for

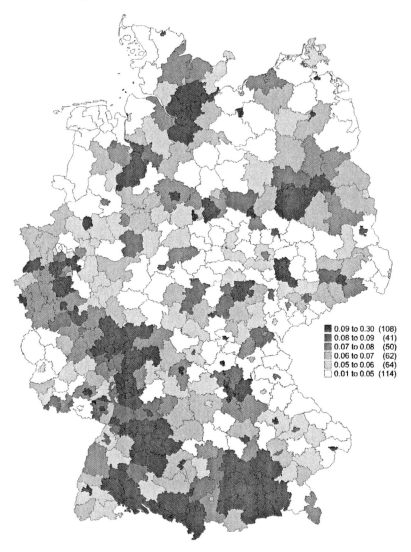

FIGURE 5.2. Startups in high-tech industries, 1998–2000, relative to population in thousands (number of regions within given range listed in parentheses)

7.5 percent of all startups in average, ranging from 1.6 percent to 17.9 percent within German Kreise. The spatial distribution of this measure is shown in figure 5.2.

A second measure of knowledge-based entrepreneurship is the startup rate in the ICT industries. This measure represents a mix of startups in ICT-oriented manufacturing and service industries. ICT entrepreneurship accounts for 7.7 percent of all startups, with a high regional variation, ranging from 1.5 percent to 19.0 percent. This measure is shown in figure 5.3.

As a "counterfactual" benchmark, a fourth measure of entrepreneurship is also used, the residual, or the aggregate, of the remaining industries, which is denoted

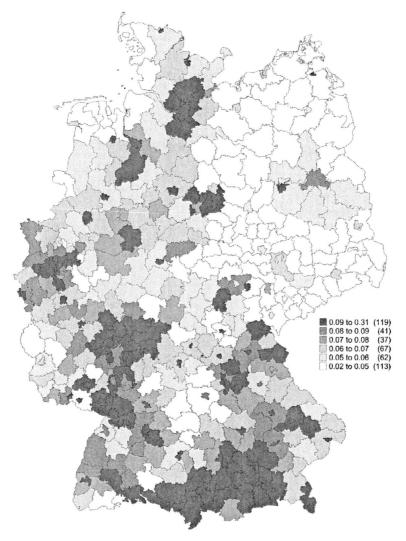

FIGURE 5.3. Startups in ICT industries, 1998–2000, relative to population in thousands (number of regions within given range listed in parentheses)

as "low-tech" entrepreneurship, which refers to the low R&D intensity of the industry and not to the degree of education or human capital of the founders. Figure 5.4 depicts the spatial distribution of this measure.

Table 5.1 shows the correlation matrix for these four measures of entrepreneurship as well as population density. This table shows that both knowledge-based measures of entrepreneurship are highly correlated with each other, while the correlations between the two measures of knowledge entrepreneurship and the low-tech measure are much weaker. The measures of general entrepreneurship and low-tech entrepreneurship are highly correlated. This reflects the high share of low-tech

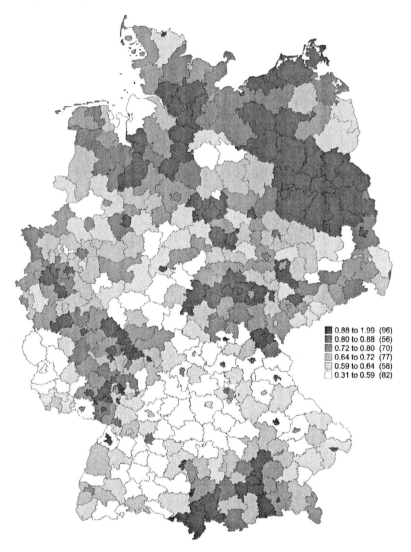

FIGURE 5.4. Startups in low-tech industries, 1998–2000, relative to population in thousands (number of regions within given range listed in parentheses)

entrepreneurship contained in the general entrepreneurship measure. Though all of the measures of entrepreneurship are significantly correlated with the regional population density of regions, the correlations between the knowledge-based entrepreneurship measures and population density are considerably stronger and are roughly twice as large as for the low-tech measure of entrepreneurship.

In the previous section, we explained the theoretical reasons, along with some of the empirical findings from previous studies, for including location-specific characteristics as influencing regional entrepreneurship. As we emphasized, each explanatory variable should reflect an aspect of either entrepreneurial opportunity,

TABLE 5.1 Correlations between Startup Rates and Population Density

	Population density	General	High-tech	ICT
General	0.3419			
High-tech	0.4325	0.6515		
ICT	0.4147	0.6063	0.8411	
Low-tech	0.2638	0.9714	0.4667	0.4110

$\dot{A}_{opp}$, or barrier to entrepreneurship, β. These factors, either generating or reflecting entrepreneurial opportunities, or else constituting a barrier to entrepreneurship, are expanded in the following list:

Economic Output: A high level of economic output implies a large market size, hence a high intensity in economic exchange and a high level of entrepreneurial opportunities. Economic output is measured as the gross value added in manufacturing. It is a stock measure of economic performance.

Economic Growth: A positive growth rate implies increasing market size, hence creates general opportunities for business including startups. It is assumed that nascent entrepreneurs derive their expectations about future opportunities from this past performance. A higher growth rate would be expected to generate a greater degree of entrepreneurial opportunities than would a stagnating economy. Rather than the stock measure of economic output, economic growth is a measure of the regions' past economic performance. This variable is computed for each region as $g_Y = \ln(Y_{t_1} - Y_{t_0})/(t_1 - t_0)$, with $t_1 = 2000$ and $t_0 = 1992$, where Y_t represents GDP at time t. This measures the regions' average growth rate between the years 1992 and 2000.

Knowledge Investment: Investments in new economic knowledge provide the source for knowledge spillovers and therefore endogenous entrepreneurship. Knowledge inputs are measured in two ways. The first is the number of R&D employees in private firms. The second measure includes R&D employees in both private firms and public institutions. These measures are divided by the variable *labor*, that is, the number of non-R&D employees in the data set. This assumes that a high regional R&D intensity reflects a greater degree of opportunities to start a new knowledge-based business. This variable is therefore more specific to knowledge opportunities as compared to GDP growth; therefore, a positive impact is expected on entrepreneurial activity.

Capital Investment: By investment, incumbent firms take on new opportunities. There are two main reasons why this variable might influence entrepreneurial activity, albeit in a contradictory manner that renders the expected sign of the estimated coefficient indeterminate. The first is that investment reflects confidence in the economic future. Hence, we would expect a positive correlation between investment and entrepreneurial opportunities. In contrast, the second is a "crowding out" effect. The measure of investment used here represents the pursuit of economic opportunities within incumbent firms rather than in startups. If this effect dominates, we expect a negative correlation between a region's level of investment and entrepreneurial opportunities. Investment in physical capital is measured for the producing sector (excluding mining) of firms with more than 20 employees (measured in 1999).

Population Density: As discussed earlier population density can be expected to increase knowledge flow and to imply a higher level of provision of ancillary services. Hence, entrepreneurial opportunities should be greater in more densely populated regions than in less densely populated regions. We measure population density as the average number of inhabitants in year 2000 relative to the regions' surface.

Entrepreneurship Policies: Public policy can be undertaken to influence entrepreneurial activity. Regional and national authorities use various subsidy schemes as instruments to achieve economic policy goals. One goal of such subsidy policies is to increase entrepreneurial activity. The variable *subsidies* measures the sum of all subsidies spent in the respective region, controlled for regional population. Startup funding is only one among a large number of subsidy schemes. This measure should reflect the role that subsidies play in a particular Standort. However, it will not provide any inferences about the effectiveness of startup funding, which would require other methodologies.[4]

Unemployment: As we previously discussed, both the theoretical relationships and empirical links between unemployment and entrepreneurship are ambiguous. Higher unemployment will reduce the opportunity cost of entrepreneurship but also may reflect a lower level of capabilities of the individual as well as a lower level of entrepreneurial opportunities at that Standort. A positive coefficient of the unemployment rate suggests that the push factors prevail, whereas a negative coefficient reflects a lower level of entrepreneurial opportunities in the region. The variable is measured as the mean unemployment rate in the region over the period from 1998 to 2000.

Taxes: As Carlton (1983) suggested, a high tax burden may reduce entrepreneurial opportunities. The German tax system does not make regional distinctions or vary systematically across regions, with the exception of the Business Tax, for which the multiplier, and hence the level, is set by regional governments. Regional governments rely on revenues from the Business Tax to finance local budgets. Such public expenditures at the regional level can conceivably generate entrepreneurial opportunities. Consequently, the relationship between business taxes and entrepreneurial opportunities may be a priori ambiguous. On the one hand, high business taxes will reduce entrepreneurial opportunities by reducing the expected profitability accruing from entrepreneurship. On the other hand, regional expenditures can be used to develop regional clusters of entrepreneurial firms, which might actually suggest a positive relationship.

Social Diversity: We take the arguments put forward by Florida (2002) (discussed in section 5.4.1) by measuring social diversity as an entropy index of the voting behavior on the occasion of the last parliament vote (1998). The measure takes into account all political parties, including the smaller ones. The entropy index is transformed to $[0, 1]$ so that 0 indicates maximum variety and 1 indicates no variety. A positive coefficient would therefore indicate that entrepreneurial opportunities are negatively related to social diversity.

Industrial Diversity: In section 5.4.1, we argued that the composition of economic activity at the Standort may also influence entrepreneurial opportunities. The impact of industrial diversity on generating entrepreneurial opportunities is reflected by including a Herfindahl index of industrial diversity in the regressions. This index is defined in the interval $[0, 1]$, where 1 implies maximal concentration (i.e., the region would be dominated by a single industry). A positive coefficient would therefore indicate that entrepreneurial opportunities are positively related to industrial specialization.

Standort Attractiveness: It has often been argued that a location that is more attractive and offers a superior quality of life will attract more knowledge workers and therefore enhance knowledge spillovers (Florida, 2002). According to this line of thinking, entrepreneurial opportunities will be greater at a more attractive Standort. The impact of the attractiveness of a Standort on entrepreneurial opportunity is reflected by including the number of a county's hotel beds relative to its surface, as a proxy measure of Standort attractiveness.

5.4.3 Empirical Results

To test the Endogenous Entrepreneurship Hypothesis, we estimated the following regression using a simple reduced form model:

$$E_i = f(\mathbf{y}_i, \mathbf{x}_i), \tag{5.1}$$

where i denotes the regions, E_i denotes *entrepreneurial activity*, $\mathbf{y}_i$ denotes measures that reflect *economic performance*, and $\mathbf{x}_i$ denotes the other factors influencing the extent of entrepreneurial opportunities.

The results in chapter 4 imply that entrepreneurial activity is positively related to economic performance. Hence, regressing a measure of entrepreneurship against measures of economic performance will lead to a simultaneity bias, that is, to inconsistent estimation results (e.g., Intriligator et al., 1992, or Greene, 2000). We therefore estimate a second equation):

$$Y_i = \alpha K_i^{\beta_1} L_i^{\beta_2} R_i^{\beta_3} E_i^{\beta_4}. \tag{5.2}$$

Estimating both equations simultaneously will correct for this inconsistency. The results of simultaneous three-stage least squares estimation of both equations are presented in table 5.2. The first column reports the results estimating general entrepreneurship, the second column for high-technology entrepreneurship, the third column for ICT entrepreneurship, and the last column for low-technology entrepreneurship. What is immediately apparent is that some of the variables differ in sign and significance for the different measures of entrepreneurship. Thus, we discuss the results for each variable individually.

Although the *economic output*, the contemporary stock measure of GDP, does not have a significant influence on entrepreneurship, *economic growth* has a significant positive impact. The positive relationship between economic growth and entrepreneurship is even stronger for the high-tech measure of entrepreneurship. Here, an increase of GDP growth by one percentage point will increase the region's startup rate by roughly 50 percent. On the other hand, GDP growth apparently does not have an impact on ICT startups. This may reflect the fact that

TABLE 5.2 Estimating Entrepreneurship (3SLS)

	Dependent variable: Entrepreneurship			
	General	High-tech	ICT	Low-tech
Economic output	−0.0022	0.0387	−0.0058	−0.0111
	(−0.12)	(1.36)	(−0.21)	(−0.59)
Economic growth	0.3205***	0.5112***	0.0718	0.3169***
	(3.74)	(3.78)	(0.55)	(3.66)
Knowledge investment	1.1184	5.6035***	5.6447***	0.3239
	(1.44)	(4.58)	(4.79)	(0.41)
Capital investment	−0.0012**	−0.0012	0.0000	−0.0012**
	(−2.28)	(−1.54)	(0.06)	(−2.26)
Population density	1.2954***	2.3897***	2.0943***	1.1616***
	(4.46)	(5.25)	(4.78)	(3.97)
Subsidies	0.0006	−0.0003	−0.0097**	0.0012
	(0.24)	(−0.06)	(−2.42)	(0.45)
Unemployment	−0.0007	−0.0425***	−0.0509***	0.0053*
	(−0.22)	(−8.83)	(−11.08)	(1.75)
Business tax	−0.1041***	−0.0730	−0.0979*	−0.1029***
	(−3.10)	(−1.38)	(−1.91)	(−3.03)
Social diversity	−0.1112	−1.0795***	−0.1794	−0.0315
	(−0.99)	(−6.06)	(−1.05)	(−0.28)
Industry diversity	0.8929***	1.1890***	1.3530***	0.8746***
	(6.49)	(5.64)	(6.68)	(6.26)
Standort attractiveness	0.0504	−0.0899	0.2170	0.0349
	(0.51)	(−0.57)	(1.43)	(0.35)
Constant	−5.6316***	−8.0169***	−8.2184***	−5.8336***
	(−19.71)	(−18.10)	(−19.28)	(−19.89)
Pseudo R^2	0.255	0.496	0.637	0.225
(p value)	(0.000)	(0.000)	(0.000)	(0.000)

	Dependent variable: GDP of German counties			
Constant	1.5601***	0.7496**	−0.1549	1.6570***
	(4.17)	(2.32)	(−0.51)	(4.05)
Capital	0.1233***	0.1388***	0.1352***	0.1073***
	(5.16)	(6.00)	(5.41)	(4.25)
Labor	0.7877***	0.7259***	0.7331***	0.8237***
	(29.02)	(27.87)	(24.89)	(27.03)
Knowledge	0.0211*	0.0262**	0.0507***	0.0249**
	(1.91)	(2.32)	(5.15)	(2.28)
General entrepreneurship	0.6195***			
	(7.12)			
High-tech entrepreneurship		0.2263***		
		(5.80)		
ICT entrepreneurship			0.0955***	
			(3.15)	
Low-tech entrepreneurship				0.6553***
				(6.72)
Pseudo R^2	0.925	0.937	0.935	0.920
(p value)	(0.000)	(0.000)	(0.000)	(0.000)
Number of observations	429	429	429	429

t statistic in parentheses.
*Statistically significant at the two-tailed test for 90% level of confidence.
**Statistically significant at the two-tailed test for 95% level of confidence.
***Statistically significant at the two-tailed test for 99% level of confidence.

ICT startups may have a more global orientation and not generated by opportunities generated at the regional level.

The impact of knowledge investment, or *R&D intensity*, is positive and significant for high-tech entrepreneurship and ICT entrepreneurship, but it is insignificant for general entrepreneurship and low-tech entrepreneurship. Hence, investments in knowledge create opportunities for localized knowledge-based entrepreneurship. This evidence supports the Endogenous Entrepreneurship Hypothesis.

Entrepreneurial opportunities tend to be greater in regions with a high *population density*. Apparently, there are more entrepreneurial opportunities in cities and surrounding areas. This effect is roughly twice as large for the knowledge-based measures of entrepreneurship. The positive relationship between population density and entrepreneurship supports the Localization Hypothesis.

As the negative and statistically coefficient of *capital investment* suggests, there is a negative relationship between capital investment and low-tech entrepreneurship. However, there is no evidence of any statistically significant relationship between capital investment and the knowledge-based measures of entrepreneurship. The negative sign indicates that the substitution effect dominates the other two effects mentioned; that is, strong investment of incumbent firms can be considered as a substitute for entrepreneurial opportunities.

The level of *subsidies* does not have a significant impact on entrepreneurship. In fact, for ICT entrepreneurship, the relationship is negative. In order to better understand and interpret this negative relationship, we did an additional analysis that revealed that the public subsidies are negatively correlated with the level of economic output, positively correlated with both regional GDP growth and investment, and at the same time negatively correlated with population density (i.e., they are relatively higher in weakly populated areas). This suggests that the estimated coefficients between the subsidy measure and entrepreneurship are statistically distorted as a result of multicollinearity. Thus, one cannot interpret this result as evidence suggesting that public policy in the form of subsidies has no impact on entrepreneurship. Nevertheless, the fact that subsidies do not exhibit a strong positive impact on entrepreneurial activity certainly does not support the existence of a positive relationship between subsidies and entrepreneurship and needs to be subjected to subsequent systematic research using microeconometric evaluation methods (e.g., Arvanitis and Keilbach, 2002).

An interesting result emerges for the relationship between *unemployment* and entrepreneurship. No statistically significant relationship appears for the general measure of entrepreneurship, but regional unemployment is negatively and significantly related to high-tech entrepreneurship. In contrast, as the positive and statistically significant coefficient suggests, unemployment is positively related to low-tech entrepreneurship. These findings suggest that the relationship between unemployment and entrepreneurship has two faces. On the one hand, high regional unemployment tends to create opportunities for entrepreneurship in low-tech industries. Apparently, such entrepreneurial opportunities provide a vehicle for moving out of unemployment. On the other hand, entrepreneurial opportunities in high-tech industries are not generated by unemployment. The high levels of human capital and knowledge that are a prerequisite for recognizing and exploiting entrepreneurial opportunities in high-tech industries simply do not respond to a high unemployment context. Rather, high regional unemployment reflects a lack of opportunities for knowledge-based startups. Therefore, public policy with the goal to encourage knowledge-based startups as a response to unemployment is probably doomed to fail.

The regression results for *business taxes* show a strongly significant negative impact on both low-tech entrepreneurship and the general measure of entrepreneurship. ICT entreprencurship is less, although still negatively, affected by taxes, while high-tech entrepreneurship is insensitive to the tax burden. The results suggest that high-tech entrepreneurial opportunities are not influenced by the regional tax burden. Rather, entrepreneurial opportunities are shaped by other factors, such as investments in new economic knowledge. Apparently, in the presence of high knowledge investment, the high tax burden does not deter the decision to start a new business.

The extent of *social diversity* does not have a statistically significant impact on general entrepreneurial opportunities. However, as the positive and statistically significant coefficient suggests, there is a positive relationship between the extent of social diversity and high-tech entrepreneurship. This result is certainly consistent with the arguments of Florida (2002), who asserts that a high level of social tolerance facilitates the creation of new ideas, which is transmitted into knowledge spillovers and ultimately entrepreneurial opportunities, at least in a high-knowledge context.

The positive and statistically significant coefficient of the measure of *industry diversity* implies that strong industry specialization has a positive impact on entrepreneurial opportunities. The statistical evidence suggests that the external effects of the Marshall-Arrow-Romer type have a positive impact on entrepreneurship.

The coefficient of *Standort attractiveness* is not statistically significant, suggesting that entrepreneurial opportunities are not related to the measure used here to reflect the desirability of the particular region. The results are insignificant for all but the ICT-oriented measure of entrepreneurship.

Finally, the regressions estimating the production function appear in the lower part of table 5.2. The results generally find positive and significant coefficients for the production factors. These results confirm the findings of section 4.1. Therefore, we do not discuss them further.

Overall, the empirical results reported here are consistent with the Endogenous Entrepreneurship Hypothesis. With other types of entrepreneurial opportunities constant, such as the level of economic growth, unemployment, social diversity, and taxes, entrepreneurial opportunities tend to be greater in contexts with greater knowledge investments. Similarly, in those contexts or regions with a paucity of knowledge investments, entrepreneurial opportunities are limited.

However, the actual impact of knowledge investment on entrepreneurship is clearly nuanced. In particular, not all types of entrepreneurship, but rather more specifically knowledge-based entrepreneurship such as high-tech and ICT entrepreneurship is an endogenous response to investments in new economic knowledge.

In contrast, low-tech entrepreneurship, which covers 85 percent of all entrepreneurial activity, does not endogenously respond to investments in new economic knowledge. Instead, low-tech entrepreneurship tends to respond to opportunities created by a strong economic performance. In addition, low-tech entrepreneurship is strongly positively correlated with the regional unemployment rate. Taxes clearly serve as a barrier to low-tech entrepreneurship. Thus, the evidence supporting the Endogenous Entrepreneurship Hypothesis extends only to knowledge-based entrepreneurship, not to low-tech entrepreneurship.

5.5 Conclusions

The prevalent and traditional theories of entrepreneurship have typically held the context constant and then examined how characteristics specific to the individual affect the cognitive process inherent in the model of entrepreneurial choice. This often leads to the view that is remarkably analogous to that concerning technical change in the Solow model: given a distribution of personality characteristics, proclivities, preferences, and tastes, entrepreneurial opportunity is actually exogenous and seemingly falls like manna from Heaven. One of the great conventional wisdoms in entrepreneurship is "Entrepreneurs are born, not made." Either you have it or you don't. This leaves virtually no room for policy or for altering what nature has created.

This chapter has presented an alternative view. We hold the individual attributes constant and instead focus on variations in the context. In particular, we consider how the knowledge context will influence the cognitive process underlying the entrepreneurial choice model. The result is a theory of endogenous entrepreneurship, where (knowledge) workers respond to opportunities generated by investments in new knowledge by starting a new firm. In this view, entrepreneurship is a rational choice made by economic agents to appropriate the expected value of their endowment of knowledge. Thus, the creation of a new firm is the endogenous response to investments in knowledge that have not been entirely or exhaustively appropriated by the incumbent firm.

In the Knowledge Spillover Theory of Entrepreneurship, the spillover of knowledge and the creation of a new, knowledge-based firm are virtually synonymous. Of course, many other important mechanisms facilitate the knowledge spillovers that have nothing to do with entrepreneurship, such as the mobility of scientists and workers and informal networks, linkages, and interactions. Similarly, certainly new firms start that have nothing to do with the spillover of knowledge. Still, the Spillover Theory of Entrepreneurship suggests that there will be additional entrepreneurial activity as a rational and cognitive response to the creation of new knowledge. Contexts with greater investment in knowledge should also experience a higher degree of entrepreneurship, ceteris paribus. Perhaps it is true that entrepreneurs are made, but more of them will discover what they are made of in a high-knowledge context than in an impoverished knowledge context. Thus, we are inclined to restate the conventional wisdom and instead propose that entrepreneurs are not necessarily made, but are rather are a response—and in particular a response to high-knowledge contexts that are especially fertile in spawning entrepreneurial opportunities.

University Spillovers and Entrepreneurial Location

6.1 University Entrepreneurship

A new literature has emerged suggesting that knowledge spills over from the firm or university producing it to another firm that commercializes that knowledge (Griliches, 1992). This view is supported by theoretical models that have focused on the role that spillovers of knowledge play in generating increasing returns and ultimately economic growth (Romer, 1986, 1990, 1994; Krugman, 1991a, 1991b; Grossman and Helpman, 1991).

An important theoretical suggestion is that geography may provide a relevant unit of observation within which knowledge spillovers occur. The theory of localization suggests that because geographic proximity is needed to transmit knowledge, especially tacit knowledge, knowledge spillovers tend to be localized within a geographic region. A wave of empirical studies by Jaffe (1989); Jaffe, Trajtenberg, and Henderson (1993); Acs, Audretsch, and Feldman (1992, 1994); Audretsch and Feldman (1996); and Audretsch and Stephan (1996) supports this theory.

Though this literature has identified the important role that knowledge spillovers play, it provides little insight into the questions of why and how knowledge spills over. What happens within the black box of the knowledge production is vague and ambiguous at best.

None of the studies suggesting that knowledge spillovers are geographically bounded and localized within spatial proximity to the knowledge source identified the actual mechanisms that transmit the knowledge spillover; rather, the spillovers were implicitly assumed to exist automatically, like "manna from heaven," but only within a geographically bounded spatial area. Based on the mixed and ambiguous findings of earlier studies, Paul Krugman (1991a, p. 53) argued that economists should abandon any attempts at measuring knowledge spillovers because "knowledge flows are invisible, they leave no paper trail by which they may be measured and tracked."

Krugman's (1991a) observation is undeniably true, but the creation of a new firm, especially in a high-technology, science-based industry, produces an event that leaves traces for penetrating the knowledge spillover process. One of the most striking features of firms making Initial Public Offerings (IPOs) in biotechnology is that they are typically able to raise millions of dollars even without a viable product when they go public. Indeed, new firms are founded and receive financing based on the prospects of transforming technological knowledge created by another source into economic knowledge at a new firm through the development and introduction of an innovative product. Thus, the establishment of a new firm in a knowledge-based industry provides a unique opportunity for examining properties of the knowledge production function, especially the links between the creation of knowledge and its commercialization.

The purpose of this chapter is to bring the two dimensions triggered by investments in knowledge—one organizational and the other geographic—together by asking whether the Knowledge Spillover Theory of Entrepreneurship also has a spatial component in that the startups tend to cluster within geographic proximity to knowledge sources, according to chapter 3's Localization Hypothesis (Audretsch, Lehmann, and Warning, 2004, 2005). However, while chapters 3, 4, and 5 generally followed the assumption in the Romer, Lucas, Krugman and Griliches studies that knowledge investments are essentially homogeneous, in this chapter we examine whether the role of location in transmitting knowledge spillovers to entrepreneurial startups is heterogeneous and varies systematically across different scientific and academic fields and for different spillover mechanisms.

The second section of this chapter explains why the Knowledge Spillover Theory of Entrepreneurship should also have a spatial component in that the knowledge startups cluster geographically around the knowledge source (Audretsch, Keilbach, and Lehmann, 2005; Audretsch and Lehmann, 2005d). The third section links entrepreneurship to university spillovers. In the fourth section, we introduce and explain a new firm-level database consisting of high-technology and knowledge-based entrepreneurial startups in Germany. This new database is drawn from the prospectus of 281 firms that made an IPO between March 1997 and March 2000 to examine the role of location in entrepreneurial access to university spillovers. The fifth section provides an empirical test within a spatial context: the region around a university. The role of geographic proximity in accessing university spillovers is measured in two ways: first, the number of firms spatially clustering within close geographic proximity to the university, and, second, the geographical distance between entrepreneurial firms and the closest university.

Finally, in the last section, we provide a summary and conclusion. In particular, the empirical evidence provides general support for the Localization Hypothesis. Universities with a greater investment in knowledge and where the regional investment in knowledge is greater tend to generate more technology startups, suggesting that university spillovers tend to be localized and spatially constrained. However, the contribution of geographical proximity to accessing and absorbing university spillovers is apparently highly nuanced and varies systematically across different scientific fields and academic disciplines as well as different spillover mechanisms. The exact role that geographic proximity plays in facilitating university spillovers depends on the degree to which the type of knowledge and actual spillover mechanism are based on tacit, rather than codified, knowledge.

6.2 Localizing the Knowledge Spillover Theory of Entrepreneurship

The degree of startup activity, or entry into industries, has an important tradition in the field of industrial organization, because such entry serves as a mechanism equilibrating the market and eroding excess profits. Thus, a large literature emerged analyzing the links between characteristics specific to industries and the extent of entrepreneurial activity, as measured by the entry of new firms (Geroski, 1995).

Entrepreneurial activity has long been observed to vary not just across industries but also across geographic space. Systematic analyses (Reynolds, Storey, and Westhead, 1994) have shown that such spatial variations in startup rates are correlated with characteristics specific to regions. Early studies (Carlton, 1983; Bartik, 1985) focused on the role of taxes in explaining variations in entrepreneurial activity across regions. More recent studies have extended this approach to including the impact of regional unemployment levels on entrepreneurship. In particular, a special issue of *Regional Studies* (Reynolds, Storey, and Westhead, 1994) was devoted toward linking characteristics specific to regions to regional startup rates. This special issue contained a series of studies from a broad spectrum of countries. For example, the study for Germany provided statistical evidence on entrepreneurial activity, measured by new-firm startups in each German region, or *Raumordungsregion* (Audretsch and Fritsch, 1994). In particular, the German study found a positive relationship between entrepreneurial activity and low levels of regional unemployment and a high population density. Other country studies contained in the *Regional Studies* special issue similarly linked regional-specific characteristics to the degree of entrepreneurial activity.

These early studies made an important contribution by highlighting that entrepreneurship varies systematically across geographic space. In addition, they provided compelling evidence that spatial variations in entrepreneurial activity are statistically correlated with characteristics specific to the region. However, the literature on regional entrepreneurship has generally not been closely attuned to the theories of entrepreneurship, and in particular, to placing entrepreneurial activities within the framework of opportunity recognition and capabilities.

The Knowledge Spillover Theory of Entrepreneurship focuses on the generation of entrepreneurial opportunities emanating from knowledge investments by incumbent firms and public research organizations that are not fully appropriated by those incumbent enterprises. It is a virtual consensus that entrepreneurship revolves around the recognition and pursuit of these opportunities (Shane and Eckhardt, 2003). Much of the contemporary thinking about entrepreneurship has focused on the cognitive process by which individuals reach the decision to start a new firm. According to Sarasvathy et al. (2003, p. 142), "An entrepreneurial opportunity consists of a set of ideas, beliefs and actions that enable the creation of future goods and services in the absence of current markets for them." Sarasvathy et al. provide a typology of entrepreneurial opportunities as consisting of opportunity recognition, opportunity discovery, and opportunity creation.

While much has been written about the key role played by the recognition of opportunities in the cognitive process underlying the decision to become an entrepreneur, relatively little has been written about the actual source of such entrepreneurial opportunities. The Knowledge Spillover Theory of Entrepreneurship identifies one source of entrepreneurial opportunities: new knowledge and ideas. The Knowledge Spillover Theory of Entrepreneurship posits that it is new knowledge and ideas created in one context but left uncommercialized or not vigorously pursued by the source actually creating those ideas, such as a research laboratory in a large corporation or research undertaken by a university, that generates entrepreneurial opportunities. Thus, in this view, one mechanism for recognizing new opportunities and actually implementing them by starting a new firm involves the spillover of knowledge. The source of the knowledge and ideas, and the organization actually making (at least some of) the investments to produce that knowledge, is not the same as the organization actually attempting to commercialize and appropriate the value of that knowledge: the new firm.

6.3 Linking Entrepreneurship to University Spillovers

6.3.1 Universities as the Source of Spillovers

University spillovers could be defined as externalities that are commercialized by firms, for which the university is the source of the spillover but is not fully compensated (Harris, 2001). Some studies focusing on university spillovers assume that geography plays no role in the cost of accessing that knowledge (Spence, 1984; Cohen and Levinthal, 1990). However, theories of localization suggest that just because university knowledge spills over does not mean that knowledge transmits without cost across geographic space. These theories argue that geographic proximity reduces the cost of accessing and absorbing knowledge spillovers. Thus, a basic tenet in the literature is that close proximity to a university lowers the cost for firms to access and absorb knowledge spillovers. If an entrepreneur decides to locate near a university, the benefits must outweigh the costs. Locating close to universities, which are typically located in urban centers, at least in the German context, is also associated with high costs of living. If the basic resources in terms of access to knowledge accruing from a university are not essential to justify or compensate for those costs, it is more advantageous to locate outside such a metropolitan area.

Theoretical reasoning and empirical evidence show that such knowledge spillovers generated by universities are not accessed and absorbed at costs that are invariant to geographic location (Bottazzi and Peri, 2003). Rather, because university spillovers tend to be spatially bounded, the costs of absorbing spillovers increases with distance from a university. So not only are knowledge spillovers spatially clustered around universities but the entrepreneurial opportunities to start a new firm are also geographically linked to the spatial distribution of knowledge spillovers. The limited geographic reach of such channels for the exchange of ideas and intellectual insights leads to a high economic value for entrepreneurship to occur within close geographical proximity of the knowledge source, such as a university. Or, as Alfred Marshall (1920) explained nearly a century ago, "The mysteries of trade become no mysteries; but are as it were in the air, and children learn many of them unconsciously" (p. 225). The further away entrepreneurial activity is from a university, the lower the access to knowledge spillovers. Thus, the Locational Hypothesis associated with the Knowledge Spillover Theory of Entrepreneurship proposes that universities with a higher output of knowledge should generate a higher degree of entrepreneurial activity within close geographic proximity.

University research, as the source of such spillovers, has been measured in various studies by the amount of money spent on R&D, the number of articles published in academic and scientific journals, and the number of employees engaged in research or patents (see Henderson, Jaffe, and Trajtenberg, 1998; McWilliams and Siegel 2000; Varga, 2000; Hall, Link and Scott, 2003). The overwhelming part of the empirical literature confirms the positive effects of university spillovers (Acs et al., 1992, 1994; Jaffe et al., 1993; Audretsch and Feldman, 1996; Anselin, Varga, and Acs, 1997; Varga, 2000; Mowery and Ziedonis, 2001).

Only a handful of studies have explicitly analyzed the link between universities and new-firm startups as conduits for knowledge spillovers. Bania, Eberts, and Fogerty (1993) analyze the frequency of high-technology startups and find only a small effect of university research funding on the startup rate. Audretsch and Stephan (1996, 1999) use joint articles written together by scientists working in the university and industry contexts. They show that the spillover of knowledge to a new firm startup facilitates the appropriation of knowledge for the individual scientist but not necessarily for the organization creating that new knowledge in the first place. Zucker, Darby, and Armstrong (1998) link universities and startups in biotechnology with academic articles. They find evidence suggesting that it is not spillover effects per se but rather the intellectual capital of star scientists that plays a major role in shaping both the location and timing of the entry of new firms. Shane (2001a, 2001b) explores the determinants of proximity to Massachusetts Institute of Technology (MIT) on new firm formation. His main finding is that universities create technological spillovers that are exploited by new firms.

However, key questions surround the role that location plays in accessing university spillovers. First, although research has identified the important role that universities play in generating knowledge spillovers, their impact on the location of entrepreneurial activity is less clear. Second, the mechanisms transmitting knowledge spillovers remain relatively unexplored. Third, the actual knowledge spillover mechanism and role that geographic proximity plays in accessing those knowledge spillovers may not be homogeneous but may be heterogeneous and may depend on the particular field and type of knowledge. Before providing answers to these questions in section 6.3.3, we address some important concepts that help in understanding the role of knowledge spillovers.

6.3.2 University Transmission of Codified
and Tacit Knowledge

An important concept in understanding the role of knowledge spillovers is the distinction between codified and tacit knowledge (Kogut and Zander, 1992). Tacit knowledge is difficult to write down in such a way that it is meaningful and readily understood (Teece, 2005). Since it is often hard to explain intuitive ideas to others, and because knowledge involves more than what can be codified and written explicitly, a key characteristic of knowledge is its tacit nature. Ambiguities inherent in the tacit nature of knowledge can be overcome only when communications take place in face-to-face situations. Errors of interpretation emanating from such ambiguities can best be corrected by a prompt use of personal feedback. Thus, tacit knowledge needs face-to-face, and even nonverbal, communication, as well as reciprocity, all of which may be ineffective or infeasible over longer distances (Teece, 1976, 1981).

By contrast, stand-alone codified knowledge can be written down, such as formulas. Thus, codified knowledge is more akin to information than to tacit knowledge. The transmission of codified knowledge, or information, does not necessarily require face-to-face contact and can carried out largely by impersonal means. Unlike tacit knowledge, codified knowledge is better structured and less ambiguous. The greater the extent to which knowledge or experience has been codified, the more economically it can be transferred. Thus, the cost of transfer of information is lower than that for tacit knowledge and is not bounded by close proximity of the source of knowledge. As Jaffe (2002) points out, geographical location is important in capturing the benefits of spillovers when the mechanism of knowledge is informal and conversational, as is the case for tacit knowledge. Then, "geographic proximity to the spillover source may be helpful or even necessary in capturing the spillover benefits" (Jaffe, 1998, p. 957).

At least two principle mechanisms facilitate the spillover of knowledge from universities to firms. The first one involves scientific research published in scholarly journals. Such published research reflects codified knowledge. Knowledge provided by articles can be transferred and transmitted with low cost across geographic space, or with costs independent of the location. For example, academic research can be downloaded from the Internet, obtained from publishers, or found in libraries.

The second type of spillover mechanism involves human capital embodied in students graduating from the university. As Saxenian (1994) points out, one of the most important mechanisms facilitating knowledge spillovers involves the mobility of human capital, embodied in graduating students, as they move from the university to a firm. Spatial proximity to universities can therefore generate positive externalities that can be accessed by the firm through the spillover mechanism of human capital. As Varga (2000) shows, university graduates may be one of the most important channels for disseminating knowledge from academia to the local high-technology industry. Such knowledge includes not only positive knowledge such as discoveries but also negative knowledge. Negative knowledge is the knowledge of failure and may contain often overlooked value. As part of the scientific method, students often learn about the failure of processes, experiments, and firm behavior. Since trial-and-error processes in firms are often associated with high costs, possessing negative knowledge can help allocate resources into more promising avenues.

In addition, other related externalities may result from close geographic proximity. For example, local proximity lowers the search costs for both firms and students. This may lead to a competitive advantage over similar firms not located close to universities, especially when highly skilled labor is a scarce resource and there is intense competition for knowledge inputs.[1] Porter and Stern (2001) point out that such geographic proximity to university spillovers can bestow a competitive advantage over similar firms not located within close geographic proximity to universities. They find that the role of geographic proximity in accessing university spillovers is especially important when there are scarce resources and there is intense competition for human capital and other knowledge inputs (Porter and Stern, 2001).

The geographic mobility of students is particularly low in Germany (Fabel, Lehmann, and Warning, 2002). Only a small percentage of students, the "high potentials," exhibit high geographic mobility. However, those students often choose to work in consulting companies or attractive multinational firms and have not traditionally been interesting in working in entrepreneurial startups.

Since academic research independent of the academic field published in scholarly journals is of a more codified than tacit nature, students and graduates may serve as a complementary factor in the knowledge production function. For example, even though a huge number of books and articles are written about engineering and managerial practices and techniques, this codified knowledge is apparently not sufficient, still demanding face-to-face instruction and real experience. Particularly in the natural sciences, articles often provide the results of laboratory experiments or studies and only a short and abbreviated description of the data-generating process. However, most of the knowledge in this context remains tacit and can not be published. The same holds for empirical studies in the social sciences. Though the results and the description of the data could be well structured and thus codified, much knowledge in social science research methods remains tacit. Such tacit knowledge could be transmitted by hiring students or graduates who are familiar with the ideas and work.

However, not all university knowledge is the same. In fact, the knowledge output of a university is heterogeneous and differs not only across academic fields but also among different universities.[2] One useful distinction differentiates between knowledge in the natural sciences and in the social sciences. This distinction might suggest that, in fact, the role of geographic proximity to access knowledge spillovers is not homogeneous across different universities, fields, and types of knowledge but is specific to each particular university as well as to the specific scientific field.

A number of reasons suggest that academic research in the natural sciences is more codified and thus does not require geographic proximity to absorb university spillovers. For example, the results of an experiment or test in the natural sciences are typically published. Those results can be characterized more like information in that they are meaningful to those who receive them and depend on whether the recipients are familiar with the information provided and the contexts in which the results are obtained and could be used.

TABLE 6.1 The Role of Geographic Proximity for Knowledge
Spillovers by Academic Field and Spillover Mechanism

	Human capital (students)	Scholarly articles
Natural sciences	High	Low
Social sciences	Low	High

By contrast, knowledge in the social sciences is less based on a unified and established scientific methodology but is instead idiosyncratic to very specific disciplines, subdisciplines, and even research approaches and trajectories. Compared to results in the natural sciences, research in the social sciences is considerably less codified. Thus, geographic proximity to high output universities may be more important for accessing social science research than for accessing natural science research, since knowledge in the social sciences is less structured and more ambiguous and cannot be transferred easily.[3]

Students in the natural sciences may be more heterogeneous in their knowledge and human capital than are their classmates in the social sciences. Social science programs are standardized throughout Germany, which results in producing graduates with a relatively homogeneous degree of human capital. However, such standardization is not found in the natural sciences, so that geographic proximity may be more important to access knowledge embodied in recent graduates in the natural sciences than in the social sciences. Therefore, the number of students graduating in the social sciences should not greatly affect the value of locating within close geographic proximity to the university.

By contrast, the specialization of universities in the natural sciences in fields such as life sciences, biochemistry, physics, or engineering results in a diverse and heterogeneous set of competencies embodied in students. Thus, the human capital of students in the natural sciences is more likely to be specific to a particular university.

Table 6.1 summarizes the different role of geographic proximity to the knowledge source according to academic field and spillover mechanism. There are two types of academic fields, natural science and social science, and two spillover mechanisms, human capital (students) and scholarly articles. Geographic proximity to the knowledge source is expected to be more important for human capital in the natural sciences and scholarly articles in the social sciences, where knowledge is more tacit and less codified. By contrast, geographic proximity is less important for accessing knowledge spillovers for human capital in the social sciences and scholarly articles in the natural sciences, which are relatively more codified and less tacit in nature.

6.3.3 University Knowledge Spillovers and Location Decision

In this section we formulate several propositions based on the questions posed at the end of section 6.3.1. As we explained in chapter 3, ideas and knowledge are particularly characterized by a greater degree of uncertainty, asymmetries, and costs of transaction, which lead to a greater variance in the expected valuation of those ideas, which in turn creates entrepreneurial opportunities. Since geographic proximity fosters access to such tacit knowledge via university spillovers, we would expect the ensuing entrepreneurial startups to be located within close geographic proximity to the university. That is, geographical proximity should dictate entrepreneurial access to university spillovers.

The question of the relative role of geographic proximity in the transmission of tacit and codified knowledge was suggested by Audretsch and Stephan (1996, 1999), who, among others, find different impacts of tacit knowledge and codified knowledge on the benefits of geographic proximity to a university. Because of its higher degree of codification, we posit that scientific knowledge can be largely accessed by (competently) reading scientific journals, resulting in the following proposition:

> Knowledge in the social sciences is more tacit and less codified, rendering geographic proximity more important in accessing knowledge spillovers. Knowledge in the natural sciences is less tacit and more codified, rending geographic proximity less important in accessing knowledge spillovers.

The second proposition is also based on the distinction between codified and tacit knowledge (Kogut and Zander, 1992). Elements of knowledge and ideas cannot be codified easily or at low cost in a blueprint, a contractual document (Mowery and Ziedonis, 2001), or a published article (Audretsch and Feldman, 1996). Thus, the limited geographic reach of such channels for the access to ideas and know-how suggests that geographic proximity to the knowledge source is important in accessing such knowledge spillovers. The university output of human capital in the form of graduating students embodies a strong component of tacit knowledge. Thus, the second proposition suggests that universities with a particularly high degree of tacit knowledge output, as measured by students graduating, will tend to have entrepreneurial firms located within close geographic proximity:

> Entrepreneurial firms are more likely to be located near universities with a large output of tacit knowledge, as measured by the number of graduating students.

The third proposition suggests that human capital embodied in graduating students as a spillover mechanism should be different from that from the spillover mechanism of published scientific articles. The transmission of tacit knowledge is facilitated by face-to-face communication, direct interaction, and reciprocity, all of which may be less effective or even infeasible over longer distances. Thus, the spillover of knowledge is associated with personal contacts, interaction, and face-to-face interactions.

If personal contacts are the main source for absorbing (tacit) knowledge spillovers, the potential for accessing such university spillovers should be directly related to the number of students graduating from any given university. The relative importance of tacit knowledge is reflected by the number of students at a university, which serves as a measure for the intense demand for labor and interpersonal communication. Ceteris paribus, a higher number of students graduating should generate a greater amount of entrepreneurship. This should be particularly true in the natural sciences, where human capital embodied in students is less codified and therefore more tacit. Thus, we posit the following proposition:

> Universities with a high output, as measured by the number of students graduating in the natural sciences, will tend to induce new startups to locate within close geographic proximity of the university in order to access university spillovers.

The fourth proposition suggests that locational proximity to a university as a means to accessing academic spillovers is not invariant to the firm life cycle. As Audretsch and Thurik (2001), among others, pointed out, the need to access university spillovers may be more important for young firms than for established firms. This is because new firms may rely on external knowledge produced by other firms or universities (Hall, Link, and Scott 2003; Link and Scott, 2003). Scherer (1991) observed that small and new firms do not tend to devote a large share of resources to formal R&D. By contrast, larger and more established enterprises are able to generate their own formal R&D and therefore are less dependent on external knowledge. This implies that geographic proximity to universities is a source of competitive advantage for young firms, when the competitive advantage is based on intangible assets, such as ideas and the human capital of the employees. So a locational strategy of geographic proximity is more important for young firms. During the innovation process, firms confront a wide range of possible problems and difficulties that may be beyond the firm's own problem-solving capacity. Thus, close location gives support to both management capacity and technological input (Schartinger, Schibany, and Gassler, 2001, p. 261).

New-technology–oriented young firms are particularly dependent on technological innovations and scientific progress and therefore more inclined than others to engage in interactions with universities. Instead, older firms were able to accumulate a stock of knowledge within the firm and thus have incorporated a vast number of fields of knowledge through their life cycles. Hence, as Link and Rees (1990) found, older firms are less dependent on external knowledge generated at universities. Thus, we suggest this proposition:

> Academic spillovers are more important for young firms than for their more mature counterparts.

6.4 Measurement Issues

To test the Locational Hypothesis that entrepreneurial activity tends to occur within close geographic proximity to a knowledge source, we use a unique data set of high-technology and other knowledge-based German firms publicly listed on the Neuer Markt, Germany's equivalent of the U.S. NASDAQ. There were 295 German firms listed on the Neuer Markt from 1997 through 2002. We excluded five banks and nine holding companies. The data set was collected by combining individual data from the prospectuses of the IPO with publicly available information from on-line data sources, including the Deutsche Boerse AG (www.deutsche-boerse.com).

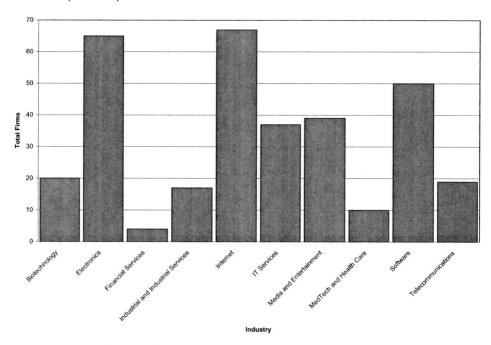

FIGURE 6.1. Firms listed on the Neuer Markt by industries in 1999

Using this data set to test the Locational Hypothesis has several advantages. The sample includes highly innovative industries, including biotechnology, medical devices, life sciences, e-commerce, and other high-technology industries, all of which are knowledge intensive. Second, studies from the United States provide strong evidence for the growth effect of clusters influenced by the presence of a strong research university (Feldman, 2000). This database enables us to follow this line of research. Third, this data set represents the technological change in the German business sector from the predominance of medium-sized firms in production and manufacturing toward the high-technology and service sector, characterized by the importance of intangible assets in contrast to fixed capital. Finally, such data in Germany is not available for privately held firms.

In figure 6.1 the distribution of firms across industries shows that the highest densities of these firms were in the Internet, electronic, and software sectors. In figures 6.2 and 6.3, firm size and employee growth rates are displayed by industrial sectors. The firms with the highest growth rates between 1998 and 1999 were those in the Internet, biotechnology, and financial service sectors. Figure 6.3 shows, in size demographics, that the largest firms were in the electronics, industrial, and IT-service industrial sectors.

Admission and reporting requirements for Neuer Markt firms are more stringent than the rules for the first (Amtlicher Handel) and second (Geregelter Markt)

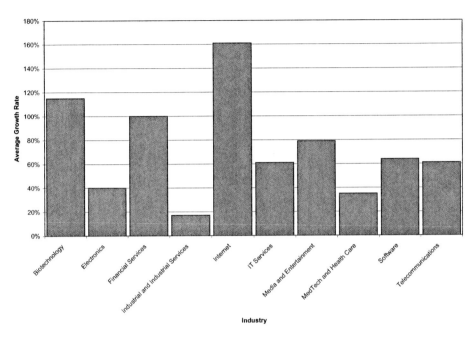

FIGURE 6.2. Employment growth of Neuer Markt firms from 1998 to 1999

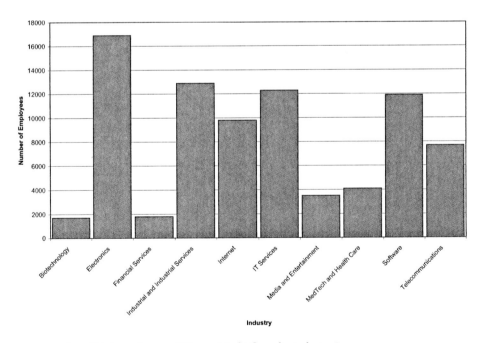

FIGURE 6.3. Total employees of Neuer Markt firms by industry in 1999

TABLE 6.2 List of the Top 20 Universities

University	Firms[a]	ϕkm[b]	#uni[c]	Staff[d]	Grants[e]	SSCI students[f]	SCI students[g]
LMU München	51	17.9	3	412,633	83,681	43,633	8,119
Uni Frankfurt	26	19.5	1	265,845	50,976	26,324	5,715
Uni Hamburg	24	13.25	3	87,924	8,870	1,361	329
Uni Stuttgart	16	16.2	1	403,180	203,489	4,779	12,104
HU Berlin	14	7.78	3	352,676	55,167	20,769	4,936
Uni Köln	12	5.9	1	299,294	51,409	47,112	9,395
TU München	10	8.8	3	462,522	205,463	1,619	14,976
Uni Karlsruhe	9	36.7	1	322,389	120,261	4,102	11,818
Uni Düsseldorf	7	18.57	1	145,912	19,382	14,697	4,762
Uni Erlangen-Nürnberg	6	14	1	290,793	103,212	12,861	7,144
Uni Freiburg	6	40.33	1	212,177	40,121	12,334	4,942
FU Berlin	5	5.5	3	435,784	73,023	30,290	6,260
TU Aachen (RWTA)	5	3.4	1	473,740	205,389	7,884	20,570
Uni Jena	5	15.8	1	198,905	34,142	7,615	2,864
U-GH Paderborn	4	17	1	161,200	40,386	6,993	8,676
Uni Bielefeld	4	15.5	1	190,698	39,114	15,831	4,400
Uni Bremen	4	25.5	1	224,573	82,507	11,749	4,800
UdB München	4	14.25	3	131,395	7,858	1,054	1,104
Uni Kiel	4	40.75	1	238,427	63,196	13,000	6,513
Uni Regensburg	4	40	1	153,090	26,069	11,192	3,696

[a]Measured by the number of firms located closest to this university.
[b]ϕkm is the average distance of the firms located closest to this university.
[c]#uni is the number of universities in this city.
[d]Staff are expenditures on personnel staff (in thousand DM).
[e]Grants are research grants.
[f]Number of students in the social sciences.
[g]Number of students in the natural sciences.

segments of the Frankfurt exchange.[4] Firms generally use the International Accounting Standards (IAS) or the U.S. Generally Accepted Accounting Principles (US-GAAP) reporting standards, but some have used a short-term exemption period during which they may follow reporting requirements from the *Handelsgesetzbuch* (HGB) or German Commercial Code (Lehmann and Lüders, 2005).

University-specific variables, which were individually collected from the 73 universities in Germany (Warning, 2004), were added to the database. For each university, the number of articles listed in the research database from the ISI (Information Sciences Institutes) was collected and added. Although this database includes only a small amount of the total number of scholarly journals in any one field, we included only the highest quality research journals.

Table 6.2 shows the output from the top 20 universities in Germany. We measured "top" by the numbers of firms from the Neuer Markt located within close geographic proximity to the respective university. "Close" is expressed by the minimum distance between a firm and a university, although this distance could be more than, say, 50 kilometers. In this case, the closest distance between a firm and a university is 50 kilometers. The number of firms located "close" to a university is thus the sum of firms for which the distance to this university is less than the distance to another university.

From the 73 public universities in Germany, only 54 universities were selected for status as the closest university for the included firms. The descriptive statistics show the highly skewed number of firms located around universities. The median distance of all firms located with close geographic proximity to a university is 7 km, and the average distance is about 16 km. The universities differ highly in their numbers of students in the natural sciences and the social sciences (see Warning, 2004, for more details).

As table 6.2 shows, the university with the greatest impact on entrepreneurial location and the most impressive impact is Ludwigs-Maximilian University (LMU) in Munich. Of the 281 firms included in the data set, 51 firms are located within close geographic proximity to LMU. This is almost twice as high as the 26 firms located within close geographic proximity to the University of Hamburg, followed by Goethe University of Frankfurt (24 firms), the University of Stuttgart (16 firms), and Humbold University (HU) in Berlin (14 firms). Thus, the spatial distribution of entrepreneurial firms is skewed with a significant concentration of entrepreneurial firms located within close geographic proximity to several of the most prolific universities in Germany. Universities not shown in the table have three or fewer firms.

This kind of ranking of universities as measured by the number of firms located closest to the respective university is consistent with rankings based on teaching quality and academic excellence as published in the business press (see *Wirtschaftswoche* No. 10, March 3, 2005, or *Focus* No. 41, October 2004). In those rankings, LMU and the technical university (TU) in Munich, the University of Köln (Cologne), the Rheinisch-Westfälische Technische Hochschule (RWTH Aachen University of Technology) in Aachen, the TU in Karlsruhe, and the Universities in Stuttgart and Frankfurt top the rankings.

The role that geographic proximity plays in accessing university spillovers for geographic proximity is evidenced by the 2004 decision of General Electric to locate a new Global Research Center in Munich. As Armin Pfoh, leader of the Global Research Center, explained, "Munich was the only city which offered us a location on the campus of the university."[5]

One way to gauge the importance of geographic proximity for entrepreneurial access to university spillovers is to measure the distance between the entrepreneurial firm and the university. If geographic proximity does not matter in accessing university spillovers, then technology-based startups will not be compelled to locate within close geographic proximity to a university. By contrast, if geographic proximity is a prerequisite for accessing university spillovers, then technology and other knowledge-based startups will tend to locate closer to the university.

Figure 6.4 shows the distribution of firms within close geographic proximity of a university, along with the output of the universities, measured by the number of students in the natural and social sciences.

Entrepreneurial proximity to a university is measured as the *distance* to the closest university as the dependent variable. Since universities in Germany are more geographically concentrated than those in the United States, a measure that is sensitive to relatively small variations is more appropriate. The distance between an entrepreneurial firm and the nearest university is measured in shortest

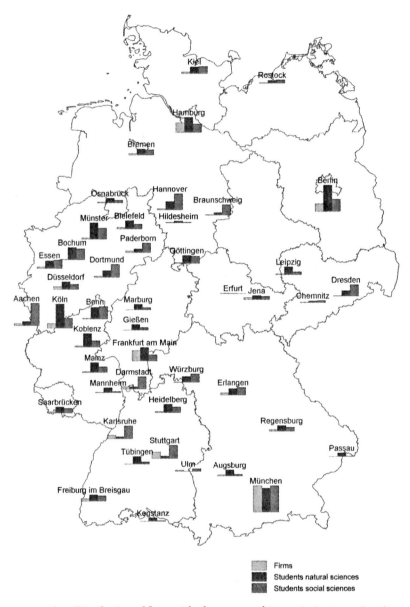

FIGURE 6.4. Distribution of firms with close geographic proximity to a university

drivable distance in kilometers using the online database of the German Automobile Club (www.adac.de) (see also Bode, 2004). All firms located within a
radius of 1.5 kilometers are classified as belonging in the distance category of one
kilometer.

However, firm location could also be measured by geographic districts, which
are comparable to the Standard Metropolitan Statistical Areas (SMSA) often used

in regional studies for the United States (Varga, 2000). This alternative measure of geographic proximity is constructed as the ordinal variable *district*. This alternative measure of geographic proximity takes on the value of 1 if the firm is located within a close radius of eight kilometers (the median value) around the university. If the firm is located within a radius of 20 kilometers, the variable takes the value 2 and 3 if the location is beyond the radius of 20 kilometers.

The previous section identified two distinct spillover mechanisms, research articles published in scholarly journals and students graduating from the university. To capture the first spillover mechanism, academic research published in scholarly journals, we follow the examples of Zucker et al. (1998) and Audretsch and Stephan (1999), by measuring the *number of articles* authored by scientists with a main affiliation with a particular university that are published in high quality journals.

The second spillover mechanism is the human capital embodied in students graduating from the university and transmitting knowledge from the university to firms for commercial application and is measured as the number of students enrolled at each university. Not only are there two distinct spillover mechanisms; the previous section also identified two distinct types of university outputs: natural science knowledge and social science knowledge. One of the main propositions suggests that the role of entrepreneurial location may vary systematically for university spillovers based on knowledge of natural science and social science.

Not all knowledge industries are based on knowledge spillovers from the natural sciences. Rather, knowledge industries, or rather knowledge services, include media and entertainment and e-commerce. Research output in the social sciences is measured by the *number of articles* published in journals listed in the Social Science Citation Index (SSCI). By contrast, the number of publications in the Science Citation Index (SCI) indicates the research activity of universities in the natural sciences. We include the number of published articles in scholarly journals from 1997 until 2000 for both the natural sciences and social sciences for each university.[6]

Table 6.3 clearly shows that research output, both in natural sciences and social sciences, varies substantially across universities. However, the number of scholarly publications in the natural sciences cannot be directly compared to those in the social sciences. Articles in the natural sciences are typically shorter and written by large teams of co-authors. This difference between the social and natural sciences is reflected by the median university output of 204 published social science articles and 4,069 published articles in the natural sciences. In both fields, the mean value of scholarly publications exceeds the median value, which suggests that some universities are more research-intensive than others.

As we did for the counterpart spillover mechanism of research published in scholarly articles, we distinguish between the two types of university outputs, students with human capital in the natural sciences and students with human capital in the social sciences. Human capital embodied in students in the natural sciences and in the social sciences is measured by aggregating the numbers of students enrolled in the relevant academic disciplines. For example, the human capital output in the natural sciences spans the academic disciplines of biology, chemistry,

TABLE 6.3 Natural and Social Science Differences across Universities

	Mean	Standard deviation	Min	Max	25%	Median	75%
Distance	16.69	23.45	1	177	1	7	21
SCI articles	5,139.43	4,603.16	0	14,176	2,179	4,069	5,924
SSCI articles	253.86	220.01	0	659	56	204	465
Science students	20,321.17	15,409.63	0	47,112	6,961	15,741	30,290
Social science students	7,304.89	3,988.45	0	20,570	4,936	7,725	9,395
Age (years)	10.27	11.11	0.1	107	3	8	14.25
Grants (thousand DM)	73,767.37	53,420.03	44	205,463	40,121	63,196	83,681
Total students	28,030.82	16,758,70	5,430	56,507	16,549	22,603	38,239
Universities	1.83	0.95	1	3	1	1	3
Staff (thousand DM)	29,3028.6	11,3090.6	5,409	473,740	212,177	299,294	412,633
Town (inhabitants)	640,441.6	897,371.4	1,850	338,700	25,000	190,000	1,195,000

physics, mathematics, computational science, agriculture, forestry, dietetics, engineering, and medicine.

By contrast, the human capital output in the social sciences includes the *number of students* in the academic disciplines of languages, cultural studies, law, economics, social sciences, and arts. These two measures of human capital based on student enrollments are for 1997. We selected this year for two main reasons. First, data is not always available for each year and each university. Second, the Neuer Markt started in 1997, and thus we take this year as the base year. Since information about university expenditures or research grants is not annually or continuously published in Germany, we restrict our data set to 1997. However, the university system in Germany has not substantially changed in the past decades, suggesting that in the period analyzed in this chapter, university investments in research, as well as the research outputs, in terms of published articles and human capital, have remained fairly stable. For example, a comparison of publications in scholarly journals between the SSCI and the SCI results in a high bivariate correlation of $r = 0.95$.

The second group of exogenous variables consists of location-specific variables for the university as well as for the firm. The number of inhabitants at the location of the university in 1997 reflects the size of the city where the university is located. No adequate data exists reflecting the costs of living at the university location, so we employ a proxy measuring the *average price of a basic single room* from the most expensive hotel in the city where the university is located. These prices differ significantly across cities, with the most expensive in Frankfurt, the most expensive city in Germany as measured by the OECD. The number of universities in the city reflects not only a cluster effect but also a competition effect among the universities.

Location-specific variables include the number of inhabitants (in the region where the firm is located) and a dummy variable that indicates that the firm is located in the former West Germany, or the western part of contemporary Germany (*West*).

To control for the size of the city and other regional cluster effects, we include the logarithm of the number of citizens (*town*) and the total number of universities (*universities*) within the same city. We also try to capture reputational effects of universities and measure this by the age of a university (*age university*). To control for regional entrepreneurial activities and the innovation infrastructure, we include a measure of knowledge (*knowledge capacity*), which is taken from Sternberg and Litzenberger (2003).

Technical universities are hypothesized to play a special role in generating university spillovers, since their focus is on engineering and the natural sciences. A dummy variable is thus included to control for this special type of university (*TU*). To reflect the life cycle of the firm, we include the age of a firm (*age*), which is measured in years from foundation to IPO. Finally, we also consider the amount of grants (*grants*), the expenditures on staff (*staff*), and the number of all students (*students*) enrolled at the respective university.

The role of locational proximity may not be invariant across industries. Thus, we control for specific industry effects by including dummy variables for the following industries: software, e-services, e-commerce, computer and hardware, telecommunication, biotechnology, medicine and life sciences, media and entertainment, and high-technology.

Table 6.3 shows that the closest locational proximity between an entrepreneurial firm and a university is 1 kilometer; the maximum distance is 177 kilometers away from the nearest university. The skewed distribution of the data is reflected by the difference between the mean and median values. While the arithmetic mean distance is about 17 kilometers, the median shows that 50 percent of the firms are located within an area within the radius of 7 kilometers. The 25th percentile (75 percent) demonstrates that 25 percent (75 percent) of the firms are located within a small radius of 1 kilometer (21). Thus, locational proximity to a university for the 281 firms in the data set is a first hint that university spillover effects influence the strategic location decision.

Tables 6.3 and 6.4 also indicate that research activities and the number of students vary considerably across the universities. A comparison between the mean and the median exhibits the skewed number of articles in both the social sciences and natural sciences. On average, each university published about 250 articles in social science and more than 5,100 articles in natural science, whereas the median number of articles published is lower. Also, the number of graduates differs across universities (see also table 6.2).[7] Interestingly, the number of articles and graduate students varies not just across universities but also across the two fields. The mean university publishes 20 times as many articles in the natural sciences as in the social sciences.

TABLE 6.4 Distribution of Universities

	Distance	Universities	West	Technical universities
Frequency (%)	1: 157 (55.9)	1: 155 (55.2)	West: 256 (91.1)	TU: 25 (8.90)
	2: 58 (20.6)	2: 16 (5.7)	East: 25 (8.9)	No TU: 91.1 (8.9)
	3: 66 (23.5)	3: 110 (39.1)		

However, articles in the natural sciences and those in social sciences differ in their length, number of co-authors, and referee time and are thus not comparable. While 50 percent of the universities publish about 200 articles in social science, there are more than 4,000 articles in the natural sciences. This is also due to the fact that departments in the natural sciences are larger than those in the social sciences.

The opposite can be found for the number of students. On average, more than 20,300 students are studying social sciences, whereas only about a third, 7,300, are enrolled in the natural sciences. However, in most fields in the natural sciences, the number of students is restricted by the numerus clauses, which places a constraint on student enrollments based on the schooling level.

The data presented in table 6.3 demonstrates that most of the firms are strikingly young. Half of the firms in our sample are eight years old or less, and 25 percent of the firms are younger than three years. About 90 percent of the firms are located in West Germany and about 9 percent are located close to one of the six technical universities. More than 55 percent of the firms are located within an 8-kilometer circle around the university, about 20 percent between the inner circle and a 20-kilometer radius, and the remaining 25 percent are located outside the 20-kilometer radius.

6.5 Results for Locational Proximity: Clustering of Firms and Proximity

This section contains the empirical estimation of both the number of firms located close to a university and geographical proximity of firms and universities. The main hypothesis to be tested, the Locational Hypothesis, suggests that geographic proximity is a prerequisite for entrepreneurial access to university spillovers. A series of ancillary propositions qualify the Locational Hypothesis by conditioning the importance of geographic proximity to a university by the type of knowledge involved in the university spillover. If the university spillover is tacit, then geographic proximity should be a prerequisite for entrepreneurial access. By contrast, if the university spillover is codified or nontacit, then location is less important for accessing university spillovers.

In order to test the Locational Hypothesis and the ancillary propositions, we estimated the following regression model and present the results in this section; we link the number of firms located within close geographic proximity to the university to both the knowledge outputs of the university and the mechanisms facilitating the university spillovers. We use three different models to test the hypotheses.

First, we include only the knowledge capacity as the exogenous variable together with control variables such as firm age or the type of a university to explain the number of firms located closest to a university:

$$\text{Number of Firms} = const. + \beta_1 knowledge\ capacity + Controlvariables + \varepsilon \quad (6.1)$$

In the second regression (6.2), we exclude the knowledge capacity and include our measures for university output, the number of students, and published articles for the natural and social sciences:

Number of Firms $= const. + \beta_1 \text{SCI Students} + \beta_2 \text{SSCI Students}$

$\qquad\qquad + \beta_3 \text{SSCI Articles} + \beta_4 \text{SCI Articles}$

$\qquad\qquad + Controlvariables + \varepsilon \qquad\qquad\qquad\qquad\qquad (6.2)$

Finally, we include all the variables in the regression (6.3):

Number of Firms $= const. + \beta_1 \text{knowledge capacity} + \beta_2 \text{SCI Students}$

$\qquad\qquad + \beta_3 \text{SSCI Students} + \beta_4 \text{SSCI Articles}$

$\qquad\qquad + \beta_5 \text{SCI Articles} + Controlvariables + \varepsilon \qquad\qquad (6.3)$

Because the dependent variable is a count variable, ordinary least squares (OLS) estimation would be inappropriate. Instead, the regression is estimated using the negative binomial regression model (Greene, 2003). An alternative candidate for estimating the regression could be the Poisson method. However, the assumption required for a Poisson estimation is the equality of mean and variance of the exogenous variable and is rejected by several tests. Thus, we apply the negative binomial regression model to overcome this problem of overdispersion. In addition, this statistical technique is designed for maximum likelihood estimation of the number of occurrence of nonnegative counts like the events of location.

The results for estimating the number of knowledge-based firms located within geographic proximity to each university are presented in table 6.5. The dependent variable is the number of firms located within close geographic proximity of a university.

In model (1), presented in the first column, neither the two types of university outputs nor the two types of spillover mechanisms are included in the estimation model. In model (2), presented in the second column, both the university outputs and spillover mechanisms are included, but the knowledge capacity of the region is excluded. All of these variables are included in model (3), which is presented in the third column.

As the positive and statistically significant coefficient of the measure of regional knowledge capacity suggests, the number of entrepreneurial startups is greater in those regions with a greater presence of knowledge inputs. There is at least some evidence that the spillover mechanism embodied in the human capital of students increases the number of startups located within close geographic proximity of the university. While the coefficient is positive and statistically significant for human capital in the social sciences, it is only statistically significant for human capital in the natural sciences in model (2), when the knowledge capacity of the region is also included.

The negative and statistically significant coefficient of research publications in the natural sciences suggests that close geographic proximity is not a prerequisite to accessing university spillovers in the natural sciences. This, however, supports the thesis that codified knowledge, as expressed in academic articles, does not require nearness to the source of such knowledge. By contrast, the positive and statistically significant coefficient for social sciences publications suggests that geographic proximity to the university is more important for the social sciences than for the

TABLE 6.5 Negative Binomial Estimating Technological Startups

	(1)	(2)	(3)
Knowledge capacity	0.03753		0.4279
	(10.19)***		(16.95)***
SCI students		0.0004	0.0001
		(3.77)***	(1.36)
SSCI students		0.00003	0.0003
		(10.03)***	(14.36)***
SSCI articles		−0.0009	−0.0009
		(8.43)***	(11.06)***
SCI articles		0.1100	0.1149
		(3.13)***	(3.99)***
Age university	−0.0004	0.0005	−0.00057
	(2.27)**	(2.30)**	(2.90)**
Technical university	−1.4786	−1.1976	−1.389
	(10.20)***	(6.65)***	(9.53)***
Town (inhabitants)	−1.17E07	−0.856E07	−3.06E07
	(1.10)	(10.09)***	(3.96)***
Number of universities	0.4047	1.1935	0.681
	(6.24)***	(20.90)***	(12.90)***
West	−0.2029	−0.6351	−0.5320
	(0.93)	(3.32)***	(3.61)***
Constant	0.4892	1.7352	0.6887
	(1.65)*	(6.65)***	(3.07)***
Pseudo R^2	0.1792	0.2067	0.3412
Log-likelihood	−897.76	−850.11	−705.998

The endogenous variable is the number of technology startups located within close geographic proximity to a university. The dataset includes 281 firms and 54 universities. Z values in brackets unless denoted otherwise.
*Statistically significant at the two-tailed test for 90% level of confidence.
**Statistically significant at the two-tailed test for 95% level of confidence.
***Statistically significant at the two-tailed test for 99% level of confidence.

natural sciences, indicating that academic research as expressed by the number of articles is less codified and thus more tacit.

The negative and statistically significant coefficient of university reputation, at least as measured by the age of the university, does not support the hypothesis that university reputation, at least measured by age, has a positive influence on startups. Rather, the younger a university is, the more entrepreneurial firms tend to locate within close geographic proximity to it.

The negative and statistically significant coefficient for technically oriented universities also suggests that locational proximity to access spillovers is not a prerequisite. This may reflect the fact that the technically oriented universities in Germany have, at least until very recently, been focused on research in traditional disciplines, such as engineering and machine tools. Scale and density apparently result in greater entrepreneurial activity but based only on the number of universities in the region and not on the population alone.

There is no reason to assume that the regression results presented in table 6.5 are homogeneous across specific industries. Thus, the model is estimated for five

TABLE 6.6 Negative Binomial Estimating Technological Startups by Industrial Sector

	Software	Technology services	Media & entertain	Hardware & technology	Biotec & medtec
Knowledge capacity	0.0437	0.0402	0.04377	0.06128	0.0706
	(7.59)***	(7.81)***	(4.50)***	(8.08)***	(2.36)**
SCI students	−1.50E06	0.0001	0.0001	0.0002	0.0003
	(0.09)	(0.98)	(2.30)***	(2.59)***	(3.04)***
SSCI students	0.00002	0.0003	0.0004	0.0004	0.0006
	(3.17)***	(8.84)***	(3.35)***	(4.49)***	(3.69)***
SSCI articles	−0.001	−0.012	−0.001	−0.0005	−0.0018
	(1.13)	(1.39)	(1.13)	(1.52)	(1.35)
SCI articles	−0.1971	0.2076	−0.0043	0.2356	0.0103
	(0.92)	(0.71)	(0.08)	(2.05)**	(1.67)*
Age university	0.00002	−0.0004	−0.006	−0.003	0.0025
	(0.05)	(1.16)	(1.12)	(2.96)***	(0.85)
TU	−1.0577	−0.9135	−2.284	−0.5618	1.468
	(3.46)***	(3.15)***	(3.01)***	(1.59)	(1.67)*
Town	−0.282E07	−4.74E07	−3.45E07	−1.17E07	−1.18E06
	(5.34)***	(2.85)***	(1.48)	(0.24)	(1.47)
West	−0.4105	−0.5606	−0.4876	−0.7883	−3.130
	(1.01)	(1.67)*	(1.12)	(0.88)	(1.45)
Number of universities	0.8234	0.9007	0.7666	0.4493	0.7164
	(5.34)***	(7.66)***	(3.42)***	(1.26)	(1.72)*
Constant	0.3309	0.7129	0.3122	0.2576	3.5109
	(0.62)	(1.41)	(0.23)	(0.22)	(2.12)*
Pseudo R^2	0.3722	0.3560	0.4042	0.3999	0.4143
Log-likelihood Ratio (χ^2)	−130.485	−164.059	−93.357	−110.326	−51.769
Number of firms	55	67	37	47	25

The endogenous variable is the number of technology startups located within geographic proximity to a university. Z values in parentheses unless denoted otherwise; we dropped all industries with less than 20 firms and matched hardware and technology as well as biotech and medtec to increase the number of firms in the regressions.
*Statistically significant at the two-tailed test for 90% level of confidence.
**Statistically significant at the two-tailed test for 95% level of confidence.
***Statistically significant at the two-tailed test for 99% level of confidence.

specific industries, and the results are presented in table 6.6. In fact, the evidence suggests that not all of the knowledge measures have a homogeneous impact on entrepreneurship across any given industry. There is no reason to think that entrepreneurship based on knowledge spillover is invariant to the type of knowledge or the industry context. Still, these results confirm that there is compelling evidence suggesting that knowledge-based startups tend to cluster within geographic proximity of the knowledge source.

An alternative approach to testing the Locational Hypothesis along with the ancillary propositions is to substitute a different dependent variable, the distance from each entrepreneurial firm to the closest university. Because of the highly skewed nature of the dependent variable, OLS estimation may not be appropriate. The quantile estimation method is more appropriate to estimate the distance between the entrepreneurial firm and the closest university.

A second advantage of quantile regressions is that they provide an estimate of the propensity for university spillovers to decay with distance.[8] While the median regression focuses on the median firm, the regression on the 92 percentile focuses on the firms 50 kilometers away from the university. Using these different estimations enables us to examine the impact of startups with greater distance from the university (compared to the median and mean).

The results of OLS and quantile regressions are reported in table 6.7. The first column shows the results from the OLS regression with the natural logarithm of kilometers as the endogenous variable. Based on the OLS estimation, neither spillover mechanism has a statistically significant impact on geographic proximity between the university and the entrepreneurial firm. In the second column, the distance measure is based on the absolute number of kilometers. Using this measure with OLS estimation, one of the spillover mechanisms, human capital in the natural sciences, has a negative and statistically significant impact on geographic proximity. The greater the human capital output in the natural sciences, the closer entrepreneurial firms tend to locate to the university.

One reason to challenge the validity of the OLS estimation is the highly skewed nature of the distribution of the distance measure. The mean distance between an entrepreneurial firm and the closest university is about 16 kilometers, whereas the median distance is only 7 kilometers. As a result of this skewed distribution, quantile regressions may be a more appropriate estimation method. The results are shown in the third and fourth columns. The third column shows the results from the median regression. As the positive and statistically significant coefficient of the number of publications in the natural sciences suggests, entrepreneurial firms do not have a high propensity to locate within close proximity to universities with a high research output in the natural sciences. In fact, as the research output increases, the distance of the entrepreneurial firm from the university also tends to increase. Thus, there is no statistical evidence suggesting that new firms locate close to research universities in order to access the spillover of knowledge using the research mechanism for the knowledge type represented by the natural sciences.

The results in the third column of table 6.7 also suggest that the magnitude of university output in the form of human capital also affects the importance of geographic proximity in accessing university spillovers. As the negative and statistically significant coefficient of human capital in the natural sciences indicates, entrepreneurial firms tend to locate more closely to universities with a large output of human capital in the natural sciences.

However, this result does not hold for the social sciences. This may indicate that human capital in the natural sciences is more specific and less general than in the social sciences. The results also indicate that the other location-specific characteristics also affect the role of geographic proximity in accessing university spillovers. Both city scale and the cost of living for the university location, as well as city scale for the firm location, are found to influence the importance of geographic proximity.

As the last column in table 6.7 indicates, the results are considerably different when the 92.5 percent quantile estimation is used. Neither the two spillover mechanisms, published research and human capital embodied in student mobility, nor the two knowledge types, the natural sciences and social sciences, have a statistically significant impact on the importance of geographic proximity. This

TABLE 6.7 Regressions on the Mean, Median, and the 92% Quantile

Variables	OLS (semi-log)	OLS	Median	0.92 Quantile
Spillover mechanism research				
SCI articles	−0.00009	−0.001	0.0012	−0.0016
	(1.05)	(0.10)	(3.22)***	(0.26)
SSCI articles	0.00093	0.0144	−0.0303	0.1116
	(0.42)	(0.39)	(3.80)***	(0.69)
Spillover mechanism human capital				
SCI students	−0.00003	−0.0006	−0.0005	−0.0002
	(1.46)	(1.95)**	(4.93)***	(0.10)
SSCI students	0.00001	−0.0007	0.0001	−0.0011
	(0.91)	(0.36)	(2.31)**	(0.88)
Location-specific variables				
Town (university)	0.0080	0.0246	0.0153	0.0323
	(0.85)	(0.94)	(11.01)***	(1.45)
Cost of living	0.0121	−0.0129	−0.00258	−0.0895
	(0.64)	(0.47)	(3.58)***	(0.56)
Number of universities	0.5340	1.5741	−2.0271	−13.822
	(3.74)***	(0.65)	(2.16)**	(0.82)
West	0.5826	−11.882	3.8011	−12.180
	(1.40)	(1.87)*	(2.31)***	(0.91)
Town (firm)	−0.0080	−0.0122	−0.0013	−0.0365
	(5.98)***	(4.34)***	(15.71)***	(2.58)***
Firm-specific characteristics				
Firm age	0.0151	0.0744	0.0507	−0.3421
	(2.06)**	(0.49)	(1.37)	(0.64)
Software	−0.0029	0.4810	0.4966	−0.3421
	(0.03)	(0.73)	(1.26)	(0.11)
Service	−0.2311	1.2914	−1.1929	9.7641
	(0.82)	(0.28)	(1.16)	(0.45)
E-commerce	0.0425	4.5571	1.8528	35.874
	(0.11)	(0.51)	(1.16)	(1.12)
Hardware	−0.0984	8.4662	−1.1422	22.321
	(0.29)	(0.86)	(0.80)	(0.85)
Telecom	−0.0066	−4.7332	0.7564	−4.315
	(0.21)	(1.22)	(0.50)	(0.25)
Biotechnology	0.5687	−7.8921	−5.0633	−4.4202
	(1.28)	(1.25)	(3.13)***	(0.12)
Medical devices	−0.9444	−13.445	−1.0453	2.8956
	(1.56)	(1.87)*	(0.55)	(0.15)
Media	−0.8593	−8.293	−4.0047	−5.9651
	(3.33)***	(2.67)**	(3.24)***	(0.25)
Constant	2.0104	32.3856	11.9244	96.441
	(3.99)***	(3.93)***	(6.05)***	(3.33)
R^2	0.1235	0.1479	0.1603	0.2848

The endogenous variable is the distance from the new firm to the closest university. T values in parentheses unless denoted otherwise; the variable for city size (for university) and city size (for firm) are multiplied by 1,000.
*Statistically significant at the two-tailed test for 90% level of confidence.
**Statistically significant at the two-tailed test for 95% level of confidence.
***Statistically significant at the two-tailed test for 99% level of confidence.

would suggest that the university spillovers are geographically bounded within a small distance from the university. The same holds for the mean regression in the second column, where the mean distance is about 16 kilometers. Thus, we prefer the median regression to capture the effect that half of the firms are located within a small circle about 7 kilometers around a university.

6.6 Conclusions

The Knowledge Spillover Theory of Entrepreneurship suggests that investment in the creation of new knowledge will generate opportunities for entrepreneurship as a mechanism for knowledge spillovers. The Locational Hypothesis places a spatial constraint on such spillovers, particularly from universities. This chapter found that, in general, those universities in regions with a higher knowledge capacity and greater knowledge output also generate a higher number of knowledge and technology startups, suggesting that university spillovers are geographically bounded. Geographic proximity is an asset, if not a prerequisite, to entrepreneurial firms in accessing and absorbing spillovers from universities.

However, this chapter has also shown that the role of geographic proximity in accessing university spillovers is considerably more nuanced than is suggested by the Locational Hypothesis. The importance of geographic proximity apparently depends on at least two factors: the particular type of university output and spillover mechanism. For those university outputs and spillover mechanisms that are more tacit in nature, geographic proximity plays a greater role in accessing and absorbing university spillovers. By contrast, for less tacit and more codified university outputs and spillover mechanisms, geographic proximity is less important.

Entrepreneurial Performance

7.1 Location and Entrepreneurial Advantage

The previous two chapters have confirmed the Localization Hypothesis. Entrepreneurial activity tends to cluster within close geographic proximity to firms and universities spawning knowledge spillovers that trigger entrepreneurship. But does such geographic proximity bestow these new entrepreneurial startups with any competitive advantage? Does the performance of those entrepreneurial startups located within close geographic proximity to knowledge sources outdo the performance of firms not enjoying locational proximity to such knowledge sources?

The purpose of this chapter is to test the Entrepreneurial Performance Hypothesis, which suggests that the performance of knowledge-based startups should be superior when they are able to access knowledge spillovers through geographic proximity to universities as a source of knowledge.

If measuring performance for established incumbent firms is complex, it is fraught with ambiguities for entrepreneurial startups. Therefore, this chapter uses two measures of entrepreneurial performance, proven standards in the literature, which are based on growth and stock market performance (Audretsch and Lehmann, 2005a, 2005b).

In fact, the last decade has seen an explosion of interest in economic growth for a diversity of units of observation. While the Endogenous Growth Theory (Romer, 1986, 1990; Lucas, 1988) and New Economic Geography (Krugman, 1991a, 1991b, 1998; Fujita, Krugman, and Venables, 1999) focus on growth at the macroeconomic level, a complementary literature has emerged examining the growth of cities (Glaeser et al., 1992; Henderson et al., 1995; Rosenthal and Stange, 2003). One of the most important findings is that knowledge externalities, or knowledge spillovers, provide a mechanism generating superior economic performance, measured in terms of growth, in spatially concentrated areas but not where economic activity is geographically dispersed. An important finding in both the endogenous growth literature as well as the studies on city growth is that agglomerations of economic activity positively affect economic growth.

However, the actual mechanisms causing this growth are less clear. An important step was made in penetrating the black box of urban space by Glaeser et al. (1992) and Feldman and Audretsch (1999), who demonstrated that growth is influenced by the spatial concentration of economic activity as well as how that activity is organized. In particular, they found that a broad spread of complementary economic activity is more conducive to growth than specialization. Still, virtually nothing is known about the impact of location on growth at the micro or firm level.

Does location make a difference in firm growth? Are there systematic differences in growth rates of firms engaged in the same industry across geographic space? Even though recent theories and empirical evidence about the linkages between agglomerations and growth at the spatial level imply that this relationship should also hold at the micro or establishment level, in fact, very little is known about the locational impact on firm performance, as measured in terms of growth. Both the conceptual framework and empirical analyses have been aggregated to spatial units such as cities or industries located in cities. Insights about the impact of location on firm growth have been limited.

This omission cannot be attributed to a lack of theories and empirical evidence about growth at the firm level. In fact, ample literature has provided a conceptual framework as well as compelling evidence as to why performance, measured in terms of growth, varies systematically across firms (Sutton, 1997; Caves, 1998). The literature on Gibrat's Law and industry dynamics has produced stylized facts about the size and age of firms and the high-tech or low-tech characteristics of industry that shape growth; however, these studies have overlooked locational aspects that influence growth.

This chapter seeks to fill these gaps in the literatures on spatial growth and firm growth by explicitly linking the performance of new technology and knowledge-based firms, measured in terms of growth, to geographic location. We combine the conceptual frameworks developed in these two distinct literatures to introduce a model of growth specific to characteristics of the location as well as the firm and industry.

The following section of this chapter explains why location and geographic proximity to knowledge sources might positively influence firm performance. In the third section, we present the model relating firm growth—not just firm characteristics but also geographic proximity—to knowledge external to the firm. In the fourth section, we link stock market performance to the location of entrepreneurial firms and to the amount and types of knowledge produced at universities. Then, in the last section, we summarize and conclude. In particular, the results of this chapter suggest that two important strands of literature need to be linked. The evidence is consistent with the Entrepreneurial Performance Hypothesis, in that geographic proximity to a knowledge source can enhance entrepreneurial performance. However, this relationship is complex and depends on a number of conditioning factors, such as the magnitude of the research output of the university, the types of research outputs, and the strength of the spillover mechanisms.

7.2 Linking Performance to Location

Locational proximity to a knowledge source might enhance entrepreneurial performance for two main reasons, both emanating from the resource theory of entrepreneurship. Barney (1986) identified access to resources as a source creating heterogeneity across firms and creating a sustainable competitive advantage (Alvarez, 2003).

The first reason why location matters for entrepreneurial performance involves accessing the knowledge triggering the startup of the new firm in the first place. As chapters 3 and 6 made clear, startups generated by a spillover from research and ideas generated by an incumbent corporation or universities may have a greater endowment of knowledge capital than startups not enjoying such access. A new firm that must generate its own knowledge capital will be limited by scale and time. It has neither the resources nor the experience to generate ideas. But a new firm that uses external knowledge and ideas can leverage its own knowledge capital by standing on the shoulders of giants.

Some evidence suggests that accessing such external knowledge does, in fact, positively affect entrepreneurial performance. Klepper and Sleeper (2000) showed how spin-offs in the automobile industry exhibited a superior performance when the founder came from a high-performing incumbent firm, rather than a low-performing incumbent firm, or even from one outside of the industry. Klepper and Sleeper interpreted this result as indicating that the experience and ability to absorb human capital within the context of the incumbent firm positively influenced the subsequent entrepreneurial performance. Agarwal et al. (2004) found similar results.

The second reason why location matters for entrepreneurial performance involves potential poststartup access to flows of external knowledge that can serve as a valuable resource and bestow a competitive advantage not enjoyed by entrepreneurial firms not located within close geographic proximity to a knowledge source. The potential flows of knowledge from external sources may not necessarily be exhausted with the act of starting up a new firm. In fact, the expectation or anticipation of a stream of poststartup knowledge flows may be influential in the locational decision. If it were just a matter of taking only the knowledge and experience garnered from an incumbent organization, perhaps the entrepreneurial locational decision would not matter as much. The expectation or anticipation of subsequent access to external knowledge may be a key factor in decisions about location.

In fact, as chapter 6 emphasized, not much is known about the actual mechanisms transmitting the spillover of knowledge. Studies have suggested that knowledge spillovers may arise from academic and industrial researchers' personal networks (Liebeskind et al., 1996; MacPherson, 1998; Feldman and Desrochers, 2003), participation in conferences and presentations, or preemployment possibilities with students as an important channel for disseminating the latest knowledge from academia to high-technology industry (Varga, 2000). University research, as the source of such spillovers, is typically measured by the amount of money spent on R&D, the number of articles published in academic and scientific journals, the number of employees or patents (see Henderson et al., 1998; McWilliams and

Siegel, 2000; Varga, 2000; Hall et al., 2003). The overwhelming majority of the empirical literature confirms the positive effects of university spillovers (Acs et al., 1992, 1994; Jaffe et al., 1993; Audretsch and Feldman, 1996; Anselin et al., 1997; Varga, 2000; Mowery and Ziedonis, 2001; Acs et al., 2002), although there are barriers to partnering such as unclear property rights (Hall et al., 2001).

A different strand of literature has focused on the capability of economic agents to recognize, assimilate, and apply new scientific knowledge. In pointing out firms that invest in R&D to generate the capacity to adapt knowledge first developed in other firms, Cohen and Levinthal (1989 and 1990) show how such R&D investments are mechanisms used to absorb external knowledge. The concept of absorptive capacity was extended by Cockburn and Henderson (1996 and 1999), who identified the potential link between a firm and the community of open science, which could be strengthened through R&D investments as a mechanism to access external knowledge spillovers. Through cultivating relationships with scientists and students at universities, participating in research consortia, and partnering with academics who do related scientific research, firms can acquire new knowledge capabilities and benefit from external knowledge.

Mansfield (1995 and 1998) identified one important source of external knowledge that can be internalized by private firms: research undertaken in university laboratories. Studies by Jaffe (1989), Acs et al. (1992), Audretsch and Feldman (1996), Feldman and Audretsch (1999), and Mowery and Shane (2002) supported the hypothesis that knowledge created in university laboratories spills over for commercial use in generating innovative activity.

A different literature focused on the role that networks and social capital can play within a geographic region. Because they can link individuals, groups, firms, industries, geographic regions, and nation states, networks span a diverse set of units of analysis. Such networks provide linkages across units of analysis resulting in a rich and complex web of interrelationships among economic agents, firms, and institutions. Considerable empirical evidence documents the characteristics of such networks (Powell, Koput, and Smith-Doerr, 1996; Florida and Cohen, 1999; Feldman et al., 2002). For example, Powell et al. document the mechanisms by which private firms can access research from universities through a set of rich linkages serving as conduits for knowledge spillovers. Examples of these linkages include attracting knowledge workers to the region in which the university is located, technology transfer, the mobility and placement of students in industry, and providing a platform for firms, individuals, and government agencies to interact (Florida and Cohen, 1999).

Much empirical work analyzes geographical proximity and university spillovers, whereas there is scarce evidence on the effects of knowledge spillovers on firm performance. One way to gauge performance is to determine whether university spillovers reduce the cost of R&D for the firms (Harhoff, 2000). Another method was introduced by Griliches (1979), who proposed using hedonic price functions to analyze whether new products have better quality than old products as a result of knowledge spillovers. One branch of research analyzes the productivity effects of spillovers (see Nadiri, 1997, for a survey). However, whether geographic proximity and access to knowledge spillovers improves firm performance remains unexplored.

Perhaps the most prevalent and established finding in the spillover literature is derived from empirical estimation of the model of the knowledge production function for spatial units of observation: innovative output and growth are higher in regions with a greater presence of knowledge inputs (Jaffe, 1989; Acs et al., 1992). However, this literature has emphasized the region or city as the unit of observation. Little is known about the impact of geographic proximity on the performance of firms. As Jaffe (1989, p. 957) points out, geographical location is just as important in capturing the benefits of spillovers when the mechanism of knowledge is informal conversation as it is for tacit knowledge: "Geographic proximity to the spillover source may be helpful or even necessary in capturing the spillover benefits."

Thus, the limited geographic reach of such channels for the exchange of ideas and know-how explains why geographic proximity improves firm performance since it leads to a competitive advantage over similar firms located farther from universities. During the innovation process, firms confront a wide range of problems and difficulties that may be beyond the firm's own problem-solving capacity. Close location supports both management capacity and technological inputs. Otherwise, large spatial distances between firms and universities pose significant barriers to interactions between university scientists and other knowledge workers and private firms (Schartinger et al., 2001).

7.3 Testing the Entrepreneurial Growth Hypothesis

The purpose of this section is to provide a link between the literatures on firm growth, on the one hand, and university-based knowledge spillovers, on the other hand. We examine whether access to university-based knowledge spillovers has an impact on firm growth (Audretsch and Lehmann, 2005b, 2005c). In the first subsection, we introduce a little model relating not just firm characteristics but also knowledge external to the firm to firm growth. In the second subsection, we discuss issues involving measurement. The results from estimating the growth rates of high-technology German firms appear in subsection three.

7.3.1 The Model

As the Caves (1998) and Sutton (1997) review articles in the *Journal of Economic Literature* confirm, the plethora of econometric studies focusing on firm growth in general, and Gibrat's Law in particular, never consider the impact of external research on the growth of firms. Instead, this entire literature consists almost exclusively of attempts to link firm-specific characteristics, principally size and age but also R&D and other types of innovative activity, to firm growth. Similarly, the literature on knowledge spillovers has concentrated mainly on performance measures such as innovation and R&D but has yet to consider the impact on firm growth.

We introduce a simple model relating firm growth to characteristics specific to the enterprise as well as external knowledge from universities. The starting point is the most prevalent model for identifying the determinants of firm growth, which has been based on Gibrat's Law (Sutton, 1997). Formalizing the relationship between size and growth, Gibrat's Law assumes that the present size of firm i in period

t may be decomposed into the product of a "proportional effect" and the initial firm size (Elston and Audretsch, 2004):

$$Size_{i,t} = (1+\varepsilon_t)Size_{i,t-1}, \qquad (7.1)$$

where $(1+\varepsilon_t)$ denotes the proportional effect for firm i in period t. Here the random shock ε_t is assumed to be identically and independently distributed. Taking the natural log and assuming that for small ε, $\ln(1+\varepsilon) \approx \varepsilon_t$,

$$\ln(Size_{i,t}) = \ln(Size_{i,0}) + \Sigma_{k=1}^{t}\varepsilon_{ik}. \qquad (7.2)$$

As $t \to \infty$ a distribution emerges that is approximately log normal with properties that $\ln(Size_{i,t}) \sim N(t\mu_\varepsilon, t\sigma_\varepsilon^2)$. Firm growth can then be measured as the difference between the natural log of the number of employees as shown:

$$Growth_{it} = \ln(S_{i,t}) - \ln(S_{i,t-1}), \qquad (7.3)$$

where the difference in size for firm i between the current period t and the initial period $(t-1)$ equals $Growth_{it}$.

This equation can be empirically estimated by the following:

$$Growth_{i,t} = B_1\ln(Size_{i,t-1}) + B_2\ln(Size_{i,t-1})^2 + B_3Age_{i,t-1} + \varepsilon_i, \qquad (7.4)$$

where growth for firm i in period t is a function of initial firm size, size^2, age, and ε_i, a stochastic error term. Sutton (1997) and Caves (1998) survey and report on the large number of empirical studies estimating equation (7.4). The evidence is systematic and compelling that both size and age are negatively related to firm growth.

Equation (7.4) considers only characteristics specific to the enterprise. We extend this approach by including knowledge spillovers from universities:

$$Growth_{i,t} = B_1\ln(Size_{i,t-1}) + B_2\ln(Size_{i,t-1})^2 + B_3Age_{i,t-1}$$
$$B_4Knowledge_{r,t-1} B_5D_{ind} + \varepsilon_i, \qquad (7.5)$$

where D_{ind} is a vector of industry dummies controlling, for example, for the knowledge intensity of production in a specific sector. Knowledge$_{(r(,t-1))}$ represents knowledge spillovers from universities. Thus, we test whether $B_4>0$.

7.3.2 Data and Measurement

The model will be estimated using the same database as that introduced in chapter 6, based on technology and knowledge-based startups that have made an IPO. To this data set, the *log growth rates* of employees one year after the IPO is included as the dependent variable.

The first two exogenous variables are firm age (*age*) and firm size (*size*). Age is measured in years from startup to IPO, and firm size by the number of employees prior to making the IPO. To capture effects from university spillovers, we include the distance to the closest university as an exogenous variable.

The descriptive statistics are depicted in table 7.1. The closest location between firms and universities is 1 kilometer and the maximum distance is 177 kilometers

TABLE 7.1 Firm Characteristics

Variable	Mean	Standard deviation	Min	Max
Distance (km)	16.69	23.45	1	177
Firm size (employees)	180.20	256.52	2	1,700
Firm age (years)	10.27	11.11	0.1	107
LN growth rates	0.4969	1.6121	−4.106	7.5183

away from the nearest university. The data also demonstrates that most of the firms are strikingly young. Half of the firms in our sample are 8 years old or younger. The firms also differ considerably in their size as measured by the number of employees prior to IPO. The mean firm before IPO employed about 180 workers. Finally, the table shows that on average the log growth rate is about 0.475.

7.3.3 Empirical Results

Table 7.2 presents the results for five specifications of the regression model estimating entrepreneurial growth. The measure of university spillovers is multiplied by (−1) to reflect that as the distance between the firm and university decreases, the higher the growth rate of the respective firm. All OLS estimations use the White-heteroskedasticity robust variance-covariance estimator.

The first two columns replicate the standard tests of Gibrat's Law. The negative and statistically significant coefficients on firm size suggest that smaller firms grow

TABLE 7.2 Regressions Estimating Entrepreneurial Growth

	OLS	OLS	OLS	OLS	2SLS	2SLS[a]
LnSize	−0.7895	−0.9290	−0.9117	−0.8537	−0.8554	−1.1272
	(2.75)**	(15.33)***	(14.10)***	(1.86)**	(10.22)***	(2.31)***
LnSize2	−0.0152			−0.0059		0.03133
	(0.47)			(0.12)		(0.58)
LnAge	0.0859	0.07390	0.0613	0.0731	0.1688	0.1929
	(1.29)	(1.40)	(1.19)	(0.96)	(2.00)**	(1.83)*
LnAge2	−0.0114			0.0092		−0.0099
	(0.41)			(0.34)		(0.31)
Distance			−0.0423	−0.0430	0.7131	0.7263
			(0.92)	(0.92)	(1.78)**	(1.79)**
Constant	4.3187	4.5762	4.4339	4.3289	5.430	6.001
	(7.03)***	(17.27)***	(13.75)***	(4.11)***	(8.25)***	(4.43)***
Adj. R^2	0.4749	0.4779	0.4856	0.4860	0.0236	0.0094

The endogenous variable is growth rates of employees one year after the IPO. T values are in parentheses. The coefficient of university spillovers is multiplied with (−1) to capture the positive effect of a close location toward the next university.

[a]University spillover is measured in log kilometers from the closest university. This variable is instrumented in the 2SLS approach by the number of research spending and the number of papers published in the natural sciences and in the social sciences.

*Statistically significant at the two-tailed test for 90% level of confidence.

**Statistically significant at the two-tailed test for 95% level of confidence.

***Statistically significant at the two-tailed test for 99% level of confidence.

faster than their larger counterparts. This finding is consistent with the plethora of previous studies linking firm size to firm growth. The coefficients of firm age as well as the squared term show no statistically significant impact on firm growth.

Including the measure of distance between the firm and the university in the third column suggests that there is no statistically significant impact of university spillovers on entrepreneurial growth. Similarly, when all of the variables are included in the fourth column, university spillovers still do not have a statistically significant impact on entrepreneurial growth.

However, one concern may involve both the theory and results from chapter 6, where we suggested that, in fact, entrepreneurial location itself is influenced by the prospects of accessing university spillovers. This would suggest that university spillovers should be treated as endogenous. Thus, in the fifth column, the measure of distance between the firm and the university is instrumented using the two-stage least squares regression method by three measures of research output of the university: the magnitude of research expenditures in the university budget, the number of research articles published in scholarly journals in the natural sciences, and the number of research articles published in scholarly journals in the social sciences. The results when the geographic proximity between the entrepreneurial firm and the university is also treated being endogenous are considerably different. In fact, as the positive and statistically significant coefficient suggests, geographic proximity to a university matters for entrepreneurial growth. The greater the geographic proximity between the firm and the nearest university, the higher the growth rate of entrepreneurial firms. These results are confirmed in the last column, which includes all of the variables in the estimation model.

At least some evidence suggests that entrepreneurial growth is not neutral to location. Rather, it is systematically greater when the entrepreneurial firms are located within close geographic proximity to a knowledge source, such as a university.

7.4 Stock Market Performance

A number of limitations and important qualifications should accompany the use of growth as a measure of entrepreneurial performance. One such important qualification is that the measure of growth does not reflect the market valuation of the enterprise. An alternative measure incorporating the market valuation of the firm is based on the stock market performance (Audretsch and Lehmann, 2005a).

We use the *log of abnormal profits* as the dependent variable. We calculated the abnormal annual log-rents on the stock market from the date of the initial public offering until the June 30 in 2002. This time period spans both the Internet bubble on the stock market as well as the rapid decline in 2001 and 2002.

The abnormal annual log-profit is measured as follows:

$$LN\ Profit = [(\text{lnprice10.06.02} - \text{lnIPOprice})$$
$$- (\text{lnNEMAX30.06.02} - \text{lnNEMAXIPO})]\frac{52}{\text{number of weeks}} \quad (7.6)$$

where *LnIPOprice* is the natural logarithm of the stock price on the day when the firm was first listed on the stock market and thus reflects the supply and demand for the firm's shares. Thus, this price is the market determined price on the first day of trading. *LnNEMAXIPO* is the logarithm of the market index at IPO. *Lnprice*(30.06.02), and *lnNEMAX*(30.June 02) are the values taken from June 30, 2002. Capital increases and dividend payments are incorporated in the stock prices. The term is divided by the number of weeks from IPO to June 30, 2002. Multiplying by 52 yields the annual abnormal profit.

The underlying performance measure of abnormal profits captures entrepreneurial performance from IPO until the first half of the year 2002. Although no new IPOs were undertaken between 2001 and 2002, the time period was extended until June 2002. This time horizon includes both the dramatic upswing, which lasted until March 2000, as well as the downswing, which subsequently occurred through March 2002.

The stock market measure of entrepreneurial performance is then linked to the measures of university knowledge outputs and spillover mechanisms introduced in chapter 6. The two types of major outputs are knowledge in the natural sciences and knowledge in the social sciences. The two types of spillover mechanisms are research articles published in scholarly journals and the mobility of human capital embodied in students graduating from the university. The spillover mechanism of published academic articles in highly ranked journals is based on the ISI database.

The impact of university knowledge outputs and spillover mechanisms should be greater if the firm is located close to the university. Thus, the same measure of this distance as that used in chapter 6 is included in the regression model, both linear and multiplicative, with the measures of university outputs and spillover mechanisms.

Size and age, the same two firm-specific characteristics found to influence entrepreneurial performance in the previous section as well as throughout the literature on Gibrat's Law, are also included as explanatory variables. We further include several control variables that may influence entrepreneurial performance. First, we include a dummy variable indicating a technical university. Technical universities are assumed to play a special role in technology transfer, since they focus on engineering and natural sciences. Technically oriented universities receive more funds than other universities to foster and promote spillovers from new technologies and research for commercialization by private firms. Finally, we include dummy variables to control for the different industries of the firms and to control for the year in which the IPO was undertaken.

The dependent variable measuring the stock market performance is highly skewed, which makes the results from OLS estimation less reliable. As an alternative, we applied the method of median regression to test the Entrepreneurial Performance Hypothesis.

The sample mean is defined as the solution to the problem of minimizing a sum of squared residuals. Similarly, the median is defined as the solution to the problem of minimizing a sum of absolute residuals. This semiparametric technique provides a general class of models in which the conditional quantiles have a linear form. In its simplest form, the least absolute deviation estimator fits medians to a linear function of covariates. The method of quantile regression is potentially attractive for the same reason that the median or other quantiles are a better measure of location than the mean. In addition, the robustness against outliers and the likelihood estimators are in general more efficient than least squares estimators. Besides these technical features, in quantile regressions, potentially different solutions at distinct quantiles may be interpreted as differences in the response of the dependent variable to changes in the explanatory variables at various points in the conditional distinction of the dependent variable. Thus, quantile regressions reveal asymmetries in the data that could not be detected by simple OLS estimations (see Fitzenberger, 1999, and Koenker and Hallock, 2001, for more details of quantile regressions).

Three nested models are estimated to identify whether the geographical proximity between a firm and university influences entrepreneurial performance:

$$
\begin{aligned}
Performance = const. &+ \beta_1 distance + \beta_2 SSCIRank + \beta_3 SCIRank \\
&+ \beta_4 SCI\ Students + \beta_5 SSCI\ Student + \beta_6 TU + \beta_7 Age \\
&+ \beta_8 Size + \beta_{9-15} industry\ dummies + \beta_{16-18} IPO \\
&\ dummies + \varepsilon
\end{aligned}
\tag{7.7}
$$

$$
\begin{aligned}
Performance = const. &+ \beta_1 distance^* SSCIRank + \beta_2 distance^* SCIRank \\
&+ \beta_3 distance^* SSCI\ Students + \beta_4 distance^* SCI\ Students + \varepsilon
\end{aligned}
\tag{7.8}
$$

$$
\begin{aligned}
Performance = const. &+ \beta_1 distance^* SSCIRank + \beta_2 distance^* SCIRank \\
&+ \beta_3 distance^* SCI\ Students + \beta_4 distance^* SSCI\ Students \\
&+ \beta_5 Age + \beta_6 Size + \beta_7 TU + \beta_{8-14} industry\ dummies \\
&+ \beta_{15-17} IPO\ dummies + \varepsilon
\end{aligned}
\tag{7.9}
$$

The results of the median regressions are presented in table 7.3.

In the first regression (7.7), distance and university output enter the regression separately. As the statistical insignificance of the coefficients implies, neither geographic proximity nor the magnitude of university research output has a significant effect on firm performance. Most of the variance in firm performance is explained either by industry effects or the time to IPO. The latter indicates the phenomenon of the "window of opportunities" (Ritter, 1991). The longer the IPO period, the lower the quality of firms brought to the stock market. The Pseudo R^2 is 0.334, which can be interpreted in the same way as the traditional R^2 in OLS regressions, since it also shows the proportion of the explained variance about the specified quantile. Thus, about 33 percent of the variance of firm performance could be explained from the estimation of this model.

In the second regression (7.8), only the interaction terms are included. Although only about 4 percent of the variance could be explained by the four variables, three of them have a statistically significant coefficient. With a given level in the output of social science research articles, firm performance improves as the geographic proximity to the university decreases. This is expressed by the negative sign: with a given amount of academic articles performance increases, the shorter the distance.

TABLE 7.3 Stock Market Performance (the endogenous variable is abnormal annual log-profits on the stock market)

	(7.7)	(7.8)	(7.9)
Distance	-0.0007^a $(0.36)^b$		
SSCI articles	0.0514 (0.28)		
SCI articles	0.1001 (0.37)		
SSCI students	−0.000001 (0.36)		
SCI students	0.00001 (0.86)		
SSCI articles * distance	—	−0.02084 $(5.06)^{***}$	−0.0104 $(2.79)^{**}$
SCI articles * distance	—	0.0270 $(5.16)^{***}$	0.0136 $(3.11)^{***}$
SSCI students * distance	—	−0.000001 (1.20)	−0.0000002 (0.29)
SCI students * distance	—	−0.000001 $(2.43)^{**}$	−0.000001 $(1.91)^{**}$
TU	−0.1236 (0.53)		0.096 (0.59)
Age	0.0066 (1.30)		0.0048 (1.26)
Size	0.00019 (1.03)		0.00019 (1.37)
Software	−0.0703 $(1.71)^*$		−0.0766 $(2.39)^{**}$
Service	−0.1712 (1.29)		−0.2171 $(2.02)^{**}$
E-commerce	−0.3214 (1.51)		−0.4096 $(2.47)^{**}$
Telecommunication	−0.21016 (1.08)		−0.2474 (1.58)
Biotechnology	−0.20204 (0.91)		−0.1481 (0.80)
MedTec	0.21509 (0.92)		0.1833 (0.96)
Media & entertainment	−0.3307 $(1.94)^*$		−0.3256 $(2.49)^{**}$
IPO 97	1.6175 $(6.20)^{***}$		1.6709 $(8.64)^{***}$
IPO 98	1.2307 $(8.11)^{***}$		1.2243 $(9.53)^{***}$
IPO 99	0.8052 (7.67)		0.7908 $(9.53)^{***}$
Constant	−2.4214 (4.83)	−1.6231 $(27.88)^{***}$	−2.0771 $(20.08)^{***}$

(*continued*)

TABLE 7.3 *(continued)*

	(7.7)	(7.8)	(7.9)
Pseudo R^2	0.334	0.0330	0.3375
N	259	259	259
Pseudo median	−1.6032	−1.6032	−1.6032

[a]Estimated median regression coefficients.
[b]Absolute *t* values in parentheses.
*Statistically significant at the 10% level.
**Statistically significant at the 5% level.
***Statistically significant at the 1% level.

However, for research output in the natural sciences, geographic proximity between the firm and the university does not apparently improve entrepreneurial performance. This result is actually consistent with findings from Audretsch and Stephan (1996, 1999) and Schartinger et al. (2001). The latter study showed that the employment of highly skilled, university-educated personnel is the most important input for the innovation process of high-tech firms. Codified knowledge, as embodied in academic articles in the natural sciences, did not need short distance to enhance firm performance.

The regression results also indicate that geographic proximity may have less of an impact on firm performance for knowledge transmitted by the mobility of human capital in the social sciences than in the natural sciences. Therefore, the amount of human capital in the social sciences may not bestow any competitive advantage to firms close to a university.

In contrast, there is considerable heterogeneity across specific research specializations of universities in the natural sciences. Universities differ in their specific research specializations, such as life sciences, biochemistry, physics, or engineering. Thus, the human capital embodied in students in the natural sciences is likely more "specific" than "general" (Acs et al., 2002).

The most important finding from linking the stock market performance of entrepreneurial firms to their geographic proximity to universities is that the role of location is complex. Geographic proximity to a university, per se, has no significant impact on entrepreneurial performance. However, entrepreneurial performance is significantly higher when a university with strong research output is in close proximity. This suggests an interactive relationship between geographic proximity and university output, on the one hand, and firm performance, on the other. Locating within close geographic proximity to a university will bestow competitive benefits to an entrepreneurial firm only if the research output and spillover mechanisms from the university are strong.

7.5 Conclusions

Recent literature has found persuasive evidence suggesting that, because of the spatially bounded nature of knowledge spillovers, economic performance, typically measured in terms of growth, is greater in cities and regions where investments in new knowledge are high. The spillover from those firms and universities investing in new knowledge results in higher rates of city and regional growth. However, this literature has remained remarkably silent about identifying the actual organizational unit of observation in which this growth occurs. Do all existing incumbent firms in the region enjoy greater growth rates, do firms moving to the region or just a certain type of firm? Though this chapter has not exhaustively inventoried the link between localized knowledge spillovers and firm performance, it has at least identified one type of firm in which performance benefits from close proximity to knowledge sources: knowledge-based entrepreneurial startups.

However, the exact relationship between location and entrepreneurial performance is complex. Whether or not geographic proximity to a knowledge source, such as a university, bestows competitive benefits to an entrepreneurial firm depends on a number of factors. In particular, the impact of geographic proximity on entrepreneurial performance is shaped by the amount and type of knowledge produced at a university. If the research output of a university is meagre, close proximity to a university will not bestow significant performance benefits. However, close proximity to a university with strong research output and spillover mechanisms enhances entrepreneurial performance. Similarly, the benefits of geographic proximity in enhancing entrepreneurial performance are not homogeneous but apparently vary across academic fields and disciplines (and, presumably, industry sector). However, this difference could also be that the spillover effects of the codified scientific knowledge are easier to anticipate by market participants and to be priced at the IPO than are spillover effects from social science knowledge.[1] Thus, the results show that spillovers matter for firm performance, depending on whether or not the impact of geographic proximity on firm performance is anticipated and priced in the IPOs.

Whether the role of location in enhancing firm performance is homogeneous across a broader and fuller range of firms' life cycles, as well as across a broader range of nonknowledge firms and knowledge-based firms, is beyond the scope of this chapter. Given the high propensity for knowledge spillovers to be commercialized and appropriated within the organizational context of a new firm, the performance benefits accruing from spatial proximity to a university may prove greater for knowledge-based entrepreneurial firms than for their more established incumbent and nonknowledge counterparts. Whether or not this conjecture holds under the scrutiny of future research, this chapter has at least found evidence consistent with the Entrepreneurial Performance Hypothesis. With a number of important conditions and qualifications, entrepreneurial performance does appear to be enhanced by close geographic proximity to knowledge sources.

Entrepreneurial Access

8.1 Entrepreneurial Strategy for Absorbing Knowledge Spillovers

Chapter 6 found that entrepreneurial firms, particularly in science-based and high-technology industries, tend to locate within close geographic proximity to a knowledge source. Chapter 7 showed why: location matters. Location matters for accessing knowledge spillovers that bestow competitive advantage. However, while geographic proximity may facilitate access to external knowledge spillovers, it does not necessarily guarantee that the entrepreneurial firm can absorb such external knowledge spillovers and transform them into a competitive advantage. An important insight introduced by Cohen and Levinthal (1989) is that firms need to invest in the capacity to access and absorb external knowledge.

The purpose of this chapter is to suggest two factors that facilitate entrepreneurial access to and absorption of external knowledge spillovers. Cohen and Levinthal (1989) focused on investments in R&D as the mechanism facilitating the absorption of external knowledge, but the size constraint of entrepreneurial start-ups may also constrain the magnitude of their R&D investments, at least in absolute terms. However, as Audretsch and Stephan (1996) identified, there is a very different mechanism facilitating the access and absorption for entrepreneurial firms in high-technology and science-based industries: board members and firm managers. Audretsch and Stephan also found compelling evidence implying that geographic proximity is a prerequisite for board members to access and absorb external knowledge.

Thus, the Entrepreneurial Access Hypothesis suggests a very different role for board members. Rather than the conventional view, which focuses on the function of boards in controlling managers to reduce problems of economic agency, we introduce a new role in the following section: to help the entrepreneurial firm access and absorb external knowledge spillovers. The composition of boards is endogenously influenced by the degree to which the firm is in a science-based or high-technology industry, as well as the potential pool of external knowledge spillovers emanating from knowledge sources within close geographic proximity (see Audretsch and Lehmann, 2005e). The results of this chapter suggest that a strategy deployed by entrepreneurial firms is to select boards and managers with the human capital and knowledge capabilities to contribute to the access and absorption of external knowledge spillovers.

8.2 Entrepreneurial Absorptive Capacity

An important assumption inherent in the Knowledge Spillover Theory of Entrepreneurship is that the knowledge embedded in a knowledge worker, such as a scientist or engineer, is exogenous and that, in an effort to appropriate the value of her knowledge endowment, the economic agent endogenously starts a new firm. Strictly considered, such an assumption would seemingly suggest that this initial endowment of knowledge suffices in generating entrepreneurial competitive advantage that should be reflected in the types of high performance analyzed in the previous chapter.

If such a strict interpretation regarding the exogeneity assumption of entrepreneurial knowledge is valid, the empirical validation of the Localization Hypothesis in chapter 6 and the Performance Hypothesis in chapter 7 is surprising, for both chapters suggest that entrepreneurial access to knowledge spillovers remains important, even after the startup of the new firm. If this were not the case, a knowledge worker might obtain the requisite knowledge in one location but then move away to a more preferable location to actually start and grow the firm. Of course, while this happens in many instances, the results from chapters 6 and 7 imply that knowledge-based and technology firms tend to locate within close geographic proximity to a knowledge source, such as a university, and that geographic proximity bestows a competitive advantage on the entrepreneur.

In order to start the firm, the founder need not access external knowledge but rather needs a knowledge endowment. As the assumption inherent in the Knowledge Spillover Theory of Entrepreneurship suggests, the knowledge was exogenously embodied in the knowledge agent confronting the entrepreneurial decision. The central feature of the model of endogenous entrepreneurship is that the spillover of knowledge is accomplished when the knowledge agent starts the new firm.

However, to access knowledge spillovers after the new-firm startup, knowledge that may be external to the entrepreneur needs to be accessed. Chapters 6 and 7 suggest that the location of the entrepreneurial startup can facilitate the access of such external knowledge spillovers. But, as Cohen and Levinthal (1989) pointed out, firms may not automatically access external knowledge but rather may require investments in absorptive capacity. A prerequisite for the continued poststartup access to knowledge spillovers is an entrepreneurial capacity for accessing and absorbing ideas generated externally by other firms and knowledge sources, such as universities and research institutions.

How can such external knowledge be accessed and absorbed by entrepreneurial firms? In a seminal article, Cohen and Levinthal (1989) focused on the role of investments in R&D as a mechanism for external knowledge access and absorption. As Henderson and Cockburn (1994) showed, considerable evidence links investments in research to the capacity of large incumbent firms to access and absorb external knowledge.

Because new firms are typically small and consist of a handful of employees, their absorptive capacity generated by investing in scientists and engineers will usually be limited. Even though science-based and high-technology firms may have a high share of employees engaged in R&D activities, and may devote a large share of their budgets to R&D, the small size of the firm will constrain the absolute magnitude of the R&D investment. Thus, in addition to investments in R&D, the entrepreneurial startup may also need mechanisms compensating for inherent size disadvantages that limit the size, scope, and scale of its initial knowledge endowment and constrain the absorptive capacity of the entrepreneurial startup.

The knowledge capabilities contributed by members of the board of directors and by the managers may provide such a mechanism. In the next two sections, we explain why and how these capabilities facilitate the absorption of knowledge spillovers into the entrepreneurial firm.

8.3 Board Composition and Entrepreneurial Access

The role of board members and their contribution to the decision-making process and efficiency of firms has merited a long tradition of scholarly scrutiny, particularly in finance. The focus of this literature is on the role that boards play in exerting control over the firm's managers (Jensen and Meckling, 1976; Hermalin and Weisbach, 1998). The result has been a number of valuable insights about the size and scope of boards required to solve the agency problem emerging when corporate control and management are separated into distinct groups. In particular, the number of outsiders and board composition have purportedly influenced the agency problem concerning corporate control. Because they are less entrenched than insiders, outsiders have a greater incentive to monitor top managers. However, as Hermalin and Weisbach (2003) report, the empirical evidence supporting the prevailing agency theory approach is mixed. As Hermalin and Weisbach suggest (2003), no clear empirical evidence shows that firm performance is enhanced by the numbers and shares of outsiders sitting on boards of U.S. firms.

The composition of boards prevalent throughout continental Europe differs considerably from their counterparts in the United States as well as in the United Kingdom. Board composition in both the United States and United Kingdom is characterized by insiders, managers, and outsiders, who cannot legally be involved in managing the firm (Allan and Gale, 2000; Fama and Jensen, 1983). The Anglo-American model has been characterized as a one-tier board.

By contrast, two-tier boards are more prevalent in continental Europe. For example, in Germany, the first tier consists of the board of managers, which includes only top managers of a firm. The second tier consists of the board of directors, which represents members whose task is to control the managers, to inform financiers, and to provide advice to the managers (Lehmann and Weigand, 2000; Frick and Lehmann, 2005).

Board size and composition in Germany is dictated by law (Frick and Lehmann, 2005). According to the Co-Determination Laws (*Mitbestmmungsgesetze*), between a third and a half of board representatives must be chosen from relevant labor unions. This restriction holds only for medium-sized and large firms and for enterprises in traditional sectors such as steel and mining. By contrast, the only restriction for the IPO firms analyzed in this chapter is that the boards of directors must include at least three members. There is little reason to think that these boards play a role substantially different from that of their counterparts serving on Anglo-American firms.

Thus, for the German IPO firms, as the prevailing literature for Anglo-American firms suggests, the main role of board members is controlling managers and reducing problems emanating from divergent interests between managers and owners, or the agency problem. In short, the board of directors has ultimate responsibility for ensuring that the firm is managed in the best interest of stockholders (Fama and Jensen, 1983).

In view of the demand for decision expertise, coupled with the requirement for detailed firm-specific knowledge, it is natural that boards contain senior managers from within the organization (Fama and Jensen, 1983). Audretsch and Stephan (1996) proposed an alternative theory of the role of board membership. Rather than focusing on the role of boards in monitoring managers, they focused instead on the role of board members as conduits facilitating and absorbing knowledge spillovers. According to Audretsch and Stephan, board members may have a very different role in addition to that of controlling managers, as suggested by agency theory. In science-based and high-technology industries, such as biotechnology, they argue that board members access and absorb external knowledge and therefore need a very different endowment of characteristics and qualifications. Scientific knowledge and other aspects involving knowledge capabilities and human capital may be more important for firms in science-based and high-technology industries, such as biotechnology. Audretsch and Stephan examine the geographic relationships of scientists serving on boards of biotechnology firms. Their results suggest that the importance of geographic proximity is clearly shaped by the role played by the scientists on the board. The scientists serving on the board are more likely to be located in the same region as the firm when the relationship involves the transfer of new economic knowledge. However, when the scientists provides a service to the company that does not involve knowledge transfer, local proximity becomes much less important. Thus, the results of Audretsch and Stephan provide compelling evidence that in a science-based or high-technology industry such as biotechnology, board members can serve to promote entrepreneurial competitiveness not just by monitoring costs but also by accessing and absorbing external knowledge.

The Entrepreneurial Access Hypothesis suggests that boards will likely have more members with the capabilities to access and absorb external knowledge when the firm is located within close geographic proximity to a knowledge source. This leads us to formulate the following proposition:

> If entrepreneurial access to external knowledge spillovers is sufficiently important in the firm's strategy to warrant geographic proximity to knowledge sources, then the

entrepreneurial firm will also tend to need mechanisms facilitating the access to such external knowledge spillovers, such as board members with high human capital.

The first empirical test of the Entrepreneurial Access Hypothesis therefore involves the composition of boards, and, in particular, the relationship between the human capital of the board members and the role of external knowledge spillovers in the firm, as represented by the geographic proximity to a university as well as the actual spillover mechanisms and output emanating from that university.

To test this hypothesis about entrepreneurial access to knowledge spillovers facilitated by board absorptive capacity, we use the same database as in chapters 6 and 7, which consists of German IPO entrepreneurial firms in knowledge and technology industries. The human capital of the board members is measured as attainment of an academic degree. As table 8.1 shows, in 49 firms, or about 18 percent, no director has an academic degree (doctorate or professor status). In 82 percent of the firms, at least one director has an academic degree.

The dependent variable to be explained is the relative importance of human capital in an entrepreneurial board. The explanatory variables should reflect the extent of potential external knowledge spillovers available to the firm. Chapters 6 and 7 identified two important interdependent factors shaping the magnitude of the external spillover pool: geographic proximity to the knowledge source and the knowledge output emanating from that knowledge source.

To measure geographic proximity and the knowledge output, we use the same variables as those in chapters 6 and 7. Geographic proximity is measured in terms of kilometers between the closest university and the firm, and the knowledge output is measured in terms of published research in scholarly journals.

We use three different estimation methods to test the hypothesis that the human capital embodied in directors is influenced by the potential access to absorb external knowledge spillovers. The first method uses the Probit model to estimate the probability that a director holds an academic degree. The second method estimates the share of members serving in the board of directors holding an academic degree. Because this variable is left censored, Tobit estimation is more appropriate. The third method estimates the number of board directors holding an academic degree. Since this is a count variable, the negative binomial regression method is appropriate.

TABLE 8.1 Frequency of Directors with an Academic Degree

Directors with an academic degree	Frequency	%	Cumulative %
0	49	17.63	17.63
1	88	31.65	49.28
2	84	30.21	79.49
3	38	13.67	93.16
4	11	3.96	97.12
5	8	2.88	100.00

TABLE 8.2 Geographic Proximity, University Spillovers, and the Selection of Directors

	Probability that a director holds an academic degree (probit)	Share of directors with an academic degree (tobit)	Number of directors with an academic degree (negative binomial)
Distance * natural science publications	-0.03978^a $(1.69)^{*b}$	-0.0088 $(1.64)^*$	-0.1789 (1.51)
Distance * social science publications	0.0451 (1.40)	0.0111 (1.31)	0.01998 (0.97)
LNAge	0.0643 (1.05)	0.0020 (0.13)	-0.0002 (0.01)
LNSize	-0.0061 (0.09)	-0.0245 (1.32)	0.0443 (1.01)
Software	0.0565 (0.63)	0.0063 (0.28)	-0.0250 (0.43)
Service	-0.2489 (1.08)	-0.0263 (0.45)	-0.0427 (0.31)
E-commerce	0.04063 (0.11)	-0.0978 (0.99)	-0.3063 (1.18)
Hardware	0.0476 (0.09)	0.0065 (0.07)	-0.0019 (0.01)
Telecommunication	-0.0422 (0.13)	-0.1671 $(1.93)^*$	-0.3912 $(1.70)^*$
Biotechnology	0.9473 $(2.28)^{**}$	0.13078 (1.41)	0.4600 $(2.17)^{**}$
Medical technology	1.001 $(2.17)^{**}$	0.2509 $(2.15)^{**}$	0.3263 (1.38)
Media & entertainment	0.0913 (0.32)	-0.0775 (1.02)	-0.1297 (0.71)
Constant	-0.4555 (1.19)	0.4915 $(4.99)^{***}$	0.3094 (1.32)
Pseudo R^2	0.062	0.061	0.025
N	278	278	278

[a]Estimated regression coefficients.
[b]Absolute $t(p)$ values in parentheses.
*Statistically significant at the 10% level.
**Statistically significant at the 5% level.
***Statistically significant at the 1% level.

The results are shown in table 8.2. The first column estimates the likelihood of a given director holding an academic degree and thus uses the Probit model of estimation. As the negative and statistically significant coefficient of the interactive variable between distance and research output in the natural sciences suggests, the likelihood that a director holds an academic degree depends on university spillovers. However, these results hold only with close geographic proximity to a university and for the natural sciences. There is no statistically significant evidence that university spillovers in the social sciences influence board selection, regardless of firm geographic proximity to the university.

The results from Probit estimation also indicate that the likelihood of a given director holding an academic degree is clearly influenced by the industry. A director is more likely to hold an academic degree in biotechnology and medical technology, the fields in which external knowledge has the highest scientific component.

The second column uses the share of directors holding an academic degree as the endogenous variable. Thus, Tobit estimation is used in the second column. As the negative and statistically significant coefficient of the multiplicative variable between distance and publications in the natural sciences suggests, the share of directors with an academic degree is significantly influenced by the university spillovers in the natural sciences, but this influence tends to decline as the geographic distance from the closest university increases. By contrast, in the social sciences, as the statistically insignificant coefficient implies, geographic proximity to a university has no impact on the composition of the board, at least in terms of human capital.

The share of board members holding an academic degree is influenced by the particular industry. In telecommunications and medical technology, more board members tend to hold an academic degree than in other industries.

The third column uses the number of directors as the dependent variable, which is estimated using negative binomial estimation. The only statistically significant coefficients are for the industry dummies, suggesting that the number of directors tends to be systematically higher for firms in both the biotechnology and medical technology fields.

Whereas firm age and size have no significant impact in the three different estimates based on different measures for the dependent variables, the results also show that the selection of directors is not independent of the specific industry. Especially in high-technology and science-based industries such as biotechnology and medical technology, there is a statistically significant higher likelihood that the directors hold an academic degree. These findings strongly support the results from Audretsch and Stephan (1999) that show that, particularly in science-based industries, members of a board may serve a role that is distinct from the traditional function of controlling and monitoring the directors. In such high-technology and science-based industries, there is a different role for board members: to serve as conduits for accessing and absorbing external knowledge spillovers (Audretsch and Lehmann 2004b).

We estimated separate regressions to identify whether geographic distance or university output, but not interactively as specified in the estimates in table 8.2, may have a significant impact on the selection of scientists as directors. The results are not statistically significant. This leads us to conclude that both factors, geographic proximity and a strong university output in the natural sciences, are necessary to change the composition of the board of directors to include directors with a greater degree of human capital.

8.4 Manager Selection and Entrepreneurial Access

Directors serving on the board are not the only possible conduits for accessing and absorbing external knowledge spillovers. Representatives serving on the board of managers provide a second conduit for accessing and absorbing external knowledge spillovers. In the strategy literature, a key task of the managers is to

TABLE 8.3 Number of Directors on the Board of
Managers Holding an Academic Degree

Managers with an academic degree	Frequency	%	Cumulative %
0	168	60.43	60.43
1	70	25.18	85.61
2	32	11.51	97.12
3	5	1.78	98.90
4	2	0.72	99.64
5	1	0.36	100.00

accumulate and protect valuable knowledge or capability (Wernerfelt, 1984; Teece, Pisano, and Shuen, 1997). Such knowledge defines a firm's capacity to efficiently convert its input into valuable outputs (Nelson and Winter, 1982, pp. 59–60). Thus, managers enhance the firm's capacity to produce efficiently by advancing their knowledge. Managers must decide how to access relevant knowledge and transform it into valuable output (Nickerson and Zenger, 2004).

Only one prescribed legal restriction constrains the selection of the board of managers. One of the board members must be the CEO of the firm. Thus, the minimum size of the board is one, whereas the prescribed maximum is seven. The median size of the board is three managers. The distribution of firms with managers holding academic degrees is summarized in table 8.3. This distribution of managers holding academic degrees varies considerably from the distribution for the board of directors. Less than 40 percent of the firms in the IPO sample employ a manager with an academic degree. In 70, or about 25 percent, of the firms, only one manager of the board of managers holds an academic degree. This gives a first hint that for managing a firm, holding an academic degree is certainly not a prerequisite.

To test the Entrepreneurial Access Hypothesis for this second conduit potentially facilitating the access and absorption of external knowledge spillovers, managers, we use the same three model specifications used in the previous section, except that managers are substituted for directors.

The results are shown in table 8.4. The coefficient of the interactive variable of distance multiplied by research output in the natural science is statistically significant for the share of managers holding an academic degree as well as for the number of managers holding an academic degree, but not for the likelihood that a given manager holds an academic degree. There is no evidence that university spillovers in the social sciences influence the selection of managers in terms of human capital, regardless of geographic proximity.

As the positive and statistically significant coefficient of firm size suggests for all three dependent variables, having mangers with a higher level of human capital increases along with the size of the firm. This is consistent with the Jovanovic (1982) model of learning and evolution, which suggests that the primary function of new startups is to learn whether the underlying idea on which the firm is founded

TABLE 8.4 Geographic Proximity, University Spillovers, and the Selection of Managers

	Probability that a manager holds an academic degree (probit)	Share of managers with an academic degree (tobit)	Number of managers with an academic degree (negative binomial)
Distance * natural science publications	−0.0315[a] (1.36)[b]	−0.1712 (1.65)*	−0.0435 (1.66)*
Distance * social science publications	0.0343 (1.07)	0.01846 (1.23)	0.0465 (1.27)
LNAge	0.0555 (0.90)	0.0224 (0.78)	0.0838 (1.21)
LNSize	0.1633 (2.29)**	0.0678 (2.05)**	0.1911 (2.45)**
Software	−0.4173 (1.56)	−0.2054 (1.64)*	−0.3536 (1.44)
Service	−0.4921 (1.93)*	−0.2373 (2.00)**	−0.4418 (1.70)*
E-commerce	−0.4278 (1.06)	−0.1632 (0.85)	−0.1165 (0.26)
Hardware	−0.2954 (0.86)	−0.0494 (0.31)	−0.1282 (0.39)
Telecommunication	−0.771 (2.12)**	−0.3756 (2.16)**	−0.7283 (1.70)*
Biotechnology	0.7683 (1.72)*	0.3516 (1.93)**	0.7838 (2.35)**
Medical technology	0.7678 (1.57)	0.3186 (1.65)*	0.5994 (1.69)*
Media & entertainment	−0.6075 (1.90)*	−0.3276 (2.16)**	−0.7699 (2.00)**
Constant	−0.695 (1.73)*	−0.2482 (1.31)	−1.2551 (2.83)**
Pseudo R^2	0.0941	0.0952	0.0699
N	278	278	278

[a]Estimated regression coefficients.
[b]Absolute $t(p)$ values in parentheses.
*Statistically significant at the 10% level.
**Statistically significant at the 5% level.

is viable and compatible with the market; only subsequently will the firm grow and then need to absorb external knowledge spillovers.

The statistical significance of only the science-based and high-technology industries again supports the findings of Audretsch and Stephan (1999), suggesting that possessing the qualifications to access and absorb external knowledge is more important in contexts with a greater prevalence of tacit knowledge. In contrast to other industries, such as e-commerce, software, services, or media and entertainment, science-based industries such as biotechnology and medical technology require a greater level of academic training to access and absorb external knowledge.

8.5 Conclusions

The previous chapters have shown that the potential access to external knowledge spillovers influences entrepreneurial location, which in turn influences the entrepreneurial competitive advantage. External knowledge spillovers can be accessed by geographic proximity to a knowledge source through an entrepreneurial firm's choice of location.

The results of this chapter suggest, however, that providing entrepreneurial access to knowledge spillovers through geographic proximity to knowledge sources is not sufficient; external knowledge spillovers need to be absorbed. This chapter has identified two factors facilitating the absorption of external knowledge spillovers: a spillover conduit, such as a board director or manager, and close geographic proximity.

These findings suggest not only that the composition of boards is endogenous to the relative importance of absorbing external knowledge spillovers for the entrepreneurial firm but also that the composition of boards may be influenced by factors other than their role in controlling managers to reduce agency problems. The evidence in this chapter suggests that board directors and managers can also play an important role by facilitating the access to and absorption of external knowledge spillover, thus enhancing the competitive advantage of entrepreneurial firms. However, to facilitate the entrepreneurial access and absorption of such external knowledge spillovers, the entrepreneurial firm must not only be in the right place but also have the right board composition.

Entrepreneurial Finance

9.1 Entrepreneurship and Capital Markets

The previous chapters explained that entrepreneurial access to external resources matters. The ability of entrepreneurial firms to access and absorb external knowledge spillovers shapes not just their decisions about location but also their competitive advantage and ultimately their performance. However, access to external knowledge spillovers does not necessarily guarantee that the entrepreneurial firms can transform such external knowledge into a competitive advantage. One necessary and critical resource is access to external finance (Gompers and Lerner, 2001).

The purpose of this chapter is to analyze the role that accessing external finance plays for entrepreneurial firms (Audretsch and Lehmann, 2004a). We differentiate between access to bank loans and equity provided by venture capital. The Entrepreneurial Access Hypothesis suggests a very different role for these two different sources of entrepreneurial finance. Although banks are able to finance young firms with low-risk projects, they are reluctant to finance entrepreneurial firms in high-technology and science-based industries. In contrast, venture capitalists provide equity but the entrepreneur may lose ownership and control of the firm.

The notion that capital markets are inherently distinct from other markets has long been noted in the economics literature. What makes capital markets distinct is the added feature of risk associated with the demand side of the market. Yet only recently has one of the main implications of this risk inherent in loaning credit been emphasized: capital markets do not, in fact, always clear.

As Fazzari, Hubbard, and Petersen (1988, p. 141) point out, "Empirical models of business investment rely generally on the assumption of a 'representative firm' that responds to prices set in centralized security markets. Indeed, if all firms have equal access to capital markets, firms' responses to changes in the cost of capital or tax-based investment incentives differ only because of differences in investment demand." That is, the financial structure of a firm does not play an important role in investment decisions, for the firm can substitute external funds for internal capital without cost. Under the assumption of perfect capital markets, then, firm-specific investment decisions are generally independent of the financial condition of that firm.

Of course, the assumption of perfect capital markets has been rigorously challenged. And once capital markets are no longer assumed to be perfect, external capital cannot be assumed as a costless substitute for internal capital. Thus, the availability of internal finance, access to new debt or equity finance, and other financial factors may shape firm investment decisions.

The second section of this chapter examines the link between the mode of finance and the nature of the firm's economic activity. Entrepreneurial firms based on knowledge spillovers may have a higher propensity for equity financing by venture capital and a lower propensity for debt financing by banks. The third section tests this hypothesis. The fourth section links the performance of entrepreneurial firms to the mode of finance. Finally, the last section of this chapter provides a summary and conclusions. The results of this chapter suggest that equity finance and bank finance are substitutes for knowledge-based entrepreneurial firms. In addition, the likelihood of an entrepreneurial firm being financed by venture capital is positively related to the degree of human capital incorporated in the board of management. Similarly, entrepreneurial firms in high-technology and science-based industries are more likely to be financed by venture capital.

9.2 Financing Entrepreneurship by Banks and Venture Capitalists

There are compelling reasons why liquidity constraints become more severe as firm size decreases. Stiglitz and Weiss (1981) point out that, unlike most markets, the market for credit is exceptional because the price of the good—the rate of interest—is not necessarily at a level that equilibrates the market. They attribute this to the fact that interest rates influence not just demand for capital but also the risk inherent in different classes of borrowers. As the rate of interest rises, so does the riskiness for borrowers, leading suppliers of capital to limit the quantity of loans they make at any particular interest rate. The amount of information about an enterprise is generally not neutral with respect to size. Rather, as Petersen and Rajan (1994, p. 3) observe, "Small and young firms are most likely to face this kind of credit rationing. Most potential lenders have little information on the managerial capabilities or investment opportunities of such firms and are unlikely to be able to screen out poor credit risks or to have control over a borrower's investments." If lenders are unable to identify the quality or risk associated with particular borrowers, credit rationing results (Neuberger, 1998; Burghof, 2000). This phenomenon is analogous to the lemons argument advanced by Akerloff (1970). The existence of asymmetric information prevents the suppliers of capital from engaging in price discrimination between riskier and less risky borrowers. But, as Diamond (1989) argues, the risk associated with any particular loan is also not neutral for the duration of the relationship because information about the underlying risk inherent in any particular customer is transmitted over time. With experience, a lender will condition the risk associated with any class of customers by characteristics associated with the individual customer.

Larger firms can finance capital expenditures from internal resources, issuance of equity, or debt. By contrast, internal earnings and the potential for issuing equity are limited for entrepreneurial firms. Since gathering information is costly, banks will expand their search for information until the expected marginal benefit of search equals zero. If the remaining information asymmetry induces a risk premium,[1] firms with fewer signaling opportunities will have to pay higher loan rates. The degree of information asymmetry depends on borrower characteristics such as firm size, firm age and governance, or legal form (Lehmann and Neuberger, 2001). Typically, new and small firms provide less information to outside financiers than do their larger counterparts. This reflects the fixed costs of information disclosure or the absence of disclosure rules.

In addition, the lack of reputation constrains the borrowing capacity of entrepreneurial firms (Martinelli, 1997). As the firm ages, the extent of information asymmetries decreases, and the firm may earn a positive reputation through a proven credit history. As a result, entrepreneurial firms are often associated with higher loan rates and less access to financial resources. As Petersen and Rajan (1994) point out, one way to overcome frictions is for firms to build close relationships with the suppliers of capital. These relationships allow the lender to collect information about the borrowers and their investments and to monitor the actions of the borrowers.

Ample literature has identified the importance of lending relationships for small and new firms as a mechanism compensating for their lack of a credit history (Berger and Udell, 1990, 1995, 1998; Petersen and Rajan, 1994; Harhoff and Körting, 1998; Machauer and Weber, 1998; Degryse and Van Cayseele, 2000; Lehmann and Neuberger, 2001; Lehmann, Neuberger, and Raethke, 2004). The costs of gathering information about a borrower may be prohibitively high if borrower and lender transact only once, but those costs are reduced by learning in repeated transactions (Neuberger, 1995, 1998).

To the degree that relationship banking is important in providing finance to small and new firms, Germany would seem to have an advantage. Two institutional features of the German financial system sharply contrast with practices in the United States and the United Kingdom, both of which may affect liquidity constraints. First, companies in Germany typically rely almost exclusively on banks for external sources of finance. The external capital market remains relatively underdeveloped. And, second, banks not only represent the major financial intermediary supplying capital to firms but are also extensively represented on the firm's supervisory boards (see Lehmann and Weigand, 2000; Frick and Lehmann, 2005).

This financial institution infrastructure, generally oriented with providing the German *Mittelstand* with finance, supposedly defuses the problem of liquidity constraints confronting smaller enterprises in the United States, as found by Evans and Jovanovic (1989b), among others.

Although there is overwhelming evidence that banks, as financial intermediaries, play a major role in the reduction of agency costs (Diamond, 1984), they may fail in providing debt when the degree of asymmetric information is too high. This failure, however, is the case in entrepreneurial firms in high-tech and science-based industries. In this case, a profit-maximizing bank cannot capture the expected costs of debt by the interest rates of the loan (Stiglitz and Weiss, 1981).[2] In particular, small firms are more likely to be subject to credit rationing. Fazzari et al. (1988) found that smaller publicly traded firms in the United States face liquidity constraints and experience difficulties obtaining capital.

Of course, as the famous Modigliani-Miller (1958) theorem shows, firm performance should be independent of the mode of finance. The Modigliani-Miller theorem implies that whether knowledge-based firms are financed by debt or equity will make no difference. However, an implicit assumption of the Modigliani-Miller theorem is the assumption of perfect capital markets, along with the absence of taxes[3] and incentive problems. Since the propensity for entrepreneurial firms to rely on debt over equity cannot be attributed to taxes, an alternative explanation may lie with the greater incentive problems resulting from information asymmetries.

Especially in science-based and high-tech industries, new firms suffer from insufficient capital (Kortum and Lerner, 2000; Audretsch, Lehmann, and Warning, 2004). Such firms are associated with high-risk, large informational asymmetries and lack of marketable collaterals (Lehmann and Neuberger, 2001). As a consequence, such capital constraints limit the innovative capabilities of entrepreneurial startups.

Aghion and Bolton (1992) show that the double moral hazard problem in financing entrepreneurship is particularly exacerbated in high-technology and science-based industries. As the relationship between the financier and the entrepreneur develops over time, eventualities arise that could not easily have been foreseen or spelled out in an initial contract. Neither the entrepreneur nor the venture capitalist may undertake first-best actions in order to enhance the expected outcome of the project. This creates a two-sided moral hazard problem in which the entrepreneur and the venture capitalist must be induced to undertake effort (Gompers, 1995, 1996; Kaplan and Strömberg, 2003, 2004; Lehmann, 2005).

However, the very nature of entrepreneurship prevents startups and their financiers from writing complete contracts in which obligations are specified in all relevant conceivable future contingents (Hart and Moore, 1998). Thus, optimal contracts between entrepreneurial firms in knowledge-based industries and their financiers differ from those between venture capitalists and banks for four main reasons.

First, because venture capitalists take an equity-linked stake in the firms they finance, they also share in both upside and downside risks. Whereas banks can profit from financing projects only by a repayment of their credits, venture capitalists can also benefit from an increased firm value that may exceed the amount of credits offered by banks.

Second, venture capitalists also contribute technological expertise, which allows them to identify projects better than banks can and to undertake the projects without the original entrepreneur (Bergloef, 1994; Ueda, 2004). This creates the double moral hazard problem: entrepreneurs may underinvest in their firm after receiving the necessary financial resources, but also the venture capitalist has an incentive to replace the entrepreneur. Though banks cannot credibly commit to contributing to the managing of the firm, the technical expertise of venture capitalists enables them to replace the original founder with a new and more appropriate CEO (Gorman and Sahlman, 1989; Lerner, 1994; Hellmann and Puri, 2000).

Third, the role played by venture capitalists in staging the investments serves to reduce agency and verifiability problems (Gompers, 1995; Bergemann and Hege, 1998). After their initial investment, venture capitalists provide entrepreneurs with access to consultants and accountants, play active roles as monitors (Lerner, 1995), and provide information for other stakeholders in the firm.

Fourth, venture capitalists take an active part in guiding the exit decision either by selling their shares directly to other firms or investors or by making an IPO (Lerner, 1994; Gompers, 1995; Cumming and MacIntosh, 2003).

Gompers and Lerner (2001) have identified the important role that venture capital plays in financing young and innovative firms in the United States. However, virtually nothing is known about whether this role is the same or different in a bank-based country such as Germany. In fact, the role of venture capital may vary between countries with bank-based systems and those with more specialized markets (Black and Gilson, 1998). On the one hand, Germany has a long tradition of specific regional and national financial institutions financing the German Mittelstand, or small- and medium-sized enterprises. On the other hand, a new generation of venture capitalists has emerged who provide finance to highly innovative firms. Although Germany is the largest venture capital market in continental Europe, there is scarce evidence about the impact of venture capital in financing young and innovative firms in a bank-based country. Black and Gilson point out the importance of an active stock market for the development of venture capital, which is not the case in a bank-based country like Germany.

The increasing importance of bringing firms to the public and thus the necessity of a stock market has been explained and documented by several studies focusing on venture capital–backed firms (Bottazzi and Da Rin, 2002; Cumming and MacIntosh, 2003).[4] For example, Becker and Hellmann (2003) analyze the rise and fall of the first German venture capital company, founded in 1974. They show that an active stock market, as proposed by Black and Gilson (1997), may be a necessary condition but is by no means sufficient. Similarly, Bascha and Walz (2002) confirm that Germany differs from Anglo-Saxon countries in that public-private venture capitalists (with private and state-owned banks as the major shareholders) are the dominant form of venture capitalists; they also underperform compared to private partnerships. The underperformance of public venture capitalists compared to independent venture capitalists is analyzed by Tyková and Walz (2003). Dittmann, Maug, and Kemper (2004) focus on the different evaluation methods used by venture capitalists and their different impact on performance. Also, Tykvová (2003) examined the differences of venture capitalists' impact on firm performance. Franzke (2001) shows that venture capital–backed IPOs appear to be more underpriced than IPOs not backed by venture capital. Schefczyk and Gerpott (2001) analyze the relationship between the experience and educational attainment levels of managers and performance measures for a sample of portfolio companies in Germany. They find that manager qualification significantly correlates with the performance of the portfolio companies. Finally, Bottazi and Da Rin (2002) analyze the role of venture capital in several European countries and find evidence suggesting that venture capital–backed companies do not grow faster than those that are not backed by venture capital.

9.3 Hypotheses on the Mode of Entrepreneurial Finance

The previous section makes it clear that the literature focusing on entrepreneurial access to financial resources is fraught with ambiguities, especially in the German context. In this section, we try to resolve some of these ambiguities by analyzing whether entrepreneurial firms differ in their access to financial resource and, if so, how. This section links the mode of finance to the role of knowledge and innovation in the firm's output.

The first null hypothesis is that financing by venture capitalists is independent of firm age and innovative activity. There are at least two alternative hypotheses. The first alternative hypothesis is that venture capitalists prefer to invest in young and innovative companies. Those firms have higher risk and are also associated with higher expected returns in the future. Since venture capitalists also act as monitors in related firms, each investment lowers the costs of monitoring[5] but also generates external effects that can be used in the assisting and mentoring of other firms. In addition, the specific technological and managerial expertise of venture capital firms generates higher marginal returns than bank-based finance. Thus, venture capitalists can presumably assess the potential profitability of the projects more accurately than can a bank (Ueda, 2003). The second alternative is that venture capitalists are also responsible to their own investors and may thus be reluctant to invest in young and highly innovative firms (Hellmann and Puri, 2000). According to this alternative, venture capitalists will prefer firms for which business concepts are easier to comprehend and communicate as well as firms having some experience in the relevant product market.

The second null hypothesis, from the perspective of the entrepreneurial firm, posits that the likelihood of being funded by venture capital is independent of a firm's debt. Although both theoretical and empirical arguments claim that financial constraints may lead to a financial pecking order (Myers and Majluf, 1984), the alternative hypothesis is formulated so that the choice of a venture capitalist to invest depends on a firm's amount of debt. If a bank, as the outside financier, is better protected by law than the equity holders, the bank has recourse against the entrepreneur personally and other equity holders up to the amount of debt they owe. Consequently, the venture capitalist as the provider of equity has only a small possibility to sell some assets to reduce his loss in the case of firm failure. The first alternative hypothesis is that the higher the amount of debt, the lower the likelihood of receiving venture capital. In this case, debt and venture capital equity are substitutes because the firm receives either venture capital equity or debt.

The second alternative hypothesis refers to the complementary argument presented by Lel and Udell (2002), who suggest that the amount of debt held by an entrepreneur signals both her capability and personal guarantees. Venture capitalists may interpret debt as a quality signal and therefore be more willing to invest in a company with greater debt.

The third hypothesis refers to the role of intangible assets such as human capital and intellectual property. The proposition underlying this hypothesis is that neither human capital nor intellectual property influences the likelihood of obtaining venture capital. The alternative hypothesis is that human capital and intellectual property will positively influence the likelihood of venture capital funding.

In knowledge-based industries, competitive advantage largely emanates from nonphysical intangible assets, such as human capital, ideas, and intellectual property rights (Audretsch and Stephan, 1996; Rajan and Zingales, 2000; Fabel, 2004). As the Knowledge Spillover Theory of Entrepreneurship suggests, knowledge plays a dominant role in founding new firms in the high-technology sector (Bates, 1990; Audretsch and Stephan, 1996), suggesting that intangible assets, such as human capital and intellectual property, also are a decisive factor in the decision-making process of venture capitalists.

To test the Entrepreneurial Finance Hypothesis, we use the same database introduced in chapters 6, 7, and 8. This database consists of German IPO entrepreneurial firms in knowledge and technology industries. The role of venture finance is measured by both the presence of one or more venture capitalists (*venture-backed*) and the amount of equity held by venture capitalists (*venture capital ownership*). The role of banks in financing new economy firms is expressed by the amount of *debt* and the equity held by banks on those firms (*bank equity ownership*). The variable debt is measured by *Log of (Short term + long term + advances payable.)*

Because major decisions are made by the board of managers, we take the academic degree of the board of managers (*executive human capital*) and of the board of directors (*human capital directors*), as introduced in chapter 8. Intellectual property is measured by the number of patents (*firm patents*). The data is taken from the Deutsche Patentamt (www.dpma.de) to identify and patent activity. Using the name of the firm as well as the name of the executives provides information about the number of patents and the underlying property rights.

The *number of employees* is used as a measure for the firm size before IPO. The difference in size before and after the IPO of the firm constitutes the *growth rates* of the firm (as measured by the difference of the natural logarithm).

The use of balance sheet data to compare the firms prior to the IPO is not without problems, since firms have the choice between US-GAAP and IAS as the main accounting system as one criterion for being publicly listed on the Neuer Markt. Thus, we include a dummy variable to correct for the main accounting system, which takes the value 1 for IAS and 0 respective for US-GAAP. In addition, the ownership concentration of the CEO, the board of directors, friends and families, and venture capitalists is included. Ownership concentration is measured by the Herfindahl Index.

As in the previous chapters, we include dummy variables to control for the year of the IPO and for industry-specific fixed effects. To facilitate an international comparison, the data set is expanded in this chapter to 341 firms, which includes foreign-owned firms. Since it is often argued that German firms have a lower propensity for using venture capital than their counterparts in the United States and United Kingdom, we include a dummy variable identifying firms based in Germany. (The data set includes 292 firms located in Germany, about 85 percent, with the rest being non-German firms.)

We use two different methods to estimate the determinants of venture capital financing. The first is based on a Probit approach with a dummy variable indicating whether the firm is venture financed or not. For the Probit model, we assume an underlying variable y_i^* defined by the regression relationship, as follows:

$$y_i^* = \beta' x_i + u_i, \tag{9.1}$$

and y_i^* is unobservable. Only the dummy variable can be observed:

$$y = 1 \quad if \ y_i^* > 0$$
$$y = 0 \quad otherwise \tag{9.2}$$

Hence, the realizations of y follow a binomial process with probabilities $\text{Prob}(y_i = 1) = \text{Prob}(u_i > -\beta' x_i) = 1 - F(-\beta' x_i)$, where F is the cumulative distribution function for u. The probability varies from trial to trial depending on x_i. In the following Probit estimation, y indicates the observable dummy variable for a venture-backed firm. Thus, we provide the following estimation:

$$\text{Prob}(y = 1) = f(debt, \ ownership \ structure, \ size, \ age, \ industry,$$
$$IPO \ Year, \ accounting \ system) + u. \tag{9.3}$$

The determinants on the amount of venture capital a firm receives can be tested using a two-limit Tobit model. Since the endogenous variable is truncated at both high and low values (minimum zero percent equity ownership of venture capitalists and maximum 100 percent), the Tobit model is used instead of the OLS-approach. Let

$$y_i^* = \beta' x_i + u_i, \tag{9.4}$$

with y_i^* as the latent variable (desired or potential equity holding by venture capitalists). Further, x_i is a vector of exogenous variables (see equation 9.3) and u_i are disturbances with $E(u_i) = 0$. The observed variable y_i is given by the following:

$$y_i = \begin{cases} \underline{c}_i & if \ y_i^* \leq \underline{c}_i \\ y_i^* & if \ \underline{c}_i < y_i^* < \bar{c}_i \\ \bar{c}_i & if \ \bar{c}_i \leq y_i^* \end{cases} \tag{9.5}$$

where $\underline{c}_i$, $\bar{c}_i$ are fixed numbers representing the censoring points of equity ownership by a venture capitalist before IPO. Thus, we estimate the following equation:

$$y(equity \ held \ by \ venture \ capitalists) = f(debt, \ ownership \ structure, \ size,$$
$$age, \ industry, \ IPO \ Year, \ accounting$$
$$system) + u \tag{9.6}$$

The descriptive statistics for the main variables are shown in table 9.1. About half of the firms in the enlarged data set are financed by venture capitalists. The descriptive statistics presented in table 9.1 indicate that venture-backed firms have significantly less debt. Thus, equity provided by venture capital appears to be a substitute rather than a complement to debt.

The equity held by banks is also lower in the venture-backed group of firms. Both findings suggest that banks play a minor role in financing and controlling knowledge-based entrepreneurial firms compared to traditional small and medium-sized enterprises. The descriptive statistics also provide initial evidence suggesting that, on average, venture-backed firms are younger, are smaller, and have significantly more patents than other firms.

Finally, the data shows that the entrepreneurial decision to increase the equity base of the firm includes not only venture capital but also friends and families. Thus, the mode of finance selected by the entrepreneur is not likely to be independent of the type of equity chosen. Table 9.1 also shows that venture capitalists typically specialize in a small group of targeted industries, including biotechnology, medicine and life sciences, and technology, all industries in which the technological expertise can be leveraged for greater returns for both the firms and venture capitalists.

Table 9.2 provides the results of estimating the determinants of venture-capital financing using the Probit and Tobit models.

The negative and statistically significant coefficient of *debt* in the Probit estimation model indicates that the likelihood of obtaining venture capital is inversely related to the extent to which the firm is financed by debt. Similarly, as the same coefficient shows for the Tobit estimation, the amount of venture capital obtained is also negatively related to the degree of debt finance. This effect may be typical for bank-based countries like Germany where debt holders are more strongly protected by law than equity holders. If an entrepreneur is financed by both banks and venture capital, the bank has the priority claim accruing from the sales of assets or collateral owned by the entrepreneur or the firm. Thus, debt reduces the incentive of a venture capitalist to invest in such firms. In any case, these results support the basic hypothesis that debt and equity are substitutes rather than complements in financing knowledge entrepreneurship.

The human capital embodied in the board of directors is found to have a positive impact on the likelihood of obtaining venture capital as well as on the amount of venture finance. High ownership shares held by executives and other firms—in contrast to other shareholders—reduces the likelihood of obtaining venture capital and the amount of venture finance obtained. The negative coefficient on the dummy variable for Germany indicates a lower likelihood of obtaining venture capital and a lower level of venture-capital funding for German-based firms.

The type of accounting system used by the firm also affects its ability to attract venture capital. Those firms relying on the International Accounting Standard (IAS) rather than the U.S. Generally Accepted Accounting Principles (GAAP) exhibit a lower propensity for attracting venture capital.

Thus, the empirical evidence suggests that the likelihood of equity-based entrepreneurial finance, as well as the magnitude of equity invested by venture

TABLE 9.1 Descriptive Statistics for Model Variables

	Mean		Standard deviation	
Variable	Nonventure-backed (N = 188)	Venture-backed (N = 157)	Nonventure-backed	Venture-backed
Debt***	48.65	11.11	206.368	21.825
Patents**	2.94	5.56	12.331	15.80
Human capital executives**	.46	.64	.719	.922
Human capital directors	1.42	1.52	1.204	1.267
Size pre IPO***	239.89	182.35	314.02	325.59
Size post IPO	325.80	287.07	416.67	391.27
Growth rate	.39	.58	1.68	1.44
Age	11.14	9.26	12.87	8.46
Ownership venture capitalists	—	29.42	—	22.89
Ownership banks	3.41	1.74	13.76	5.77
Ownership firms***	20.25	7.28	34.56	18.77
Ownership executives**	38.31	32.58	34.07	29.13
Ownership friends & family**	23.49	18.58	29.16	22.79

	%	
Variable (Observations)	Nonventure-backed (N = 188)	Venture-backed (N = 157)
IAS (106)***	.63	.37
Germany (292)**	.56	.43
IPO 1997 (14)	.64	.36
IPO 1998 (44)**	.68	.31
IPO 1999 (137)	.59	.41
IPO 2000 (138)**	.46	.53
IPO 2001 (12)***	.25	.75
Software (63)*	.65	.35
Service (78)	.55	.45
E-commerce (25)	.52	.48
Computer (27)	.53	.47
Telecommunication (26)	.53	.47
Biotechnology (18)***	.16	.84
Life science & medicine (13)**	.31	.69
Entertainment (40)**	.67	.33
Technology (34)	.47	.53
Others*	.59	.41

The table provides the descriptive statistics for the explanatory variables. The first part of the table shows the mean and the standard deviation of both groups, the venture-backed firms, and the firms financed without venture capital. The table also presents the results of a two-tailed test of equal means. The second part of the table presents the included dummy variables and their distribution between both groups.
A test of independence between both groups is made using Pearson's chi-square as the underlying test statistic. t values in parentheses.
*Statistically significant at the two-tailed test for 90% level of confidence.
**Statistically significant at the two-tailed test for 95% level of confidence.
***Statistically significant at the two-tailed test for 99% level of confidence.

TABLE 9.2 The Determinants of Venture Capital Finance

	Probit	Tobit
Debt	−.0125	−.2125
	(2.63)***	(1.86)**
Firm patents	−.0021	.1018
	(0.17)	(0.4)
Human capital executives	−.0701	.4443
	(0.57)	(0.16)
Human capital directors	.2225	4.647
	(2.49)**	(2.36)**
Size	−.0463	−1.960
	(0.51)	(0.90)
Age	−.0623	−.9069
	(0.87)	(0.52)
Ownership banks	−.0027	−.5942
	(0.17)	(1.53)
Ownership executives	−.0143	−.5362
	(4.33)***	(6.74)***
Ownership firms	−.0215	−.6918
	(5.24)***	(6.68)***
Germany	−.6808	−10.1883
	(2.65)***	(1.74)*
IAS	−.6443	−11.6730
	(3.27)***	(2.52)**
Software	.1389	4.0451
	(0.75)	(1.42)
Service	.3372	5.1019
	(1.08)	(0.71)
Computer & hardware	.4602	16.0843
	(1.14)	(1.69)*
Telecommunication	.4261	19.152
	(1.06)	(2.01)**
Biotechnology	1.1627	21.7168
	(1.98)**	(2.00)**
Life science & medicine	.6135	25.1667
	(1.07)	(2.04)**
Entertainment	.1261	8.3305
	(0.35)	(0.97)
Technology	.6708	19.8960
	(1.61)*	(2.21)**
IPO 2000	1.1034	20.374
	(1.83)*	(1.33)
IPO 1999	.4844	8.6645
	(0.82)	(0.57)
LL	−137.586	−672.439
LR χ^2	92.85***	121.69***
Pseudo R^2	.2523	.0830

This table provides estimates of equations (9.3) and (9.6). The dependent variable in the probit model is "VC_backed," a dummy variable indicating whether venture capitalists are involved in the investment or not. The dependent variable in the (left censored) Tobit model is "Ownership Venture Capital," the amount of equity ownership of venture capitalists.

Standard deviations are in parentheses. The definitions of the explanatory variables are given in table 9.1. The likelihood ratio (LR) chi-square test statistic is statistically significant at 1% in both estimations.

*Statistically significant at the two-tailed test for 90% level of confidence.
**Statistically significant at the two-tailed test for 95% level of confidence.
***Statistically significant at the two-tailed test for 99% level of confidence.

capitalists, is negatively related to the amount of debt finance but positively related to the degree of human capital embodied in the board of management. Entrepreneurial firms utilizing higher levels of knowledge tend to have a greater reliance on venture capital.

9.4 Linking Venture Finance to Entrepreneurial Performance

The previous section shows that the mode of finance is not independent of the knowledge activity of entrepreneurial firms. This section examines the degree to which the mode of finance is linked to entrepreneurial performance.

One view, posited by Bottazzi and Da Rin (2002), is that entrepreneurial performance should be invariant to the mode of finance. By contrast, Brander, Amit, and Antweiler (2002) argue that venture capital–financed firms should exhibit a superior performance, since such firms receive not only financial resources but also value-enhancing advice. In addition, because banks cannot accrue the higher returns associated with higher risk-higher return new ventures, they will tend not to finance knowledge-based entrepreneurial firms.

To examine the impact of the mode of finance on entrepreneurial performance, we use two different kinds of estimations. First, a simple OLS regression is estimated, like that used by Bottazzi and Da Rin (2002). Applying the same estimation method ensures some comparability of the results:

$$y(growth\ rate) = f(debt,\ ownership\ structure,\ size\ age,\ industry,$$
$$IPO\ Year,\ accounting\ system) + u. \qquad (9.7)$$

In addition, we follow the example from the labor market literature using the method of quantile regression estimation. This semiparametric technique provides a general class of models in which the conditional quantiles have a linear form. In its simplest form, the least absolute deviation estimator fits medians to a linear function of covariates. The method of quantile regression is potentially attractive for the same reason that the median or other quantiles are a better measure of location than the mean. Other useful features are the robustness against outliers and the likelihood that the estimators are in general more efficient than least square estimators. Besides the technical features, quantile regressions allow that potentially different solutions at distinct quantiles may be interpreted as differences in the response of the dependent variable, namely, the growth rates, to changes in the regressors at various points in the conditional distinction of the dependent variable. Thus, quantile regressions reveal asymmetries in the data, which could not be detected by simple OLS estimations.[6]

Let (y_i, x_i), $i = 1, \ldots, n$, be a sample of firms, where x_i is a $K \times 1$ vector of regressors. Assume that $Quant_\theta(y_i, x_i)$ devotes the conditional quantile of y_i, conditional on the regressor vector x_i. The distribution of the error term $u_{\theta i}$ satisfies the quantile restriction $Quant_\theta(u_{\theta i}, x_i) = 0$. Thus, we estimate $y_i = Quant_\theta(y_i, x_i) + \mu_{\theta i}$, or with $Quant_\theta(y_i, x_i) = x_i' \beta_\theta$:

$$y_i = x_i' \beta_\theta + \mu_{\theta i}. \qquad (9.8)$$

TABLE 9.3 Performance of Venture-Backed Firm

	OLS	0.20 Quantile	.50 Quantile	.80 Quantile
Ownership VC	.0072	.0139	.0098	.0022
	(1.76)*	(1.85)*	(3.63)***	(0.58)
Debt	.0002	.0009	.0001	−.0003
	(0.33)	(1.13)	(0.50)	(1)
Firm patents	−.0045	−.0128	.0091	.0011
	(0.56)	(0.69)	(1.90)*	(0.22)
Human capital executives	−.1132	.1017	.1715	−.0245
	(1.15)	(0.79)	(1.24)	(0.29)
Human capital directors	.0626	−.1633	.0633	.0848
	(0.92)	(0.93)	(13.19)*	(1.53)
Size	−.8583	−.8637	−.8498	−.8187
	(12.35)***	(6.40)***	(17.74)***	(12.81)***
Age	.0070	.03464	.0350	−.0300
	(0.12)	(0.34)	(0.88)	(0.64)
Ownership banks	−.0016	−.01039	−.0001	.0088
	(0.17)	(0.69)	(0.02)	(1.24)
Ownership exec.	.0078	.0083	.0086	.0122
	(2.69)**	(1.41)	(4.3)***	(4.69)***
Ownership firms	.0059	.0068	.0046	.0056
	(1.90)**	(1.11)	(2.19)**	(2.24)**
Germany	−.5081	−.4233	−.4657	−.6450
	(2.43)**	(1.11)	(3.27)***	(3.94)***
IAS	−.07929	−.2583	−.0745	−.1619
	(5.11)	(0.93)	(0.69)	(1.23)
Software	−.1245	−.1012	−.1639	−.1950
	(1.09)	(1.48)	(5.87)***	(6.44)***
Service	.1086	.2902	.1641	.2160
	(0.44)	(0.66)	(1.01)	(1.07)
E-commerce	−.3221	−.0436	−.4716	.4109
	(0.90)	(0.07)	(1.95)*	(1.50)
Computer	.1836	.0090	.0215	.3189
	(0.53)	(0.02)	(0.10)	(1.33)
Telecom	−.3980	−1.007	−.0738	−.2457
	(1.17)	(1.61)*	(0.33)	(0.88)
Biotechnology	.1289	−.0709	−.5678	.3985
	(0.32)	(0.10)	(2.07)**	(1.48)
Medical technology	.2300	.2584	−.3459	.5573
	(0.51)	(0.28)	(1.15)	(2.28)**
Entertainment	−.0511	−.3198	.0483	.2711
	(0.17)	(0.61)	(0.25)	(1.10)
Technology	−.0002	.2180	−.0864	.0738
	(0.00)	(0.34)	(0.39)	(0.26)
IPO 2000	.9911	.0540	.0098	1.2333
	(1.79)*	(0.05)	(3.63)***	(4.97)***

(continued)

TABLE 9.3 (*continued*)

	OLS	0.20 Quantile	.50 Quantile	.80 Quantile
IPO 1999	−.1175	−.3165	.8799	1.4154
	(0.76)	(0.28)	(2.82)***	(6.12)***
Pseudo R^2		.2895	.2982	.3609
Adj. R^2	.4501			

This table provides estimates of the equations (9.7) and (9.8). The dependent variable in all specifications is GROWTH, as measured by the difference of the log of employees before and after the IPO. The second column reports the results from the OLS regression. The results from the quantile regressions are presented in columns 3 and 4. To limit the number of columns, we report the results for the 0.20. the 0.80. and the median quantile. Standard deviations are in parentheses. The definitions of the explanatory variables are given in table 9.1.
* Statistically significant at the two-tailed test for 90% level of confidence.
** Statistically significant at the two-tailed test for 95% level of confidence.
*** Statistically significant at the two-tailed test for 99% level of confidence.

The variables included in the estimate of equation (9.8) are the same as those used in the OLS regression. We analyze three different quantiles. The 0.20 quantile includes the lower performing firms based on column (3) in table 9.3.[7] The median quantile is based on the 0.50 quantile in column (4) of table 9.3. This regression is closest to the OLS approach, where the expected mean value is used in the estimation instead of the median. Finally, we use the .80 quantile with the higher performing firms. As one increases θ from 0 to 1, one traces the entire conditional distribution of the endogenous variable y, conditional on x. The quantile's coefficient could be interpreted using the partial derivative of the quantile of y with respect to one of the regressors, say, j. This derivative can be interpreted as the marginal change in the θth conditional quantile due to marginal change in the jth element of x.

The results of the three different estimations appear in table 9.3. The positive and statistically significant coefficient on venture capital ownership indicates that growth rates are in general higher in venture-backed firms. The one exception is in the high performing cohort, where venture capital ownership has no influence on performance. Thus, it seems that growth rates in the lower quantile group react more sensitively toward an increase in venture capital. This is consistent with other empirical evidence documenting the disciplining influence of venture capitalists in poorly performing firms (Hart, 2001; Kaplan and Strömberg, 2004).

There is at least some evidence suggesting that intellectual property, as measured by firm patents, has a positive impact on firm growth, at least for the median quantile. This also holds for the human capital of the board of directors, which is positively related to firm growth for the median quantile.

The positive and statistically significant coefficients of ownership concentration by executives and other firms indicate not only a superior performance when CEOs and external firms have a high degree of ownership but also that the control group, firms owned predominantly by friends and family, exhibits a systematically lower level of performance. Interestingly and in contrast to the equity held by venture capitalists, growth rates in the higher quantiles react more sensitively toward an increase in equity held by firms as well as by executives. This may be a hint that equity provided by outside investors, such as firms and venture capitalists, may be substitutes rather than complements.

The variable indicating equity ownership by banks is not significant in all estimates. Once again, German firms exhibit systematically lower levels of performance. Control variables reflecting industry effects, the IPO date, and firm size contribute to explaining firm growth. The quantile regressions also document some asymmetries in the data set.

9.5 Conclusions

An important finding by Gompers and Lerner (2001) suggests that banks are not the appropriate financial intermediary for financing innovative firms, in general, and, in particular, high-technology startups. They show how equity-based venture capital has proven to be a superior form financing entrepreneurship. The findings of Gompers and Lerner pose a challenge to bank-based finance countries, such as Germany. Is it possible to sustain high growth and generate innovative startups in countries dominated by traditional banking systems?

The evidence provided by this chapter is that it is not. As long as finance is restricted to the traditional banks, innovative firms and, in particular, technology-based startups, will suffer a lower performance. However, to the degree to which new institutions can be developed facilitating entrepreneurial access to venture capital or some functional equivalent, high-growth innovative firms can be generated. Thus, the constraint on innovation is not necessarily specific to the country but rather to its institutions, in this case, the need to develop an equity market facilitating the development of venture capital finance.

The findings of this chapter also suggest that institutions such as the former Neuer Markt make an important contribution to generating an entrepreneurial economy, because venture capital is apparently a substitute for and not a complement to bank-based debt. Banks play only a minor role in providing entrepreneurial access to financial resources.

A great debate has raged about the efficacy of debt finance relative to equity (Myers, 2001). The results of this chapter suggest this may be the wrong question for knowledge-based entrepreneurship. What is clear is that, whatever the mode of finance, entrepreneurial firms need access to financial capital as well as knowledge capital to generate both a competitive advantage and superior performance.

The Emergence of Entrepreneurship Policy

10.1 A Changing Paradigm

Confronted by not just economic stagnation but also the worst job creation performance of any modern U.S. president, George W. Bush responded with a policy to promote economic growth that focused on entrepreneurship and small business:

> 70 percent of the new jobs in America are created by small businesses. I understand that. And I have promoted during the course of the last four years one of the most aggressive, pro-entrepreneur, small business policies.... And so in a new term, we will make sure the tax relief continues to be robust for our small businesses. We'll push legal reform and regulatory reform because I understand the engine of growth is through the small business sector.[1]

In fact, neither the current president nor his political party has a monopoly in advocating entrepreneurship policy as an engine of growth and job creation. The 1990s saw the reemergence of competitiveness, innovative activity, and job generation in the United States. Not only was this economic turnaround largely unanticipated by many scholars and members of the policy community, but what was even more surprising than the resurgence itself was the primary source: small and new firms. As scholars began the arduous task of documenting the crucial role played by small firms and entrepreneurship in the United States as a driving engine of growth, job creation, and competitiveness in global markets, policy-makers responded with a bipartisan emphasis on policies to promote entrepreneurship.[2]

For example, in his 1993 State of the Union Address, President Bill Clinton proposed:

> Because small business has created such a high percentage of all the new jobs in our nation over the last 10 or 15 years, our plan includes the boldest targeted incentives for small business in history. We propose a permanent investment tax credit for the smallest firms in this country, with revenues of under $5 million. That's about 90 percent of the firms in America employing about 40 percent of the work force, but creating a big majority of the net new jobs for more than a decade.[3]

The Republican response to Clinton was, "We agree with the President that we have to put more people to work, but remember this: 80 to 85 percent of the new jobs in this country are created by small business. So the climate for starting and expanding businesses must be enhanced with tax incentives and deregulation, rather than imposing higher taxes and more governmental mandates."[4]

Entrepreneurship policy to ignite economic growth has not been restricted to the United States. On the other side of the Atlantic, in the Lisbon Accord of 2000, the European Commission made a formal commitment to becoming the entrepreneurship and knowledge leader in the world by 2020 in order to foster economic growth and prosperity throughout the European Union.

As Bresnahan and Gambardella (2004, p. 1) observe, "Clusters of high-tech industry, such as Silicon Valley, have received a great deal of attention from scholars and in the public policy arena. National economic growth can be fueled by development of such clusters. In the United States the long boom of the 1980s and 1990s was largely driven by growth in the information technology industries in a few regional clusters. Innovation and entrepreneurship can be supported by a number of mechanisms operating within a cluster, such as easy access to capital, knowledge about technology and markets, and collaborators." Similarly, Wallsten (2004, p. 229) wrote that, "policy makers around the world are anxious to find tools that will help their regions emulate the success of Silicon Valley and create new centers of innovation and high technology."

It is no doubt surprising that such a consensus in the public policy community could emerge concerning the appropriate policy to generate economic growth and employment that could cross party lines within a country as well as a broad spectrum of disparate nations and regions. But what is even more striking is the focus of this emerging public policy approach: entrepreneurship. Just a few years earlier, new and small firms were viewed as imposing a burden on the economy. For example, the Small Business Administration in the United States was created with a clear and compelling mandate to protect and preserve firms that were burdened with size-inherent inefficiencies that rendered them uncompetitive. Rather, the public policy focus on economic growth has traditionally revolved around macroeconomic instruments involving monetary and fiscal policies.

During the postwar era, a heated debate raged about the appropriate public policy to spur economic growth. On the one hand, the Keynesians advocated fiscal policy instruments; on the other hand, the Monetarists supported monetary in-struments. Despite what at times became an acrimonious debate, a virtual con-sensus reigned about the appropriate realm for public policy: macroeconomics.

By the 1980s, a new policy approach began to appear with a greater focus on a very different set of instruments, such as R&D, university research, and invest-ments in human capital. Though these instruments were certainly not new, the attention they drew in public policy debates was certainly a contrast to the more macroeconomic focus of an earlier generation.

More recently, public policy has again refocused, this time toward en-trepreneurship as an engine of growth. Trying to promote entrepreneurship in order to foster economic growth might have seemed unfathomable just a few years earlier.

The purpose of this chapter is to explain how and why public policy has turned to entrepreneurship as a mechanism generating economic growth and employment. The following section reviews the public policy approach consistent with the capital-driven, or Solow economy. The third section turns toward the knowledge-based, or Romer economy. In the fourth section, we define entrepreneurship policy and distinguish it from SME policy. We identify the mandate for entrepreneurship policy and the sources of market failure for entrepreneurship, which provide an economic rationale for public policy intervention. We also explain why entrepreneurship policy is diffusing across many different national and regional contexts.

The chapter concludes by suggesting that entrepreneurship policy is a purposeful attempt to create an entrepreneurial economy. Thus, this chapter does not advocate any particular policies and certainly no specific policy instruments to promote entrepreneurship. As Gordon Moore, who is "widely regarded as one of Silicon Valley's founding fathers" (Bresnahan and Gambardella, 2004, p. 7), and Kevin Davis warn, the policy rush to emulate the Silicon Valley success is somewhat misguided: "The potential disaster lies in the fact that these static, descriptive efforts culminate in policy recommendations and analytical tomes that resemble recipes or magic potions such as: combine liberal amounts of technology, entrepreneurs, capital, and sunshine; add one (1) university; stir vigorously" (Moore and Davis, 2004, p. 9). Apparently, creating the next Silicon Valley is not so simple. Still, the purpose of this chapter is not to reveal the recipe but rather to suggest that the framework provided by the Knowledge Spillover Theory of Entrepreneurship explains why the public policy community is looking for the recipe to create an entrepreneurial economy.

10.2 The Solow Economy

The view of the economy characterized by the Solow model framed the policy debate focusing on economic growth. The main mechanism for inducing higher growth rates was almost universally viewed as investments in physical capital. After all, the economy characterized by the Solow model was capital-driven. Increasing labor could increase the level of economic output but not the rate of economic growth.

As we emphasized in the second chapter, technical change shifted the production function; in the Solow model, it was considered exogenous, and therefore beyond the reach of policy. Thus, the policy debate during the postwar era, which may be reflected best by the Solow model, did not dispute the mechanism, physical capital, but rather the instruments. A vigorous dispute emerged in the economics literature and among the public policy community about which particular instruments were more conducive to inducing investments in physical capital.

On the one hand, there were advocates of monetary policy, focusing mainly on interest rates to induce capital investment. On the other hand were advocates of fiscal policy instruments who felt that taxes and government expenditures were the means to generate short-term growth, eventually inducing investments in new physical capital, thereby ensuring long-term growth. The choice of the particular instrument remained at the center of an intellectual and public policy storm, but a near consensus left the actual policy mechanism to achieve economic growth virtually unchallenged.

Though the context was considerably different, the choice of policy mechanisms to foster economic growth was not so different for developing countries. The intellectual and policy focus on how to foster growth and prosperity in developing countries revolved around instruments to foster inward foreign direct investment (Kindleberger and Audretsch, 1983). The context of developing countries may have suggested different instruments uniquely suited for the development context, but the mechanism used to attain the policy goal of economic growth remained the same: investment in physical capital.

The policy focus on capital as the driving input for economic growth after the World War II era generated a concomitant concern about the organization of that capital, both at the industry and firm level. The emerging field of industrial organization, in particular, was charged with the task of identifying how the organization of capital, or structure of an industry, influenced economic performance. A generation of scholars produced theoretical and empirical evidence suggesting that physical capital in many, but certainly not all, industries dictated a concentration of production resulting in an oligopolisitic market structure characterized by a concentration of ownership in relatively few producers (Scherer, 1970).

Scholars spanning a broad spectrum of academic fields and disciplines generated a massive literature that attempted to sort out the perceived trade-off between economic efficiency, on the one hand, and political and economic decentralization on the other. The large corporation purportedly had superior productive efficiency and was the engine of technological innovation. Ironically, the literature's obsession with oligopoly was combined with an essentially static analysis. There was considerable concern about what to do about the existing industrial structure, but little attention was paid to where it came from and where it was going. Oliver Williamson's classic 1968 article, "Economies as an Antitrust Defense: The Welfare Tradeoffs," in the *American Economic Review*, became something of a final statement demonstrating that gains in productive efficiency could be obtained through increased concentration and that gains in terms of competition, and implicitly democracy, could be achieved through decentralizing policies. But it did not seem possible to have both, certainly not in Williamson's completely static model.

Public policy toward business in this period revolved around finding solutions to the perceived trade-off between scale and efficiency, on the one hand, and decentralization and inefficiency on the other hand. The three main policy instruments deployed to achieve the required balance in the industrialized countries were antitrust (or competition policy, as it was called in Europe), regulation, and public ownership of business.

The key public policy question of the day was, How can society reap the benefits of the large corporation in an oligopolistic setting while avoiding or at least minimizing the costs imposed by a concentration of economic power? The answer centered on constraining the freedom of large firms to contract through public ownership, regulation, and antitrust. Different countries blended these three policy instruments in very different proportions. France and Sweden were in the vanguard of government ownership of business. The Netherlands and Germany, by contrast, emphasized regulation. The United States emphasized antitrust. Although these differences loomed large to scholars at the time, at this removed date, they are better seen as manifestations of a common policy approach that aimed to restrict the power of the large corporation.

Of course, each country adapted its own mix of policy instruments to try to obtain the benefits of large-scale production and concentrated ownership while, at the same time, restricting and constraining those firms to avoid political and economic abuse. For example, ever since its famous economic miracle of the 1950s (*Wirtschaftswunder*), Germany had been associated with remarkable prosperity and stability, providing both high employment and high wage rates. The German model of a social market economy (*Sozialmarktwirtschaft*) had generated a standard of living (*Wohlstand*) that created not only the material wealth found on the other side of the Atlantic but also the high degree of social services and security found elsewhere in Europe. The German Economic Model provided a unique policy approach to balancing economic efficiency accruing from large-scale production along with political safeguards to preempt abuses of that power.

This consensus consisted of three principle actors: the industry employer associations (*Arbeitgeberverbände*), labor unions (*Gewerkschaften*), and the government. Through a broad spectrum of institutions, such as the Work Councils (*Betriebsrat*), industry-wide wage agreements, and the apprentice system (*Lehrstellen*), these actors provided the basis for unparalleled success in generating high wages and levels of employment. Under this consensus, labor fulfilled its obligation in the social contract by supplying highly skilled and disciplined workers. For their part, the employers associations—the leading German industrial firms— provided stable and generous employment, including a rich array of social services. With labor and industry working together under this consensus facilitated by the government, industries such as automobiles and metalworking were more competitive in Germany than anywhere else in the world. The task of the major political parties was to shift the fruits of this enviably productive consensus either more toward labor Social Democratic Party (SPD) or toward the status quo firms in the "employers associations" Christian Democratic Union (CDU).

Similarly, in what was called the Polder Model of the Netherlands, a consensus emerged among the labor unions, large corporations, such as Phillips, and the government. In contrast, the Swedish and French models involved a greater share of ownership by the government.

The policy focus on large-scale corporations as the engine of economic growth was also prevalent in Europe. In advocating a new public policy approach to promote growth and international competitiveness in Europe, Servan-Schreiber (1968, p. 153) warned of the "American Challenge" in the form of the "dynamism, organization, innovation, and boldness that characterize the giant American corporations." Because giant corporations were considered to be the engine of growth and innovation, Servan-Schreiber advocated the "creation of large industrial units which are able both in size and management to compete with the American giants" (p. 159). According to Servan-Schreiber (p. 159), "The first problem of an industrial policy for Europe consists in choosing 50 to 100 firms which, once they are large enough, would be the most likely to become world leaders of modern technology in their fields. At the moment we are simply letting industry be gradually destroyed by the superior power of American corporations." Ironically, the 1988 Cecchini Report identified the gains from European integration as largely accruing from increases in scale economies.

The focus of public policy on the trade-off between efficiency and democracy inherent in the capital-driven economy was not limited to the West. For example, the industrial policies of Japan during the postwar era offered yet another variant involving the need to promote large-scale production but prevent political and economic abuse ensuing from the concentration of production and ownership.

Which of these policy approaches was most effective is not the point of this book. What was striking was the common public policy response to an economy where growth was seemingly dictated by not just investments in physical capital but also an organization of firms and industries that seemingly precludes the checks and balances inherent in competitive markets.

Whereas a heated debate emerged about which approach best promoted large-scale production while simultaneously constraining the ability of large corporations to exert market power, there was much less debate about public policy toward small business and entrepreneurship. The only issue was whether public policy-makers should simply allow small firms to disappear as a result of their inefficiency or should intervene to preserve them on social and political grounds. Those who perceived that small firms contribute significantly to growth, employment generation, and competitiveness were few and far between.

Thus, in the postwar era, small firms and entrepreneurship were viewed as a luxury, perhaps needed by the West to ensure a decentralization of decision making, but in any case obtained only at a cost to efficiency. Certainly, the systematic empirical evidence, gathered from both Europe and North America, documented a sharp trend toward a decreased role of small firms during the postwar period.

Public policy toward small firms generally reflected the view of economists and other scholars that they were a drag on economic efficiency and growth, generated lower quality jobs in terms of direct and indirect compensation, and were generally on the way to becoming less important to the economy, if not threatened by long-term extinction. Some countries, such as the former Soviet Union, but also Sweden and France, adapted the policy stance of allowing small firms to gradually disappear and consequently account for a smaller share of economic activity.

The public policy stance of the United States reflected long-term political and social valuation of small firms that seemed to reach back to Jeffersonian traditions. After all, in an 1890 congressional debate, Senator Sherman vowed, "If we will not endure a King as a political power we should not endure a King over the production, transportation, and sale of the necessaries of life. If we would not submit to an emperor we should not submit to an autocrat of trade with power to prevent competition and to fix the price of any commodity."[5]

Thus, public policy toward small business in the United States was oriented towards preserving what were considered to be inefficient enterprises, which, if left unprotected, might otherwise become extinct. An example of such preservationist policies toward small business was provided by enactment and enforcement of the Robinson-Patman Act. Even advocates of small business agreed that small firms were less efficient than big companies. These advocates were willing to sacrifice a modicum of efficiency, however, because of other contributions—moral, political, and otherwise—made by small business to society. Small business policy was thus "preservationist." The passage of the Robinson-Patman Act in 1936, for instance, was widely interpreted as one effort to protect small firms, like independent retailers, that would otherwise have been too inefficient to survive in open competition with large corporations.[6] According to Richard Posner (1976, p. 46), "The Robinson-Patman Act . . . is almost uniformly condemned by professional and academic opinion, legal and economic." Similarly, Robert Bork (1978, p. 382) observed, "One often hears of the baseball player who, although a weak hitter, was also a poor fielder. Robinson-Patman is a little like that. Although it does not prevent much price discrimination, at least it has stifled a great deal of competition."

Preservationist policies were clearly at work with the creation of the U.S. Small Business Administration. In the Small Business Act of July 10, 1953, Congress authorized the creation of the Small Business Administration, with an explicit mandate to "aid, counsel, assist and protect . . . the interests of small business concerns."[7] The Small Business Act was clearly an attempt by the Congress to halt the continued disappearance of small businesses and to preserve their role in the U.S. economy.

10.3 The Romer Economy

If physical capital was at the heart of the Solow economy, knowledge capital replaced it in the Romer economy. While the policy goals remained relatively unchanged, economic growth, the Romer model reflected the emergence of a new emphasis on a strikingly different policy mechanism, knowledge capital, involving very different policy instruments.

The new policy instruments corresponding to the knowledge-driven economy, or the Romer Model, generally involved inducing investments not necessarily in physical capital but rather in knowledge capital. Though the concept of knowledge capital seemed more vague and less conducive to measurement than did the traditional factor of physical capital, it clearly involved knowledge augmenting investments in human capital and research and development. Such instruments were strikingly different from their counterparts corresponding to the Solow economy. These instruments included, but were not limited to, education at all levels, but certainly at the university level, public research support, and tax and subsidy incentives to encourage private R&D.

For example, investment in universities was not necessarily viewed as an instrument promoting economic growth in the capital-driven economy. After all, it was not at all clear how the output of universities, students and research, would contribute to augmenting investments in capital. There was an important case to be made for investing in universities for political, social, and even moral reasons, but the case was less compelling for economic reasons, particularly for economic growth. It was indeed possible to view investments in universities as actually detracting from economic growth, because they diverted resources away from physical capital. But no one can dispute the primacy of investment in universities in the Romer economy.

Other countries adapted different types of instruments to augment and increase the levels of human capital. For example, Germany used a broad spectrum of instruments to create high levels of skilled labor and human capital to produce products that, although they might cost more in globally linked markets, were of superior quality (Sorge, 1991; Streeck, 1991). The knowledge investments in Germany generated a comparative advantage in moderate-technology products in traditional industries, such as machine tools, automobile parts, metalworking, chemicals, and the food industry.

In *National Systems of Innovation*, Nelson (1992) concludes that German success in innovative activity lies in incremental improvements in products and processes of existing industries. In the German Economic Model the bias toward incremental innovation over radical innovation is the direct result of long-term commitments between workers and firms, low worker mobility, and a bias in financial' institutions toward existing firms and technologies. According to Dertouzos, Lester, and Solow (1989), Sorge (1991), and Streeck (1991), an institutional structure emphasizing consensus and long-term commitments gave Germany the capabilities to incrementally improve on existing technological trajectories.

Ergas (1987, p. 192) was among the first to classify the national system of innovation in Germany as diffusion-oriented. He defines the German approach to innovation as, "Closely bound up with the provision of public goods, the principal purpose of these policies is to diffuse technological capabilities throughout the industrial structure, thus facilitating the ongoing and mainly incremental adaptation to change." In addition, he argues that "diffusion-oriented policies seek to provide a broadly based capacity for adjusting to technological change throughout the industrial structure. They are characteristic of open economies where the state, bearing the interests of the firms in mind, aims at facilitating change rather than directing it" (p. 205).

As Sorge (1991) and Streeck (1991) have written, the most significant feature of the German public policy is the depth and breadth of investment in human capital and enhancement of workforce skills. Workers, endowed with a high level of human capital, are trained to possess the capabilities and competencies necessary to increase the value of existing technologies through incremental and continuous improvements in products and processes.

As recently as the first election of Bill Clinton, both the new president and his newly appointed secretary of labor, Robert Reich, held up the instruments of training, apprentice systems, and education of Europe, especially Germany and the Nordic countries, as models for the United States to follow to regain international competitiveness. This sentiment generally mirrored the influential study, *Made in America*, directed by the leaders of the MIT Commission on Industrial Productivity, Michael L. Dertouzos, Richard K. Lester, and Robert M. Solow, who assembled a team of 23 scholars, spanning a broad range of disciplines and backgrounds and concluded that, to restore international competitiveness, the United States must adapt the types of policies targeting the leading corporations prevalent in Japan and Germany. In particular, the MIT Commission on Industrial Productivity advocated that the United States adopt the training and education policies of Germany and Japan to regain competitiveness in the capital-based manufacturing sector.

Even as recently as a 15 years ago, there were serious concerns about the ability of the United States to withstand competition in the global economy, create jobs, and continue to develop. Lester Thurow bemoaned that the United States was "losing the economic race," because "today it's very hard to find an industrial corporation in America that isn't in really serious trouble basically because of trade problems. . . . The systematic erosion of our competitiveness comes from having lower rates of growth of manufacturing productivity year after year, as compared with the rest of the world" (1985, p. 23).

Jorde and Teece (1990) argued that the deterioration of American international competitiveness was attributable to technological sluggishness. According to them, the underlying culprit responsible for the lack of innovative activity was U.S. anti-trust legislations, which constrained the ability of American firms to attain market power and economies of scale. This echoed the view of the Reagan Administration, whose secretary of commerce asserted, "We are simply living in a different world today. Because of larger markets, the cost of research and development, new product innovation, marketing and so forth . . . it takes larger companies to compete successfully" (Baldridge, 1986, p. 29). Baldridge based his argument on the observation that the American share of the largest corporations in the world had fallen considerably between 1960 and 1984. He warned that programs promoting the large-scale enterprise must not be stopped by those who are preoccupied with outdated notions about firm size. Baldridge's concerns were more than empty rhetoric. The Reagan Administration advocated eliminating the antitrust statutes as a means of enhancing the international competitiveness of U.S. firms on the basis that "if our industries are going to survive, there will have to be additional consolidations to achieve needed economies of scale" (*New York Times*, 1985).

W. W. Rostow (1987) predicted a revolution in economic policy, concluding that "the United States is entering a new political era, one in which it will be preoccupied by increased economic competition from abroad and will need better cooperation at home to deal with this challenge." However, neither Rostow nor Thurow predicted that this new focus of public policy to restore U.S. growth and competitiveness in globally linked markets would be entrepreneurship.

In a *Harvard Business Review* article, Ferguson (1988, p. 61), argued that entrepreneurship would actually reduce rather than increase economic performance. He considered entrepreneurship in Silicon Valley a drag on economic performance, because the

> fragmentation, instability, and entrepreneurialism are not signs of well-being. In fact, they are symptoms of the larger structural problems that afflict U.S. industry. In semiconductors, a combination of personnel mobility, ineffective intellectual property protection, risk aversion in large companies, and tax subsidies for the formation of new companies contribute to a fragmented "chronically entrepreneurial" industry. U.S. semiconductor companies are unable to sustain the large, long-term investments required for continued U.S. competitiveness. Companies avoid long-term

R&D, personnel training, and long-term cooperative relationships because these are presumed, often correctly, to yield no benefit to the original investors. Economies of scale are not sufficiently developed. An elaborate infrastructure of small subcontractors has sprung up in Silicon Valley. Personnel turnover in the American merchant semiconductor industry has risen to 20 percent compared with less than 5 percent in IBM and Japanese corporations. . . . Fragmentation discouraged badly needed co-ordinated action—to develop process technology and also to demand better government support.

10.4 The Entrepreneurial Economy

10.4.1 The Mandate

The mandate for entrepreneurship policy emerged from what would appear to be two opposite directions. One direction emanates from the failure of the traditional policy instruments, corresponding to the Solow model, or those based on instruments promoting investment in physical capital, to adequately maintain economic growth and employment in globally linked markets. The second push for the entrepreneurship policy mandate is from the opposite direction: the failure of the new economy policy instruments, corresponding to the Romer model, or those promoting investment into knowledge capital, to adequately generate economic growth and employment. Although coming from opposite origins, both have in common unacceptable economic performance. Therefore, the mandate for entrepreneurship policy is rooted in dissatisfaction—dissatisfaction with the status quo, especially with the status quo economic performance.[8]

The first direction underlying the mandate for entrepreneurship policy emanates from regions and even countries that prospered during the postwar economy characterized by the Solow model but more recently have been adversely affected by globalization and loss of competitiveness in traditional industries, resulting in an adverse economic performance. Such economies developed institutions and policies consistent with the capital-driven model. For example, just as Michigan and much of the midwestern United States developed a set of institutions and public policies to channel capital and labor into the automobile industry, Pittsburgh, Detroit, and Cleveland did so for steel, and Ohio for tires.

During the capital-driven era following World War II, the midwest ranked among the wealthiest regions in the country. For example, as recently as 1965, Indiana ranked seventeenth in per capita income among the 50 states and the District of Columbia. The source of this economic success was the concentration of traditional manufacturing throughout the state. In 1970, around a third of Indiana residents were employed in the manufacturing sector, a proportion considerably higher than in the rest of the country, which propelled the American midwest to a high standard of living.

Increased globalization has triggered a shift in the competitive advantage away from capital-based traditional manufacturing. In the capital-based manufacturing economy, comparative advantage was based on combining large-scale capital-based heavy manufacturing with unskilled and semiskilled labor. Regions in North

America and Europe that have relied heavily on traditional manufacturing have lost employment and experienced significant wage declines relative to the rest of the country. For example, the Indiana share of nonfarm employment has fallen from 2.6 percent in 1960, to 2.4 percent in 1980, and to 2.2 percent in 2000.

The capital-based model of economic development proved not to be sustainable. In the last three decades, manufacturing jobs throughout the midwest have declined dramatically. For example, Indiana has maintained its national leadership in manufacturing employment shares; Indiana has the highest share of the labor force in manufacturing in the country. However, with easier access to the cheaper labor and materials in foreign countries, it is highly likely that traditional, assembly-line manufacturing jobs will only continue to decline in the midwest in the future. As Cohen and Delong (2005, p. 113) point out:

> The threat of downward mobility first hit America in a big way in the 1980s, when the old-line, unionized Midwestern manufacturing companies found themselves under enormous pressure from foreign companies such as Honda, Toyota, and Komatsu. The result was a hemorrhaging of unionized manufacturing jobs and the emergence of the Rust Belt. In addition, new technologies and consumption patterns were shifting the U.S. economy's center of gravity from skilled, unionized, mass-production industry—which fashions products from expensive materials and capital-intensive industries—to services and retailing, where barriers to the entry of competitors are lower, labor costs more significant, and competitive advantage more reliant on squeezing those labor costs.

The loss of traditional manufacturing jobs has resulted in a long-term decline in per capita income. For example, per capita income in Indiana exceeded the national average in the early 1960s but has subsequently declined over time. By the end of the 1990s, it was considerably below the national average.

The second direction contributing to the mandate for entrepreneurship policy comes from the opposite direction and involves a very different economic context— contexts where substantial investments in knowledge have been undertaken but the yield in terms of economic growth and employment creation has been disappointing.

Shifting to a policy focus involving instruments to induce investments in knowledge capital has clearly been successful in generating economic growth in many regions. However, as the Knowledge Spillover Theory of Entrepreneurship suggests, investments in knowledge capital may be a necessary but not sufficient condition to ensure that such investments are actually commercialized and generate economic growth. The existence of a severe knowledge filter will impede the spillover and commercialization of investments in new knowledge, thereby choking off the potential for economic growth.

There are certainly many examples of cities and regions exhibiting vigorous investments in new knowledge that have not, at least until now, triggered economic growth. For example, Feldman and Desrochers (2004) carefully document how large and sustained investments in research and human capital at Johns Hopkins University have failed to spawn commercialization and growth.

Perhaps the failure of knowledge investments to generate economic growth is most striking at the country level. Consider the case of Sweden. Throughout the postwar era, Sweden has consistently ranked among the leading nations in the world for investments in new knowledge. Whether measured in private R&D, levels of education, university research, or public research, Sweden has exhibited strong and sustained investment in knowledge. As recently as 2003, Sweden had the highest ratio of GDP invested in R&D. Yet, even in the face of such investments in knowledge, the return in employment creation and economic growth has been modest, at best, and disappointing to the Swedish public politicians.

Similar examples of high investments in new knowledge but low performance in economic growth can be found throughout Europe, spanning Germany and France, leading the European Union to invent a name for the European failure to commercialize investments in new knowledge: the European Paradox. According to the Commission of the European Community (1995, p. 5), "Although Europe's scientific and technological performance is comparable, if not superior, to that of its major competitors, EU member states fell behind in terms of transformation of research results into marketable products and services."

Examples of high investments in knowledge but low growth performance are not restricted to Europe. Japan is an Asian example. Japanese investments in private R&D and human capital have ranked among the highest in the world. Still, Japan has been bogged down with low and stagnant growth for over a decade. It would seem that Europe does not have a monopoly on the European Paradox.

As the traditional policy instruments targeting either physical capital or knowledge capital failed to generate sustainable economic growth, employment, and competitiveness in globally linked markets, policy-makers began to look elsewhere. The political mandate for entrepreneurship was to replace, or at least augment, physical capital and augment knowledge capital with the missing link: a mechanism facilitating the return on investments made in knowledge not accruing in economic growth and employment in regions making such knowledge investments.

The traditional public policy instruments failed to preserve employment and international competitiveness in the traditional industries in North Carolina. Furniture, textiles, and tobacco had all lost international competitiveness, resulting in declines in employment and stagnant real incomes. In 1952, only Arkansas and Mississippi had lower per capita incomes. According to Link and Scott (2003), a movement emerged to use the rich knowledge base of the region, formed by the three major universities: Duke University, University of North Carolina-Chapel Hill, and North Carolina State University. This movement, though it initially consisted only of businessmen looking to improve industrial growth, ultimately fell into the hands of the governor, who supported the efforts through fruition (Link, 1995). Empirical evidence provides strong support that the initiative creating the Research Triangle Park has led to fundamental changes in the region. Link and Scott (2003) document the growth in the number of research companies in the Research Triangle Park from none in 1958 to 50 by the mid-1980s and to more than 100 by 1997. At the same time, employment in these research companies increased from zero in the late 1950s to over 40,000 by 1997. Lugar (2001) attributes the Research Triangle Park with directly and indirectly generating a quarter of all jobs in the region between 1959 and 1990 and shifting the nature of those jobs toward high-value-added knowledge activities.

Thus, the inadequate economic performance of specific regions or entire countries and the inability of traditional policy approaches to deliver a sustainable economic performance led to a refocus of public policy toward entrepreneurship as an engine of economic growth and employment creation. Whether this disappointment was with the traditional economic policy strategy of investment in physical capital or investments in knowledge capital, apparently something had been missing in the economic growth strategy. As chapter 3 suggests, the missing link in economic growth has been entrepreneurship. Entrepreneurship policy has emerged as a cornerstone in the strategic management of places.

10.4.2 The Rationale

Not only has a mandate emerged for entrepreneurship policy but also an economic rationale for public policy intervention to create an entrepreneurial economy. That is, just because entrepreneurship capital matters and serves as the missing link to economic growth does not necessarily warrant policy intervention. After all, as Bresnahan and Gambardella (2004, p. 5) conclude, the emergence of the most prominent contemporary entrepreneurial economy that has set the standard, Silicon Valley, was not the result of public policy: "Our overall research design took seriously the proposition government policy leading and directing cluster formation might be an important part of the cluster formation story.... [W]e ultimately reject that proposition."

Rather, for an economic rationale justifying policy intervention, there must be a reason why the market will not appropriately and fully supply the good or service in question, in this case, entrepreneurship. Only with instances of market failure will an economic rationale for public policy intervention be justified. Such an economic rationale for policy intervention is based on four instances of market failure: network externalities, knowledge externalities, failure externalities, and demonstration externalities. These four sources of market failure effectively increase the value of β, or barriers to entrepreneurship, in the Knowledge Spillover Theory of Entrepreneurship, which was presented in chapter 3.

10.4.2.1 *Network Externalities* Network externalities result from the value of an individual's or firm's capabilities, and therefore potential value, conditional on the geographic proximity of complementary firms and individuals. As Saxenian (1994) pointed out, local proximity is essential for accessing these complementary inputs. This makes the value of an entrepreneurial firm greater in the (local) presence of other entrepreneurial firms. The value of any individual's or firm's capabilities is therefore conditional on the existence of partners in a network. Firms and workers place a greater value on locations within clusters that contain complementary workers and firms than on those outside of clusters. Such market failure can occur where there is a potential for geographic, intersectoral linkages, or networks.

Thus, this source of market failure involves the geographic context that provides the (potential) platform for interactions and networks. Contexts, or regions, that do not enjoy a rich density of entrepreneurial networks will be burdened with a greater value of β, or more significant barriers to entrepreneurship, because the expected value of any recognized opportunity will be correspondingly lower, resulting in a lower propensity for economic agents to decide to become entrepreneurs.

10.4.2.2 *Knowledge Externalities* The second source of market failure involves knowledge externalities. As Arrow (1962) pointed out, knowledge, which involves new ideas, can serve as a public good, and its production generates externalities. However, as shown in chapters 3 and 6, local proximity is essential for accessing these knowledge spillovers. This source of market failure involves the units of analysis of the individual scientist and firm, since these generate knowledge. It also involves the region because knowledge externalities have been spatially bounded.

Chapter 6 provided evidence supporting the Localization Hypothesis, which suggests that knowledge-spillover entrepreneurship tends to cluster within close geographic proximity to knowledge sources. Similarly, chapter 7 found evidence supporting the Entrepreneurial Performance Hypothesis, which suggests that entrepreneurial startups locating within close proximity to knowledge sources to facilitate the access and absorption of knowledge spillovers exhibit better performance than their counterparts that are geographically isolated. These findings suggest that the extent of market failure in the form of knowledge externalities is not trivial. Location matters for entrepreneurial startups for attaining competitive advantage, and, ultimately, a superior entrepreneurial performance. In the absence of a viable entrepreneurial cluster spontaneously emerging, public policy intervention may be appropriate to induce entrepreneurial location at a particular Standort to create such an entrepreneurial cluster.

10.4.2.3 *Failure Externalities* The third source of market failure associated with entrepreneurship is that positive economic value for third-party firms and individuals is created even when entrepreneurial firms fail. The high failure rate of new-firm startups has been widely documented (Caves, 1998), and the failure rates in knowledge-based activities are especially high. This is not surprising since knowledge activities are associated with a greater degree of uncertainty. However, the failure of a high-technology firm does not imply that the firm created no value. Ideas created by failed firms and projects often become integral parts of successful products and projects in other (successful) firms. Insights emerging from failed entrepreneurial episodes are rarely codified and presumably require informal interactions to access them. Once again, such learning may be more efficient and may lower cost within a geographically bounded context.

The externalities accruing from failed firms also create a market failure in the valuation of (potential) new enterprises by private investors and policy-makers. Whereas private investors can appropriate their investment only if the particular firm succeeds, a failed firm that generates positive externalities contributes to the success of other third-party firms. The private investor, however, does not appropriate anything from the original investment. Likewise, individual firms and workers would have no incentive to invest in the development of a cluster, which is the creation of other entrepreneurial firms, because they cannot appropriate returns from such a cluster.

From the public policy perspective, on the other hand, it does not matter which entrepreneurial firm succeeds, as long as some firms do, so that growth, along with the other benefits accruing from entrepreneurship, is ultimately generated for that particular Standort.

10.4.2.4 *Demonstration Externalities*   The fourth source of market failure involves the demonstration effect emanating from knowledge-based and technology entrepreneurial activity. This is particularly valuable at a Standort where entrepreneurship has been noticeably lacking and where no strong tradition of entrepreneurship exists. Entrepreneurial activity involves not just the firm or the entrepreneurial scientist making the decision to start the firm. Rather, other colleagues will observe the process of opportunity recognition and action in starting a new knowledge-based firm, along with the results accruing from this entrepreneurial activity. Manski (2000) considers that many of the interactions in R&D and human capital formation that are important to endogenous growth theory occur in nonmarket environments and are influenced by the expectations, preferences, and constraints of related economic agents. The demonstration externality is in the form of learning by third-party individuals that entrepreneurship is a viable alternative to the status quo. As a result of this demonstration effect, others will be induced to develop entrepreneurial strategies and perhaps alter their own career trajectories to include entrepreneurial activities. Thus, there is a strong and compelling positive externality associated with entrepreneurship as a result of the demonstration effect, particularly in regions without a strong entrepreneurial tradition. The demonstration effect focuses primarily on the individual scientist but is also linked to the poststartup performance of the firm. We would expect the demonstration effect to be greater within a geographically bounded regional context.

As a result of the market failures inherent in the externalities involved in knowledge spillover entrepreneurship—which stem from networks, knowledge, failure, and demonstration—a gap is created in the valuation of entrepreneurial activities between private parties and the local policy-makers. Just as Branscomb and Auerswald (2003) identified the existence of liquidity constraints in the form of what they term *the Valley of Death* and *the Darwinian Sea*, the financing constraints confronting not just the new and young high-technology and knowledge-based enterprises but also potential entrepreneurs may be even more severe in regions outside of an entrepreneurial cluster than for those within it.

The role that entrepreneurship plays in permeating the knowledge filter and serving as a conduit of knowledge spillovers, combined with the strong propensity for those knowledge spillovers to remain localized, suggests a special focus for public policy on the impact of local institutions, universities, and policies on the individual cognitive process of changing career trajectories and deciding to become a high-technology entrepreneur. By filling the gaps created by the inherent market failure, public policy can create a positive entrepreneurial feedback loop, wherein entrepreneurs network and link to each other, and can provide strong role models of high-technology entrepreneurship for the local scientific community to emulate.

The four sources of market failure associated with entrepreneurship contribute to significant barriers to entrepreneurship, or a high value of β, at least in some contexts. The economic rationale for entrepreneurship policy is to mitigate these four sources of market failure impeding the emergence of an entrepreneurial economy.

10.4.3 Instruments

With the issues of the mandate and rationale for entrepreneurship policy clarified, two remaining questions revolve around entrepreneurship policy. What constitutes a bona fide entrepreneurship policy instrument? And who actually implements entrepreneurship policy?

In distinguishing entrepreneurship policy from more traditional approaches toward business, the focus has shifted from the traditional triad of policy instruments essentially constraining the freedom of firms to contract—regulation, competition policy, or antitrust in the United States—and public ownership of business. The policy approach of constraint was sensible as long as the major issue was how to restrain large corporations in possession of considerable market power. That this policy approach toward business is less relevant in a global economy is reflected by the waves of deregulation and privatization throughout the OECD.

Instead, a new policy approach is emerging that focuses on enabling the creation and commercialization of knowledge. Probably the greatest and most salient change in small business policy over the last 15 years has been a shift from trying to preserve small businesses that confront a cost disadvantage due to size-inherent scale disadvantages toward promoting the startup and viability of new and small firms involved in the commercialization of knowledge, or knowledge-based entrepreneurship.

Entrepreneurship policy is a relatively new phenomenon. An important distinction should be made between the traditional small business policies and entrepreneurship policies. Small-business policy typically refers to policies implemented by a ministry or government agency charged with the mandate to promote and protect small businesses. The actual definition of a small business varies considerably across countries, ranging from enterprises with fewer than 500 employees in some of the most developed countries, such as the United States and Canada, to fewer than 250 employees in the European Union, to 50 employees in many developing countries.

Small-business policy typically takes the existing enterprises within the appropriate size class as exogenous, or given, and then develops instruments to promote the viability of those enterprises. Thus, small-business policy is almost exclusively targeted toward the existing stock of enterprises, and virtually all of the instruments included in the policy portfolio are designed to promote the viability of the small business.

In contrast, entrepreneurship policy has a much broader focus. Lundström and Stevenson (2001, p. 19) introduced the definition for OECD countries: "Entrepreneurship policy consists of measures taken to stimulate more entrepreneurial behavior in a region or country.... We define entrepreneurship policy as those measures intended to directly influence the level of entrepreneurial vitality in a country or a region."

Entrepreneurship policy is different from small-business policy in at least two important ways (Lundström and Stevenson, 2005). The first is the breadth of policy orientation and instruments. Whereas small-business policy focuses on the existing stock of small firms, entrepreneurship policy is more encompassing in that it includes potential entrepreneurs. This suggests that entrepreneurship policy is more focused on the process of change, regardless of the organizational unit, whereas small-business policy is more static and remains focused on the enterprise level. Entrepreneurship policy also has a greater sensitivity to framework or contextual conditions that shape the decision-making process of entrepreneurs and potential entrepreneurs.

Whereas small-business policy is primarily concerned with one organizational level, the enterprise, entrepreneurship policy encompasses multiple units of organization and analysis. These range from the individual to the enterprise, and to the cluster or network, which might involve an industry or sectoral dimension, or a spatial dimension, such as a district, city, region, or even an entire country. Just as each level is an important target for policy, the interactions and linkages across these disparate levels are also important. In this sense, entrepreneurship policy tends to be more systemic than small-business policy. However, it is important to emphasize that small-business policy still remains at the core of entrepreneurship policy.

The second way of distinguishing entrepreneurship policy from traditional small-business policy is that virtually every country has a ministry or governmental agency charged with promoting the viability of the small-business sector. These ministries and agencies have by now developed a well-established arsenal of policy instruments to promote small business. However, no such agencies exist to promote entrepreneurship. Part of the challenge of implementing entrepreneurship policy is that no country has yet to introduce an agency mandated to promote entrepreneurship. Rather, aspects relevant to entrepreneurship policy can be found across a broad spectrum of ministries and agencies, ranging from education to trade and immigration. Thus, whereas small business has agencies and ministries that champion their issues, no analogous agency exists for entrepreneurship policy.

Entrepreneurship policy is not only implemented by different agencies from those implementing either the traditional policy instruments constraining the freedom of firms to contract, or those implementing traditional small-business policy. but it involves a different, distinct set of policy instruments.

Lundström and Stevenson (2005) have meticulously classified the broad and diverse range of instruments being used around the globe to promote entrepreneurship. Examples of the emerging entrepreneurship policy abound. A new policy instrument reflecting the policy shift to enabling the creation and viability of entrepreneurial firms was created by passage by the United States Congress of the Bayh-Dole Act[9] (*Economist*, 2002):

> Possibly the most inspired piece of legislation to be enacted in America over the past half-century was the Bayh-Dole Act of 1980. Together with amendments in 1984 and augmentation in 1986, this unlocked all the inventions and discoveries that had been made in laboratories through the United States with the help of taxpayers' money. More than anything, this single policy measure helped to reverse America's precipitous slide into industrial irrelevance. Before Bayh-Dole, the fruits of research supported by government agencies had gone strictly to the federal government. Nobody could exploit such research without tedious

negotiations with a federal agency concerned. Worse, companies found it nigh impossible to acquire exclusive rights to a government owned patent. And without that, few firms were willing to invest millions more of their own money to turn a basic research idea into a marketable product.

An even more enthusiastic assessment suggested that "the Bayh-Dole Act turned out to be a strong drive to campus innovation. Universities that would previously have let their intellectual property lie fallow began filing for—and getting—patents at unprecedented rates. Coupled with other legal, economic and political developments that also spurred patenting and licensing, the results seems nothing less than a major boom to national economic growth."[10]

The president of the Association of American Universities claimed, "Before Bayh-Dole, the federal government had accumulated 30,000 patents, of which only 5% had been licensed and even fewer had found their way into commercial products. Today under Bayh-Dole more than 200 universities are engaged in technology transfer, adding more than $21 billion each year to the economy."[11] Similarly, the Commission of the U.S. Patent and Trademark Office claimed:

> In the 1970s, the government discovered that inventions that resulted from public funding were not reaching the marketplace because no one could make the additional investment to turn basic research into marketable products. That finding resulted in the Bayh-Dole Act, passed in 1980. It enabled universities, small companies, and nonprofit organizations to commercialize the results of federally funded research. The results of Bayh-Dole have been significant. Before 1981, fewer than 250 patents were issued to universities each year. A decade later universities were averaging approximately 1,000 patents a year.[12]

Mowery (2005, p. 2) argues that such an enthusiastic assessment of the impact on Bayh-Dole is exaggerated: "Although it seems clear that the criticism of high-technology startups that was widespread during the period of pessimism over U.S. competitiveness was overstated, the recent focus on patenting and licensing as the essential ingredient in university-industry collaboration and knowledge transfer may be no less exaggerated. The emphasis on the Bayh-Dole Act as a catalyst to these interactions also seems somewhat misplaced."

Still, the point to be emphasized here is not so much the efficacy of the policy but the clearly stated goal: to promote the spillover of knowledge from universities for commercialization that would foster innovation and ultimately economic growth. That such a policy goal did not have a high enough priority to come to fruition in the postwar era, characterized by the Solow Model, reflects the shift in policy priorities and, ultimately, instruments, as the economy evolved from being capital-driven to knowledge-driven and finally becoming the entrepreneurial economy.

Another example of the enabling approach inherent in entrepreneurship policy instruments is provided by the Small Business Innovation Research (SBIR) program, which was enacted in the early 1980s. The SBIR was a response to the loss of American competitiveness in global markets. Congress mandated that each federal agency allocate about 4 percent of its annual budget to funding innovative small firms as a mechanism for restoring American international competitiveness

(Wessner, 2000). The SBIR provides a mandate to the major R&D agencies in the United States to allocate a share of the research budget to innovative small firms. In 2001, the SBIR program amounted to around $1.4 billion. The SBIR program consists of three phases for involved firms. Phase I is oriented toward determining the scientific and technical merit along with the feasibility of a proposed research idea. A Phase I award provides an opportunity for a small business to establish the feasibility and technical merit of a proposed innovation. The duration of the award is 6 months and cannot exceed $100,000. Phase II extends the technological idea and emphasizes commercialization. A Phase II Award is granted to only the most promising of the Phase I projects based on scientific/technical merit, the expected value to the funding agency, company capability, and commercial potential. The duration of the award is a maximum of 24 months and cannot exceed $750,000. Approximately 40 percent of the Phase I Awards continue on to Phase II. Phase III involves additional private funding for the commercial application of a technology. A Phase III Award is for the infusion and use of a product into the commercial market. Private sector investment, in various forms, is typically present in Phase III. Under the Small Business Research and Development Enhancement Act of 1992, funding in Phase I was increased to $100,000, and in Phase II to $750,000.

The SBIR represents about 60 percent of all public entrepreneurial finance programs. Taken together, the public small-business finance is about two-thirds as large as private venture capital. In 2004, the sum of equity financing provided through and guaranteed by public programs financing SMEs was around $3.0 billion, which amounted to more than 60 percent of the total funding disbursed by traditional venture funds in that year. Equally as important, the emphasis on SBIR and most public funds is on early-stage finance, which is generally ignored by private venture capital. Some of the most innovative American companies that received early-stage finance from SBIR include Apple Computer, Chiron, Compaq, and Intel.

There is compelling evidence that the SBIR program has had a positive impact on economic performance in the United States (Lerner, 1999; Wessner, 2000). The benefits have been documented as follows:

- The survival and growth rates of SBIR recipients have exceeded those of firms not receiving SBIR funding.
- The SBIR induces scientists involved in biomedical research to alter their career path. By applying the scientific knowledge to commercialization, these scientists shift their career trajectories away from basic research toward entrepreneurial activities.
- The SBIR awards provide a source of funding for scientists to launch startup firms that otherwise would not have had access to funding.
- SBIR awards have a powerful demonstration effect. Scientists commercializing research results by starting companies induce colleagues to consider applications and the commercial potential of their own research.

Sternberg (1996) has shown that a number of government-sponsored technology policies in four countries—the United Kingdom, Germany, the United States, and Japan—has triggered the startup of new firms. The majority of the startup programs are targeted toward eliminating particular bottlenecks in the development and financing of new firms. Analyzing the impact of 70 innovations centers on the development of technology-based small firms, Sternberg (1990) finds that the majority of the entrepreneurs find a number of advantages from locating at an innovation center.

An analytical approach common among most studies examining the impact of universities on entrepreneurship is to analyze the influence of various university programs, such as incubators or technology transfer offices, on firms that already exist. Yet a different type of impact from the programs may arise by inducing scientists and engineers to become entrepreneurs who otherwise would never have become involved in commercialization. For example, *Nature Magazine* (2003, p. 988) reports, "Jeff Alberts, a psychology professor, was trained as a scientist, not an entrepreneur. But with the help of government funding, he turned his knack for designing animal cages and other experimental apparatus into a successful small business. Alberts made the move in the 1980s after working on part of a space project that involved developmental biology experiments using rats. The only problem was that Alberts knew little about business, so he turned to the recently established SBIR programme for help in getting his company off the ground."

Such impact on the career trajectories of scientists could be an important aspect of public policy, because, as chapter 3 suggested, entrepreneurship can serve as a key mechanism permeating the filter impeding knowledge spillovers. Because entrepreneurship can serve as an important mechanism facilitating knowledge spillovers, policies that induce scientists, engineers, and other knowledge workers to become entrepreneurs may have a significant impact on economic growth.

Not only are entrepreneurship policy instruments decidedly distinct from those traditionally used toward business, and small business in particular, but the locus of such enabling policies is also different. The instruments constraining the freedom of firms to contract—antitrust regulation and public ownership—were generally controlled and used at the federal or national level. By contrast, the instruments of entrepreneurship policy are generally applied at the decentralized level of a state or city level.

For example, the Advanced Research Program in Texas provided support for basic research and the strengthening of the infrastructure of the University of Texas, which has played a central role in developing a high-technology cluster around Austin (Feller, 1997). The Thomas Edison Centers in Ohio, the Advanced Technology Centers in New Jersey, and the Centers for Advanced Technology at Case Western Reserve University, Rutgers University, and the University of Rochester have supported generic, precompetitive research. This support has generally provided diversified technology development involving a mix of activities encompassing a broad spectrum of industrial collaborators. The Edison Technology Program of Ohio was established by the state of Ohio as a means of transferring technology from universities and government research institutes to new firm start-ups. Carlsson and Braunerhjelm (1999) explain how the Edison BioTechnology Center serves an important dual role as a "bridging institution" between academic research and industry and between new startups and potential sources of finance. The Edison Centers, in particular, try to link the leading universities and medical institutions, businesses, and foundations to civic and state organizations in Ohio in order to create new business opportunities. Numerous centers exist across the state. Similarly, the Edison Program has established a bridging institution to support polymer research and technology in Ohio. Carlsson and Braunerhjelm (1999) credit the program with the startup of new high-technology firms in Ohio.

Other examples of enabling policies are evidenced by the plethora of science, technology, and research parks. Lugar and Goldstein (1991) conducted a review of research parks and concluded that such parks are created to promote the competitiveness of a particular region. Lugar (2001, p. 47) further noted that "the most successful parks . . . have a profound impact on a region and its competitiveness." A distinct exemplar of this effect is found in the Research Triangle Park in North Carolina.

These programs promoting entrepreneurship in a regional context are typical of the new enabling policies to promote entrepreneurial activity. While these entrepreneurial policies are evolving, they are clearly gaining in importance and impact in the overall portfolio of economic policy instruments.

In fact, as Lundström and Stevenson (2005) point out, entrepreneurship policy ranges across a broad spectrum of instruments spanning taxes, immigration, education, and more direct instruments such as the provision of finance or training. If entrepreneurship policy can be viewed as the purposeful attempt to create an entrepreneurial economy, entire institutions that were the cornerstone of the Solow Economy are being challenged and reconfigured to create the entrepreneurial economy. According to Powers (2005, p. 126), "The cultural sameness and conformity that prevailed after World War II—the era of Father Knows Best and Betty Crocker— have been replaced by popular pursuit of difference and self-expression."

10.4.4 Diffusion

The first sighting of the entrepreneurial economy was California's Silicon Valley in the 1980s. As Gordon Moore, the co-founder of Intel, who has been said to rank among the founding fathers of Silicon Valley, and Davis (2004, p. 7) suggest, "We hold that the central element in the history of Silicon Valley is the founding of a previously unknown type of regional dynamic, high-technology economy." Certainly at that point in time, innovation and new technology were generally associated with the large flagship corporations, such as IBM, Wang, and DEC, which seemed invincible with their large armies of engineers and scientists. These scientists demonstrated undying loyalty to their employers, forged from lifetime contracts, and had a generally paternalistic stance toward their employees.

In the 1984 bestseller by Peters and Waterman, *In Search of Excellence*, which documented the top 50 U.S. corporations, these characteristics not only placed IBM at the top of the list but also served as a shining example for corporate America to learn from and imitate. The incipient entrepreneurial economy of Silicon Valley provided a striking contrast, where people were quick to leave their companies to start new firms and, on occasion, entirely new industries.

While IBM was large and bureaucratic with rules and hierarchical decision making, the emerging Silicon Valley entrepreneurial economy thrived on spontaneity, participation, openness, and a general disdain for rules and hierarchy. If obedience and conformity were trademarks of the capital-driven economy corresponding to the Solow Model, the entrepreneurial economy values above all creativity, originality, independence, and autonomy.

The entrepreneurial economy subsequently diffused to places such as Route 128 around Boston, Research Triangle Park in North Carolina, and Austin, Texas. More recently, the diffusion of the entrepreneurial economy in the United States has been more pervasive, including not just the Washington, D.C., region (northern Virginia and Maryland), San Diego, Los Angeles, Salt Lake City, and Seattle but also smaller cities such as Madison, Wisconsin.

The flagship entrepreneurial economy institutions chiefly focus on networks and linkages and include research universities, such as technology parks, and nontraditional sources of early-stage capital, such as angel capital and venture capital. These institutions are a departure from the Solow economy stalwarts, which were unions, big government programs, and corporate hierarchy.

Diffusion of the entrepreneurial economy has in some cases occurred organically, in the absence of dedicated and targeted public policies. In other cases, public policy, including a broad spectrum of public-private partnerships, has been directed to foster the transition to an entrepreneurial economy.

The emergence and diffusion of entrepreneurship policy has not been restricted to the United States. For example, the European public policy stance toward the entrepreneurial economy has evolved through five distinct stages: denial, recognition, envy, consensus, and attainment.

The first stage was denial. During the 1980s and early 1990s, European policymakers looked to Silicon Valley with skepticism and doubts. After all, in 1968 Jean Jacques Servan-Schreiber had warned Europeans to beware the "American Challenge" in the form of the "dynamisms, organization, innovation, and boldness that characterize the giant American corporations" (p. 159). Because giant corporations were needed to amass the requisite resources for innovation, Servan-Schrieber advocated a European policy targeting the creation of large corporations to compete with the American leading corporations in a global economy.

Europe was used to looking across the Atlantic and facing a competitive threat from large multinational corporations, such as General Motors, U.S. Steel, and IBM, not nameless and unrecognizable startup firms in exotic industries such as software and biotechnology. In fact, the Cecchini Report to the European Commission in 1988 documented the economic gains in terms of the scale economies to be achieved from the anticipated European integration. The emerging firms such as Apple, Microsoft, and Intel seemed interesting but lacking sufficient relevance for the mainstay businesses in the automobile, textile, machinery, and chemical industries, which were the obvious engines of European competitiveness, growth, and employment. The high performance of Silicon Valley was generally condemned as suffering from a short-term perspective, where long-term investments and commitments were sacrificed for short-term profits.

The second stage, during the mid-1990s, was recognition. Europe recognized that the high performance exhibited by the entrepreneurial economy in Silicon Valley did, in fact, deliver sustainable long-run performance. The theory of comparative advantage typically evoked during this phase was that Europe would provide the automobiles, textiles, and machine tools. The entrepreneurial economy of Silicon Valley, Route 128, and the Research Triangle Park would produce the software and microprocessors. Each continent would specialize in its comparative advantage and then trade with each other. Thus, Europe held to its traditional institutions and policies that channeled resources into traditional moderate-technology industries.

The third stage, envy, was characterized by two components. The first involved economic performance, in particular, growth and unemployment. The second involved the perceived ability to deploy the now recognized mechanism essential for attaining that performance: entrepreneurship. By the mid-1990s, Europe exhibited a floundering economic performance, but at the same time it was widely thought that its traditions, cultures, and institutions precluded the shift to an entrepreneurial economy. Thus, the German Economic Model, discussed earlier in this chapter, demonstrated that capitalism could generate a high and equitable *Wohlstand* and also have a friendly face.

That the bottom would drop out of such a successful national economic model, which was responsible for postwar German Wohlstand, sent shock waves through the country and across Europe. Early in 1998, the unemployment rate reached nearly 13 percent, representing 4.8 million people (*New York Times*, 1998, p. A8), which was the highest unemployment level since the pre-Nazi Weimar Republic.[13] One of Germany's most widely read weekly magazines, *Stern*, responded with the headline, "Germany before the Crash?" and warned of unemployment levels exceeding 5 million people (*Stern*, 1997). By 2005, the number of 5 million had been passed.

Unemployment of such proportions threatens the once solid economic basis on which postwar German democracy was built. One of the most serious daily newspapers in the country, *Die Zeit*, alarmingly asked: "Will Bonn become the Weimar Republic?" Such concerns reflect a troubled, questioning social mood. The public's confidence in the economy and the government's ability to manage the crisis has eroded considerably. In the September 1998 election, this shaken confidence led to the defeat of the CDU and the reigning *Bundeskanzler*, Helmut Kohl, and the election of the SPD challenger, Gerhard Schröder. Schröder was reelected in 2002.

As economic growth stalled and unemployment began to ratchet upward in the early 1990s, German reunification was frequently cited as the culprit. However, it is clear that the burden imposed on the West German economic model by absorbing 18 million people from the former communist German Democratic Republic (GDR) is not singularly responsible for Germany's current problems. At the heart of the German crisis is an economic model that once served as the engine driving the Wirtschaftswunder, and proved to be a great success with the capital-driven Solow economy, but actually imposes a high value of β, or significant barriers to entrepreneurship, thus impeding the shift to the entrepreneurial economy. An economic system that is no longer viable in West Germany was rigidly imposed on the five new Bundesländer.

As European unemployment in countries such as Germany, France, and Spain soared into double digits and growth stagnated, the capacity of the entrepreneurial economy in places like Silicon Valley to generate both jobs and higher wages became the object of envy. The United States and Europe seemed to be on divergent trajectories. The *separate but equal* doctrine from the concept of comparative advantage yielded to the *different but better* doctrine of dynamic competitive advantage. This was reflected by the strikingly divergent rates of economic growth and corresponding unemployment rates between the two sides of the Atlantic during the 1990s. At the start of the decade, in 1991, per capita GDP barely differed between the United States and the leading European counterparts. For example, GDP per capita was only $1,000 higher in the United States than in France. The gap was somewhat higher, $2,000, with Italy and Germany, and $5,000 with the United Kingdom.[14]

However, by 2001, the trans-Atlantic gap in GDP had exploded to $11,000 with the United Kingdom, $12,000 with Germany, $13,000 with France, and $16,000 with Italy. Taken as a whole, the trans-Atlantic gap in the standard of living, as measured by GDP per capita, was greater at the turn of the century than it had been in nearly four decades during the postwar era (Thurow, 2002). The trans-Atlantic gap in economic growth was reflected in divergent unemployment rates. Even as unemployment sank to the lowest levels since the 1960s in the United States, on the other side of the Atlantic, unemployment skyrocketed to postwar highs. This divergence in economic performance in the 1990s was reflected by the creation of 22 million net new jobs in the United States, while no new net jobs were created in Europe.

As the entrepreneurial economy continued to diffuse across the United States, most policy-makers despaired that European traditions, institutions, culture, and values were seemingly inconsistent and incompatible with the entrepreneurial economy. For example, Joschka Fischer, a Green Party member, and more recently the foreign minister of Germany, mourned in 1995 that "a company like Microsoft would never have a chance in Germany"(*Economist*, 1995b, pp. 75–76).

In fact, it was not just the newly created entrepreneurial companies such as Microsoft, Intel, and Apple Computers that seemed to elude Germany as well as the rest of Europe. Thurow (2002) points out that 20 percent of the largest firms that did not grow large as a result of mergers in the world in 2002 are new companies founded in the United States subsequent to 1960. By contrast, there is only one European startup included in the list of the largest enterprises in the world: SAP, which ranked as number 73.[15] As Thurow (2002, p. 35) concludes, "Europe is falling behind because it doesn't build the new big firms of the future."

The year 1989 brought unification to Germany and also accelerated the process of globalization by enabling previously excluded countries to participate in the global economy. Globalization, combined with the telecommunications revolution, has shattered the viability of the social contract inherent in the consensus demanded of the German *Sozialmarktwirtschaft*. Pressed to maintain competitiveness in traditional industries, where economic activity can be easily transferred across geographic space to access lower production costs, the largest and most prominent German companies have deployed two strategic responses. The first was to offset greater wage differentials between Germany and low-cost locations by increasing productivity through the substitution of technology and capital for labor.

The second was to locate new plants and establishments outside of Germany. What both strategic responses have in common is that the German flagship companies have been downsizing employment in the domestic market, resulting in levels of unemployment not seen in Germany since World War II.

Why has structural change proven so difficult to implement in Germany? *Der Spiegel* observes, "Global structural change has had an impact on the German economy that only a short time ago would have been unimaginable: Many of the products, such as automobiles, machinery, chemicals and steel are no longer competitive in global markets. And in the industries of the future, like biotechnology and electronics, the German companies are barely participating" (1994, pp. 82–83).

None of the prevailing actors in the industry-labor-government consensus has an interest in championing the ability of individuals to move outside of the status quo institutions to start new firms. New firms in new industries pose a threat to the large, established firms by generating not just new competition in product markets but also competition for the best employees with the best new ideas. Similarly, new firms in new industries may generate new employment, but those jobs may not be compatible with union practices.

Part of the envy associated with this stage emanated from what could be characterized as the industry-union-government cartel inherent in the model of consensus (Audretsch, 1999). The interests in preserving the profitability of the status quo in German flagship companies and wage levels of unionized workers associated with those firms provided a strong common interest to block the requisite reforms in deregulation and labor market flexibility to trigger the startup and growth of new firms in knowledge-based industries.

The fourth stage, during the final years of the last century, was consensus. European policy-makers reached a consensus that not only was the entrepreneurial economy superior to the managed economy but a commitment had to be forged to create a European entrepreneurial economy.

Rather than despairing that the United States had achieved what Europe could not, European policy-makers instituted a broad set of policies to create a European entrepreneurial economy. These European policy-makers looked across the Atlantic and realized that if places such as North Carolina, Austin, and Salt Lake City could implement conscious targeted policies to create the entrepreneurial economy, cities such as Munich, Helsinki, Stockholm, and the Netherlands' Randstad (the region between Rotterdam and Amsterdam) could as well. After all, Europe had a number of assets and traditions, such as a highly educated and skilled labor force and world-class research institutions. In addition, Europe had a long tradition of government-industry-worker partnerships that, when redirected, could be well suited for the entrepreneurial economy. Perhaps most important, Europe had traditions dating back to the Enlightenment focusing on creativity, originality, and independence of thinking and action.

The fifth stage will be attainment. While Europe may not be there quite yet, there are definite signs that an entrepreneurial economy is emerging on the continent. Consider the cover story (*Der Spiegel*, 1994, p. 110) of one of the most serious German weekly magazines, *Der Spiegel*, which recently proclaimed,

"Handys, Hightech and Reform: Good Morning, Europe—How the Old Continent Is Attacking the Economic Power USA."

Still, the relevant point to be emphasized here is not whether or not Europe has succeeded or will succeed in attaining an entrepreneurial economy but the shift in policy focus within the past 15 years, away from the status quo in industrial structures and toward a vigorous commitment to creating an entrepreneurial economy. Thus, entrepreneurship policy as a bona fide approach to generating economic growth has not only emerged in a few places but diffused across a broad spectrum of national, regional, and local contexts.

10.5 Conclusions

There is no assured recipe for public policy to create an entrepreneurial economy. But the effort to do so has resulted in the emergence of a distinct new public policy approach to generate economic growth: entrepreneurship policy. Although the goals remain the same, economic growth and employment creation, or at least maintenance, the mechanism used (entrepreneurship) and accompanying instruments are strikingly different.

The downsizing of federal agencies charged with the regulation of business combined with widespread privatization throughout the OECD countries has been interpreted by many scholars as the eclipse of government intervention. But to interpret deregulation, privatization, and the decreased emphasis of competition policies as the end of government intervention in business ignores an important public policy shift. Rather, the public policy approach to constraining the freedom of firms to contract, through the policy instruments of regulation, public ownership, and antitrust, has given way to a new, more diffused and decentralized set of enabling policies with a focus on the creation and commercialization of new ideas, especially in new firms—entrepreneurship policy.

As, first, the capital-driven Solow model and, more recently, the knowledge-driven Romer model have not delivered the expected levels of economic performance, a mandate for entrepreneurship policy has emerged and begun to diffuse not just across regions of the United States but throughout the entire globe. Whether or not specific policy instruments will work in their particular contexts is not the point of this book. What is striking, however, is the emergence and diffusion of an entirely new public policy approach to generate economic growth: entrepreneurship policy. On this new mantel of entrepreneurship policy, Standorts, ranging from communities to cities, states, and even entire nations, hang their hopes, dreams, and aspirations for prosperity and security.

11

Entrepreneurship as Creative Construction

A quiet and virtually unnoticed revolution has transformed public policy. Where policy to ensure economic growth and job creation once looked to fiscal and monetary stimulation, on the one hand, and the large corporation, on the other, a new approach has emerged focusing on entrepreneurship. What once seemed anathema to economic efficiency and prosperity in the postwar era—small and new firms—has become the engine of economic growth and job creation not just in one economy but around the world. This book has attempted to explain why the goal of creating an entrepreneurial economy has become the priority of public policy.

This book raises four principal questions: (1) What is the impact of entrepreneurship on economic growth? (2) Why does entrepreneurship influence growth? (3) How does entrepreneurship affect growth? (4) Why has entrepreneurship become more important over time?

To answer these questions, we used the framework provided by the Knowledge Spillover Theory of Entrepreneurship, introduced in chapter 3, to derive a series of main hypotheses: the Endogenous Entrepreneurship Hypothesis, Growth Hypothesis, Localization Hypothesis, Entrepreneurial Performance Hypothesis, and Entrepreneurial Access Hypothesis. In particular, chapter 3 suggests why entrepreneurship might influence economic growth. As the well-established Griliches model of the knowledge production function suggests, firms will purposefully invest in activities to generate new economic knowledge that can, in turn, generate innovative output.

However, as Arrow (1962) pointed out, the appropriation of investments in new ideas is not so straightforward. Burdened with high levels of uncertainty, imposing asymmetries, and significant costs of transaction, the potential economic value of a new idea is not always obvious and certainly not unanimous across economic agents. Thus, the production, or simply the existence, of new ideas can result in a difference in their valuation not only across economic agents but also between knowledge workers and the decision-making hierarchies of incumbent organizations.

Divergent valuation of new ideas may make it difficult and prohibitively costly for an incumbent firm to pursue all or even most of the new ideas at its disposal. What happens to those ideas not pursued by the firm for commercialization?

Here again, Griliches (1992), but also Romer (1986), Lucas (1993), and Krugman (1991a, 1991b), provided an important answer: knowledge spills over for use by other, third-party firms. In the case of knowledge spillovers, the commercialization of new ideas will be enacted not by the firm producing those ideas through purposeful and targeted investments in new knowledge but by another firm.

The insight by Arrow (1962) that knowledge is nonexcludable and non-exhaustive has triggered a vast literature and policy concern about the role of intellectual property rights and other instruments to protect and facilitate the appropriation of returns accruing from investments in new economic knowledge. But what if a new idea is not valued by any incumbent firm, whether the firm originally generating the new knowledge or any other incumbent organization? There are many reasons to expect a positive correlation across firms in evaluating new ideas. First and foremost, the same challenge confronting the firm producing the new idea may confront all firms: the high degree of uncertainty, asymmetries, and costs of transaction. Often the knowledge workers who had the idea in the first place and understand the idea the best value its potential differently than incumbent organizations do.

In this case, there will be no knowledge spillover. Investments were made in creating new knowledge, both privately from within the firm, but also publicly, if generation of the new knowledge used any public knowledge emanating from research at universities or publicly provided investments in human capital. However, in the absence of knowledge spillover, such investments will not be appropriated either by the firm or by society. The social investments of education and research are also expected to generate a return in growth and employment.

Thus, the spillover of knowledge that exists by assumption in the Griliches (1992), Romer (1986), Lucas (1993), and Krugman (1991a, 1991b) models, may, in fact, not be so automatic but may be impeded by a filter, or what is referred to in chapter 3 as the knowledge filter. The knowledge filter serves to impede, if not preempt, the spillover and commercialization of knowledge.

Entrepreneurship can contribute to economic growth by serving as a mechanism that permeates the knowledge filter. It is a virtual consensus that entrepreneurship revolves around the recognition of opportunities along with the cognitive decision to commercialize those opportunities by starting a new firm. If investments in new knowledge create asymmetric opportunities, because they are more apparent or valued more highly by economic agents (potential entrepreneurs) than by the incumbent firms themselves, the only organizational context for commercializing that new idea will be a new firm. Thus, by serving as a conduit for knowledge spillovers that might otherwise not exist, entrepreneurship permeates the knowledge filter and provides the missing link to economic growth.

Confronted with the nontrivial knowledge filter, investments in labor, physical capital, and knowledge capital may not result in adequate levels of economic growth and employment creation. Entrepreneurship makes a unique contribution to economic growth by permeating the knowledge filter and commercializing ideas that would otherwise remain uncommercialized. Thus, the Growth Hypothesis posits that, ceteris parabus, entrepreneurship will have a positive impact on economic performance.

However, as the literature on the new economic geography has found, knowledge spillovers tend to be geographically localized. Thus, the Localization Hypothesis posits that the link between entrepreneurship and economic growth will be geographically bounded, since the entrepreneurial response to the creation of new opportunities emanating from investments in knowledge will also be spatially localized.

Empirical evidence supporting the Growth Hypothesis was provided in chapter 4. Evoking the model of growth accounting as pioneered by Robert Solow (1956), entrepreneurship capital is included in a production function model along with the traditional factors of labor and physical capital but also knowledge capital. The econometric estimation is based on linking these factors to economic performance in German regions in the 1990s. Robust and consistent results provide empirical evidence consistent with the Growth Hypothesis. Regions exhibiting a greater degree of entrepreneurial activity also generate higher levels of economic growth and performance.

Entrepreneurial opportunities are not at all exogenous, or given, in the Knowledge Spillover Theory of Entrepreneurship. Rather, they are endogenously generated by the extent of investments in new knowledge. Thus, a context rich in knowledge will generate more entrepreneurial opportunities than a context with impoverished knowledge.

The Endogenous Entrepreneurship Hypothesis challenges, or at least provides an alternative to, the prevailing view in the entrepreneurship literature that assumes entrepreneurial opportunities are given. The tradition in the entrepreneurship literature has been to focus on variations across individual-specific characteristics, inclinations, and proclivities in explaining entrepreneurial activity. We certainly do not want to contest whether entrepreneurs are born or made, but the findings of chapter 5 are consistent with the Endogenous Entrepreneurship Hypothesis and suggest that context matters. In particular, those contexts that are rich in knowledge generate more entrepreneurial opportunities; contexts with impoverished knowledge have fewer entrepreneurial opportunities.

Thus, while the entrepreneurship literature has not addressed where entrepreneurial opportunities come from but takes them as given, the Knowledge Spillover Theory of Entrepreneurship identifies at least one important source. Investment in new knowledge and ideas systematically generates more entrepreneurial opportunities, because these new ideas are not fully or completely commercialized by the incumbent organizations. Of course, whether such entrepreneurial opportunities will be pursued and ultimately be translated into economic growth depends on the value of β, or the extent to which barriers to entrepreneurship impede the decision to actually become an entrepreneur.

How entrepreneurship matters is explained in chapters 6, 7, 8, and 9. In addressing the Localization Hypothesis, chapter 6 showed that the role of knowledge spillovers tends to shape the location of entrepreneurial firms. In particular, when spillovers involve tacit knowledge, geographic proximity to the knowledge source becomes more important. In contrast, when spillovers involve codified knowledge, geographic proximity becomes less important. Thus, the actual role of geographic proximity in accessing knowledge spillovers seems to depend on the type of knowledge as well as the spillover mechanism. Why geographic location matters for entrepreneurial firms was made clear in chapter 7. In an empirical test of the Entrepreneurial Performance Hypothesis, the results suggest that geographic proximity to a knowledge source bestows competitive advantage resulting in a superior performance in firm growth.

However, location alone may not suffice in providing access to knowledge spillovers. Chapter 8 examined the Entrepreneurial Access Hypothesis. The empirical evidence suggests external knowledge spillovers need to be accessed and absorbed. In particular, we identified two factors that facilitate the absorption of external knowledge spillovers: a spillover conduit, such as a board director or manager, and close geographic proximity. Similarly, chapter 9 examined the Entrepreneurial Finance Hypothesis. The empirical evidence suggested not only that entrepreneurial firms have a high propensity for equity-based finance rather than traditional bank-based finance but also that entrepreneurial firms financed by venture capital exhibit systematically higher rates of growth.

Chapters 6, 7, 8, and 9 identify key strategies deployed by entrepreneurial firms that ultimately render them as conduits of knowledge spillovers. These strategies involve locational proximity to knowledge sources, roles for boards and managers that involve accessing and absorbing external knowledge spillovers, and nontraditional equity-based sources of finance, such as venture capital.

Neither the Knowledge Spillover Theory of Entrepreneurship presented in chapter 3 nor the empirical results presented in the ensuing chapters explain why entrepreneurship has become more important over time. They do, however, suggest an interpretation that can be used to infer what has triggered the growing importance of entrepreneurship.

The framework presented in chapter 3 argues that entrepreneurship contributes to economic growth by serving as a conduit of knowledge spillovers, thereby commercializing knowledge and new ideas that might otherwise remain uncommercialized. The increased importance of new knowledge as an important factor not just of production but also of international comparative advantage in the leading developed economies suggests that more entrepreneurial opportunities are being generated. A Standort with a low β, or low barriers to entrepreneurship, and a high endowment of entrepreneurship capital is able to transform those knowledge investments into concomitant economic growth, employment creation, and international competitiveness. By contrast, a Standort with a high β, or high barriers to entrepreneurship, and a low endowment of entrepreneurship capital is ineffective in appropriating the value of knowledge investments in growth and employment. The greater the role of knowledge and ideas, the greater the potential contribution of entrepreneurship to economic growth.

In the postwar economy characterized by the Solow Model, technical change was exogenous, delivered as manna from Heaven, so that neither entrepreneurship nor anything else predictable could generate its provision. With a focus on physical capital as the engine of economic growth, employment, and global competitiveness, there seemed to be little contribution to be made by the startup of a new firm. Although entrepreneurial opportunities may have been bountiful, they did not seem to have much to do with the perceived sources of not only efficiency but also growth: size and scale economies. Thus, though small firms may have been valued in certain countries, such as the United States, they did not seem to be important for economic growth but for social and political reasons. And, as we said in chapter 2, small firms were not universally recognized as an essential element of society throughout the West, let alone throughout the world.

With the emergence of knowledge as a recognized factor generating growth, entrepreneurship seemed even less relevant. As the Griliches model of the knowledge production function suggests, innovation and new knowledge are the result of large investments in R&D, which seemed to bestow the large corporation with an even greater competitive advantage than had been the case with scale economies in production. After all, Schumpeter (1942, p. 132) had concluded that, due to scale economies in the production of new economic knowledge, large corporations would have the innovative advantage over small and new enterprises, and the economic role of small and new firms would diminish and perhaps disappear: "Innovation itself is being reduced to routine. Technological progress is increasingly becoming the business of teams of trained specialists who turn out what is required and make it work in predictable ways."

The "routinization" of R&D reflects a focus on the role of knowledge on the large, fairly established, and mature corporations and industries, which dominated the postwar industrial landscape, such as automobiles, steel, textiles, and even mainframe computers. Such routinized R&D may be more appropriate for incremental innovations that improve existing products rather than create entirely new industries.

It may be that globalization has jolted the comparative advantage, so that production based on such routinized R&D can be increasingly outsourced to lower-cost locations, as Vernon (1966) had predicted. What he did not predict in his model, however, were revolutions in both technology and politics, both accelerating and extending the degree to which relatively standardized activity could be outsourced. This would suggest that perhaps the comparative advantage of Standort in the contemporary global economy is shifting toward not only knowledge but types of knowledge and ideas that are increasingly focused on the earlier stage of innovative activity. Those conditions generating entrepreneurial opportunities — high uncertainty, asymmetries, and transaction costs — are even more prominent in earlier stage activity. As economic activity involves earlier stages of innovative activity, the knowledge filter becomes more severe. Thus, entrepreneurship gains in importance as the missing link in the process of economic growth. Globalization has resulted in the emergence of the entrepreneurial economy as the mechanism by which (public) investments in knowledge can be appropriated in growth, employment, and competitiveness.

We would not want to argue that the view of the youthful Schumpeter (1911 [1934, p. xxvii]) was wrong about "a perennial gale of creative destruction is going through capitalism." However, it does seem that twenty-first-century entrepreneurship has more to do with *creative construction* than with creative destruction. By facilitating the spillover of knowledge investments that might otherwise remain uncommercialized, entrepreneurship takes little away from the incumbent enterprises, but instead creates alternative opportunities for employment. Rather, as we suggested in chapter 2, the *destruction* comes from the side of globalization that presents competitive alternatives to standardized production in high-cost Standort. This destructive element, emanating from globalization, comes with or without entrepreneurship. The exposure of a Standort to global competition has less to do with its endowment of entrepreneurship capital and more to do with its traditional source for economic activity.

By contrast, the *construction* comes from an entirely different source: the entrepreneurship capital of that Standort. Perhaps because he dealt with a singular closed and unglobalized economy in both his early (1911) and later (1942) writings, Schumpeter did not consider that the *destructive force* would actually come from opportunities coming from outside of the domestic economy. In contrast, the entrepreneurial opportunities that might not otherwise have been pursued come from within the Standort. Thus, rather than serving as a force for destruction of the status quo, entrepreneurship serves as a *constructive force* for a new economic alternative from knowledge and ideas that otherwise might have not been commercialized.

To the individual, the knowledge accessed to reach the entrepreneurial decision is virtually a free good. To the firm or nonprofit organization, the knowledge has no a priori economic value. Whereas Schumpeter's (1942) pronouncement that innovation is becoming routinized may have been correct, the generation of entrepreneurial opportunities and their concomitant assessment by economic agents are anything but routine. Thus, entrepreneurship is a constructive force because it increases the value of knowledge and ideas that might otherwise not be pursued and commercialized. The Endogenous Entrepreneurship Hypothesis, as confirmed through the econometric analyses of chapters 5 and 6, suggests that by serving as a conduit of knowledge spillovers, entrepreneurship serves not to detract from the incumbent firms and industries but to create new alternatives.

In terms of the two disparate policy directions underlying the mandate for entrepreneurship policy, identified in chapter 10, the first policy direction emanating from the Solow model reflects the destruction inherent in the loss of traditional capital-based firms and entire industries based on the factor of capital. In contrast, the second direction emanating from the Romer model reflects the creative construction of a viable and sustainable alternative: knowledge-based economic activity. Exposure to globalization is attributable for the destruction; entrepreneurship is attributable for the sustainable alternative: *creative construction*.

Thus, the perspective of the singular or effectively closed economy at the turn of the last century may have led Schumpeter (1911) to conclude that the contribution of entrepreneurship is through the destruction of the status quo by displacement by new firms, but in the globalized economy of the twenty-first-century economy, the destruction comes from global competition. Creative construction of new possibilities and sources of growth comes from entrepreneurship.

Perhaps the role of entrepreneurship in generating creative construction rather than creative destruction explains the emergence of entrepreneurship policy at the heart of the strategic management of places, or *Standortpolitik*. As the comparative advantage in physical capital is lost, investments in knowledge, both private and public, are needed to create new jobs. Whether or not such knowledge investments at a Standort, both private and public, actually result in a public return in growth and employment may depend on the existence of entrepreneurship capital. Thus, the effort to create an entrepreneurial economy shifts the focus of public policy to reducing β, or barriers to entrepreneurship. As chapter 10 suggests, the emergence of entrepreneurship policy can be interpreted as an effort to create an entrepreneurial economy, which can be defined as one in which entrepreneurship plays a key role in generating economic growth.

Perhaps the recognition that investments in knowledge may not suffice and that entrepreneurship can serve as the missing link to permeating the knowledge filter impeding economic growth is not so new. As Johann Wolfgang von Goethe observed some two centuries ago, "Es ist nicht genug zu wissen, man muss es auch anwenden; es ist nicht genug zu wollen, man muss es auch tun" (Knowledge alone does not suffice, it must also be applied: wanting is not enough, one has to actually do it).

Notes

4. Entrepreneurship Capital and Economic Performance

1. According to Gartner and Carter (2003), "Entrepreneurial behavior involves the activities of individuals who are associated with creating new organizations rather than the activities of individuals who are involved with maintaining or changing the operations of on-going established organizations" (p. 195).

2. Firms with low credit requirements, with a low number of employees, or with illimited legal forms are registered only with a time lag. These are typically retail stores or catering firms. See Harhoff and Steil (1997) for more detail on the ZEW foundation panels.

3. Cobb and Douglas (1928) estimated a production elasticity of 0.75 for labor and 0.25 for capital, implying that an increase of labor (capital) input by 1 percent increases output by 0.75 percent (0.25 percent). Virtually all subsequent estimates that have been done for different regions or industries have found results in ranges between 0.66 to 0.75 for labor and 0.25 and 0.33 for capital.

4. See, for example, Barro and Sala-i-Martin, 1995, p. 384, and the subsequent literature on convergence.

5. See Barrow and Sala-i-Martin, 1995.

5. Endogenous Entrepreneurship

1. See, for example, Glaeser et al., 1992; Henderson, Kuncoro, and Turner, 1995; Henderson, 1997; or Ellison and Glaeser, 1997, for a discussion of these types of externalities and the underlying processes. Keilbach (2000) gives a summary of this literature.

2. For a discussion of this measure, see section 4.2.

3. Here, we follow the classification used in the reports of the Federal Ministry of Education and Research. See, for example, Grupp et al. (2000).

4. The impact of funding schemes can be measured, for example, using micro-econometric evaluation procedures, for example, Arvanitis and Keilbach (2002).

6. *University Spillovers and Entrepreneurial Location*

1. See also Stephan et al. (2002), analyzing the firm's placement of doctoral students.

2. Abundant empirical evidence shows that universities differ extremely in the amount and quality of their academic and teaching output (see Winston, 1999, and Thursby, 2000, for the United States; Lehmann and Warning, 2004, for the U.K.; and Fabel et al., 2002, for Germany).

3. This does not necessarily hold when the results are clearly structured by formulas as is the case in economic theory.

4. While the rules of the Neuer Markt are more stringent than those of most exchanges in Europe, they remain both more relaxed and less frequently enforced by the *Bundesau- sichtsamt fuer den Wertpapierhandel* (BAWe) than the SEC equivalent.

5. *Focus*, No. 41, October 2004, p. 118.

6. Over time, publications in social science and natural science did not vary across the universities (see Warning, 2004).

7. The University of Ulm (University of Erfurt) has no students in social science (natural sciences).

8. This semiparametric technique provides a general class of models in which the conditional quantiles have a linear form. In its simplest form, the least absolute deviation estimator fits medians to a linear function of covariates. The method of quantile regression is potentially attractive for the same reason that the median or other quantiles are a better measure of location than the mean. Other useful features are the robustness against outliers and more efficient likelihood estimators than least square estimators. Besides the technical features, quantile regressions allow that potentially different solutions at distinct quantiles may be interpreted as differences in the response of the dependent variable, namely, the distance, to changes in the regressors at various points in the conditional distinction of the dependent variable. Thus, quantile regressions reveal asymmetries in the data, which could not be detected by simple OLS estimations (see Buchinsky, 1998).

7. *Entrepreneurial Performance*

1. In fact, it seems that codified knowledge could be more easily priced. If we use the IPO returns (difference between the fixed price before IPO and the first market determined price), the results differ in that the coefficients of the interaction terms show the opposite signs. Another explanation is that firms overestimate their future returns from spillovers in the sciences, which are then reflected by higher IPO prices.

9. *Entrepreneurial Finance*

1. This compensation device has the drawback that rising loan rates aggravate moral hazard and adverse selection problems. Thus, the supply curve of loans may bend backward (Stiglitz and Weiss, 1981). However, better information increases the ability to raise loan rates, since the bank's loan offer curve is less likely to bend backward.

2. Dybwig and Wang (2002) show that the choice between debt or equity depends on the relative severity of the induced incentive problems.

3. As mentioned by Hart (2001), if taxes are the main factors influencing the debt-equity ratio, we should see much higher debt-equity ratios than we actually do. See also Myers (2001) for a recent survey on the determinants of capital structure.

4. However, financing high-tech startups and bringing them to the public are high positively correlated since venture capitalists tend to reinvest gains from the IPO to

fund new firms. This explains the fact that the financing of small firms by venture capitalists could be explained more by waves than a continuous process (Gompers and Lerner, 2001).

5. The effect of decreasing costs of monitoring is one explanation of the intermediation of banks.

6. See Buchinsky (1998) for a survey of the method and some application in the labor markets.

7. As an example, the 0.20 quantile divides the data set into two parts, whereas 20 percent of the included firms have growth rates less or equal the 0.20 quantile and 80 percent of the firms have higher growth rates.

10. *The Emergence of Entrepreneurship Policy*

1. President George W. Bush, news conference, November 4, 2004. Transcript available online at http:www.whitehouse.gov/news/releases/2004/11/200411045.html.

2. For example, *U.S. News and World Report* (August 16, 1993) reported, "What do Bill Clinton, George Bush and Bob Dole have in common? All have uttered one of the most enduring homilies in American political discourse: That small businesses create most of the nation's jobs."

3. This is cited from Davis, Haltiwanger, and Schuh (1996b, p. 298).

4. This is from Representative Robert Michel, House Minority Leader, in the Republican Response to the 1993 State of the Union Address, cited from Davis et al. (1996b, p. 298).

5. This quotation is from Scherer (1977, p. 980).

6. According to the Robinson-Patman Act, "It shall be unlawful for any person engaged in commerce, in the course of such commerce, either directly or indirectly, to discriminate in price between different purchasers of commodities of like grade and quality." For example, A&P was found in violation of the Robinson-Patman Act for direct purchases from suppliers and for performing its own wholesale functions. While these activities resulted in lower distribution costs, the gains in efficiency were seen as irrelevant because small businesses were threatened.

7. This quotation was found at http://www.sba.gov/aboutsba/sbahistory.html.

8. A third direction contributing to the mandate for entrepreneurship policy may be in the context of less developed regions and developing countries. Such regions have had endowments of neither physical capital nor knowledge capital but still look to entrepreneurship capital to serve as an engine of economic growth.

9. Public Law 98-620.

10. Cited in Mowery (2005, p. 2).

11. Cited in Mowery (2005, p. 2).

12. Cited in Mowery (2005, p. 2).

13. "Recession Looms in Germany," *International Herald Tribune*, November 22, 2001, p. 1, cited in Thurow (2002).

14. "Recession Looms in Germany," *International Herald Tribune*, November 22, 2001, p. 1, cited in Thurow (2002).

15. "Fortuyn Dared to Touch Hot Topic," *International Herald Tribune*, May 10, 2002, p. 1, cited in Thurow (2002).

References

Abramovitz, M. (1952). Economics of Growth. In A *Survey of Contemporary Economics*, vol. 2. Homewood: American Economic Association, 132–178.

Abramovitz, M. (1956). Resource and Output Trends in the United States since 1870. *American Economic Review*, 46, 5–23.

Acs, Z., and Audretsch, D. (1988). Innovation in Large and Small Firms: An Empirical Analysis. *American Economic Review*, 78, 678–690.

Acs, Z., and Audretsch, D. (1990). *Innovation and Small Firms*. Cambridge: MIT Press.

Acs, Z., and Audretsch, D. (1993). *Small Firms and Entrepreneurship: An East-West Perspective*. Cambridge: Cambridge University Press.

Acs, Z., and Audretsch, D. (2003). *Handbook of Entrepreneurship Research*. Dordrecht: Kluwer Academic Publishers.

Acs, Z., Audretsch, D., Braunerhjelm, P., and Carlsson, B. (2004). *The Missing Link: The Knowledge Filter and Endogenous Growth* (Discussion paper). Stockholm: Center for Business and Policy Studies.

Acs, Z., Audretsch, D., and Feldman, M. (1992). Real Effects of Academic Research: Comment. *American Economic Review*, 82, 363–367.

Acs, Z., Audretsch, D., and Feldman, M. (1994). R&D Spillovers and Innovative Activity. *Managerial and Decision Economics*, 15, 131–138.

ADT (Arbeitsgemeinschaft Deutscher Technologie- und Gründerzentren e.V.). (1998). *Ausgründungen technologieorientierter Unternehmen aus Hochschulen und ausseruniversitären Forschungseinrichtungen*. Report prepared for the BMBF (Bundesministerium fuer Bildung, Wissenschaft, Forschung und Technologie). Berlin: Arbeitsgemeinschaft Deutscher Technologie- und Gründerzentren e.V.

Aghion, P., and Bolton, P. (1992). An Incomplete Contracts Approach to Financial Contracting. *Review of Economic Studies*, 59, 473–494.

Agrawal, R., Echambadi, R., Franco, A., and Sarkar, M. (2004). Knowledge Transfer through Inheritance: Spin-out Generation, Development and Performance. *Academy of Management Journal*, 47, 507–522.

Akerloff, G. (1970). The Market for Lemons: Quality Uncertainty and the Market Mechanism. *Quarterly Journal of Economics*, 89, 488–500.

Aldrich, H., and Martinez, M. (2003). Entrepreneurship as Social Construction: A Multi-level Evolutionary Approach. In Z. Acs and D. Audretsch (eds.), *Handbook of Entrepreneurship Research* (pp. 359–399). Dordrecht: Kluwer.

Allan, F., and Gale, D. (2000). Corporate Governance and Competition. In X. Vives (ed.) *Corporate Governance. Theoretical and Empirical Perspectives* (pp. 23–94). Cambridge: Cambridge University Press.

Almus, M., and Nerlinger, E. (1998). *Beschäftigungsdynamik in jungen innovativen Unternehmen: Ergebnisse für West-Deutschland.* ZEW Discussion Paper No. 98-09.

Almus, M., and Nerlinger, E. (2000). Testing Gibrat's Law for Young Firms: Empirical Results for West Germany. *Small Business Economics*, 15, 1–12.

Alvarez, S. (2003). Resources and Hierarchies: Intersections between Entrepreneurship and Strategy. In Z. Acs and D. Audretsch (eds.), *The Handbook of Entrepreneurship Research* (pp. 247–263). Dordrecht: Kluwer.

Amin, A. (2000). The Economic Base of Contemporary Cities. In *The Companion to the City* (pp. 115–129). Malden: Blackwell.

Anselin, L., Varga, A., and Acs, Z. (1997). Local Geographic Spillovers between University Research and High Technology Innovations. *Journal of Urban Economics*, 42, 422–448.

Arrow, K. (1962). Economic Welfare and the Allocation of Resources for Invention. In *The Rate and Direction of Inventive Activity* (pp. 609–626). Princeton: Princeton University Press.

Arvanitis, S., and Keilbach, M. (2002). Microeconometric Models. In *RTD Evaluation Toolbox, Assessing the Socio-Economic Impact of RTD-Policies*. Sevilla: IPTS, 101–118.

Audretsch, D. (1991). New Firm Survival and the Technological Regime. *Review of Economics and Statistics*, 73, 441–450.

Audretsch, D. (1995). *Innovation and Industry Evolution.* Cambridge: MIT Press.

Audretsch, D. (1999). How Germany Can Create Jobs. *Wall Street Journal Europe*, January 12, p. 10.

Audretsch, D., Come, M., von Stel, A., and Thurik, R. (2002). Impeded Industrial Restructuring: The Growth Penalty. *Kyklos* 55, 81–98.

Audretsch, D., and Elston, J. (2002). Does Firm Size Matter? Evidence on the Impacts of Liquidity Constraints on Firm Investment Behavior in Germany. *International Journal of Industrial Organization*, 20, 1–17.

Audretsch, D., and Feldman, M. (1996). R&D Spillovers and the Geography of Innovation and Production. *American Economic Review*, 86, 630–640.

Audretsch, D., and Feldman, M. (1999). Innovation in Cities: Science-based Diversity, Specialization, and Localized Competition. *European Economic Review*, 43, 409–429.

Audretsch, D., and Fritsch, M. (1994). The Geography of Firm Births in Germany. *Regional Studies*, 28, 359–365.

Audretsch, D., and Fritsch, M. (1996). Creative Destruction: Turbulence and Economic Growth. In E. Helmstädter and M. Perlman (eds.), *Behavioral Norms, Technological Progress, and Economic Dynamics: Studies in Schumpeterian Economics* (pp. 137–150). Ann Arbor: University of Michigan Press.

Audretsch, D., and Fritsch, M. (2002). Growth Regimes over Time and Space. *Regional Studies*, 36, 113–124.

Audretsch, D., and Keilbach, M. (2004a). Entrepreneurship Capital and Economic Performance. *Regional Studies*, 38, 949–959.

Audretsch, D., and Keilbach, M. (2004b). Entrepreneurship and Regional Growth: An Evolutionary Interpretation. *Journal of Evolutionary Economics*, 14, 605–616.

Audretsch, D., and Keilbach, M. (2004c). Does Entrepreneurship Capital Matter? *Entrepreneurship Theory and Practice, Fall*, 419–429.

Audretsch, D., Keilbach, M., and Lehmann, E. (2005). The Knowledge Spillover Theory of Entrepreneurship and Technological Diffusion. In G. D. Libecap (ed.), *University Entrepreneurship and Technological Transfer: Process, Design and Intellectual Property* (pp. 69–91). Advances in the Study of Entrepreneurship, Innovation and Economic Growth, vol. 16. Amsterdam: Elsevier.

Audretsch, D., and Lehmann, E. (2004a). Debt or Equity: The Role of Venture Capital in Financing High-Tech Firms in Germany. *Schmalenbach Business Review, 56,* 340–357.

Audretsch, D., and Lehmann, E. (2004b). Ownership, Knowledge, and Firm Survival. *Review of Accounting and Finance, 4(4),* 13–33.

Audretsch, D., and Lehmann, E. (2005a). Do Locational Spillovers Pay? Empirical Evidence from IPO Data. *Economics of Innovation and New Technology* (forthcoming).

Audretsch, D., and Lehmann, E. (2005b). Mansfield's Missing Link: The Impact of Knowledge Spillovers on Firm Growth. *Journal of Technology Transfer, 30(1/2),* 207–210.

Audretsch, D., and Lehmann, E. (2005c). Do University Policies Make a Difference? *Research Policy, 34,* 343–347.

Audretsch, D., and Lehmann, E. (2005d). Does the Knowledge Spillover Theory of Entrepreneurship Hold for Regions? *Research Policy, 34,* 1191–1202.

Audretsch, D., and Lehmann, E. (2005e). University Spillover and Board Composition. Discussion paper, MPI, Jena.

Audretsch, D., Lehmann, E., and Warning, S. (2004). University Spillovers: Does the Kind of Knowledge Matter? *Industry and Innovation, 11,* 193–205.

Audretsch, D., Lehmann, E., and Warning, S. (2005). University Spillovers and New Firm Location. *Research Policy, 34,* 1113–1122.

Audretsch, D., Santarelli, E., and Vivarelli, M. (1999). Start-up Size and Industrial Dynamics: Some Evidence from Italian Manufacturing. *International Journal of Industrial Organization, 17,* 965–983.

Audretsch, D., and Stephan, P. (1996). Company-Scientist Locational Links: The Case of Biotechnology. *American Economic Review, 86,* 641–652.

Audretsch, D., and Stephan, P. (1999). Knowledge Spillovers in Biotechnology: Sources and Incentives. *Journal of Evolutionary Economics, 19,* 97–107.

Audretsch, D., and Thurik, R. (2001). What's New about the New Economy? Sources of Growth in the Managed and Entrepreneurial Economies. *Industrial and Corporate Change, 19,* 795–821.

Baldridge, M. (1986). Statement of the Honorable Malcolm Baldridge, Secretary, Department of Commerce, in Merger Law Reform: Hearings on S. 2022 and S. 2160, Before the Senate Committee on the Judiciary, 99th Congress, 2nd Session.

Bania, N., Eberts, R., and Fogerty, M. (1993). Universities and the Start-up of New Companies: Can We Generalize from Route 128 and Silicon Valley? *Review of Economics and Statistics, 75,* 761–766.

Barney, J. (1986). Strategic Factor Markets: Expectations, Luck and Business Strategy. *Management Science, 42,* 1231–1241.

Barro, R., and Sala-i-Martin, X. (1992). Convergence. *Journal of Political Economy, 100,* 223–251.

Barro, R., and Sala-i-Martin, X. (1995). *Economic Growth.* Cambridge, MA: McGraw-Hill.

Bartik, T. (1985). Business Location Decisions in the United States: Estimates of the Effects of Unionization, Taxes, and other Characteristics of States. *Journal of Business and Economic Statistics, 3,* 14–22.

Bates, T. (1990). Entrepreneur Human Capital Inputs and Small Business Longevity. *Review of Economics and Statistics, 72,* 551–559.

Baumol, W. (2002). *Free Market Innovation Machine: Analyzing the Growth Miracle of Capitalism.* Princeton: Princeton University Press.

Bascha, A., and Walz, U. (2002). *Financing Practices in the German Venture Capital Industry. An Empirical Assessment.* CFS Working Paper, No. 2002/08.

Becker, R., and Hellmann, T. (2005). The Genesis of Venture Capital—Lessons from the German Experience. In C. Keuschnigg and V. Kanniainen (eds.), *Venture Capital, Entrepreneurship, and Public Policy* (pp. 33–67). Cambridge: MIT Press.

Bergemann, D., and Hege, U. (1998). Venture Capital Financing, Moral Hazard, and Learning. *Journal of Banking and Finance*, 22, 703–735.

Berger, A., and Udell, G. (1990). Collateral, Loan Quality and Bank Risk. *Journal of Monetary Economics*, 25, 21–42.

Berger, A., and Udell, G. (1995). Relationship Lending and Lines of Credit in Small Firm Finance. *Journal of Business*, 68, 351–381.

Berger, A., and Udell, G. (1998). The Economics of Small Business Finance: The Role of Private Equity and Debt Markets in the Financial Growth Cycle. *Journal of Banking and Finance*, 22, 613–673.

Berglof, E. (1994). A Control Theory of Venture Capital Finance. *Journal of Law, Economics, and Organization*, 10, 247–267.

Berman, E., Bound, J., and Machin, S. (1997). *Implications of Skill-Biased Technological Change: International Evidence.* Cambridge: National Bureau of Economic Research Inc.

Birch, D. (1979). *The Job Generation Process.* MIT Program on Neighborhood and Regional Change. Cambridge: MIT.

Birch, D. (1981). Who Creates Jobs? *Public Interest*, 65, 3–14.

Birch, D. (1999). *Entrepreneurial Hot Spots.* Boston: Cognetics Inc.

Black, B., and Gilson, R. (1997). Venture Capital and the Structure of Capital Markets: Banks versus Stock Markets. *Journal of Financial Economics*, 47, 243–277.

Blanchflower, D., and Meyer, B. (1994). A Longitudinal Analysis of Young Entrepreneurs in Australia and the United States. *Small Business Economics*, 6, 1–20.

Blanchflower, D., and Oswald, A. (1990). *What Makes an Entrepreneur?* NBER Working Paper 3252. Cambridge, MA: National Bureau of Economic Research.

Blau, D. (1987). A Time Series Analysis of Self-Employment in the United States. *Journal of Political Economy*, 95, 445–467.

Blinder, A. (1988). The Challenge of High Unemployment. *American Economic Review*, 78, 1–15.

BMWi. (1999). The Economic Report 1999. Berlin: Bundesministerium für Wirtschaft und Technologie.

BMWi. (2000). Annual Report 2000. Berlin: Bundesministerium für Wirtschaft und Technologie.

Bode, E. (2004). The Spatial Pattern of Localized R&D Spillovers: An Empirical Investigation for Germany. *Journal of Economic Geography*, 4, 43–64.

Boegenhold, D. (1985). *Die Selbständigen.* New York: Springer.

Bork, R. (1978). *The Antitrust Paradox.* New York: Basic Books.

Bottazzi, L., and Da Rin, M. (2002). Venture Capital in Europe and the Financing of Innovative Companies. *Economic Policy*, 17, 229–270.

Bottazzi, L., and Peri, G. (2003). Innovation and Spillovers in Regions: Evidence from European Patent Data. *European Economic Review*, 47, 687–710.

Bowen, H., Leamer, E., and Sveikauskas, L. (1987). Multicountry, Multifactor Rests of the Factor Abundance Theory. *American Economic Review*, 77, 791–809.

Brander, J., Amit, R., and Antweiler, W. (2002). Venture-Capital Syndication: Improved Venture Selection versus the Value-Added Hypothesis. *Journal of Economics and Management Strategy*, 11, 423–452.

Branscomb, L., and Auerswald, P. (2003). Start-Ups and Spin-offs: Collective Entrepreneurship between Invention and Innovation. In D. M. Hart (ed.), *The Emergence of Entrepreneurship Policy: Governance, Start-Ups, and Growth in the Knowledge Economy* (pp. 61–91). Cambridge: Cambridge University Press.

Bresnahan, T., and Gambardella, A. (2004). *Building High-Tech Clusters: Silicon Valley and Beyond*. Cambridge: Cambridge University Press.

Brock, W., and Evans, D. (1989). Small Business Economics. *Small Business Economics*, 1, 7–20.

Broesma, L., and Gautier, P. (1997). Job Creation and Job Destruction by Small Firms: An Empirical Investigation for the Dutch Manufacturing Sector. *Small Business Economics*, 9, 211–224.

Brown, C., Hamilton, J., and Medoff, J. (1990). *Employers Large and Small*. Cambridge: Harvard University Press.

Brown, C., and Medoff, J. (1989). The Employer Size Wage Effect. *Journal of Political Economy*, 97, 1027–1059.

Brüderl, J., and Preisendörfer, P. (1998). Network Support and Success of Newly Founded Businesses. *Small Business Economics*, 10, 213–225.

Buchinsky, M. (1998). Recent Advantages in Quantile Regression Models. *Journal of Human Resources*, 33, 88–126.

Bürgel, O., Fier, A., Licht, G., and Murray, G. (1999). The Internationalisation of British and German Start-up Companies in High-Technology Industries. In R. Oakey and W. During (eds.), *New Technology Based Firms in the 1990s* (pp. 226–245). London: New Technology Based Firms Bd. VI.

Burghof, H.-P. (2000). Credit and Information in Universal Banking. *Schmalenbach Business Review*, 52, 282–309.

Callejon, M., and Segarra, A. (1999). Business Dynamics and Efficiency in Industries and Regions: The Case of Spain. *Small Business Economics*, 13, 253–271.

Carlton, D. (1983). The Location and Employment Choices of New Firms: An Econometric Model with Discrete and Continuous Endogenous Variables. *Review of Economics and Statistics*, 54, 440–449.

Carree, M., van Stel, A., Thurik, R., and Wennekers, A. (2001). Economic Development and Business Ownership. *Small Business Economics*, 19, 271–290.

Carter, N., Gartner, W., Shaver, K., and Gatewood, E. (2003). The Career Reasons of Nascent Entrepreneurs. *Journal of Business Venturing*, 18, 13–39.

Caves, R. (1982). *Multinational Enterprise Economic Analysis*. Cambridge: Cambridge University Press.

Caves, R. (1998). Industrial Organization and New Findings on the Turnover and Mobility of Firms. *Journal of Economic Literature*, 36, 1947–1982.

Carlsson, B., and Braunerhjelm, P. (1999). *Industry Clusters*. Stockholm: IUI.

Chandler, A. (1977). *The Visible Hand: The Managerial Revolution in American Business*. Cambridge: Belknap Press.

Chandler, A. (1990). *Scale and Scope: The Dynamics of Industrial Capitalism*. Cambridge: Harvard University Press.

Chirinko, R. (1993). Business Fixed Investment Spending: Modeling Strategies, Empirical Results, and Policy Implications. *Journal of Economic Literature*, 31, 1875–1911.

Ciccone, A., and Hall, R. (1996). Productivity and the Density of Economic Activity. *American Economic Review*, 86, 54–70.

Clark, G., Feldman, M., and Gertler, M. (2000). *The Handbook of Economic Geography*. Oxford: Oxford University Press.

Cobb, C., and Douglas, P. (1928). Theory of Production. *American Economic Review*, 18, 139–165.

Cockburn, I., and Henderson, R. (1996). Scale, Scope, and Spillovers: The Determinants of Research Productivity in Drug Discovery. *RAND Journal of Economics*, 27, 32–59.

Cockburn, I., and Henderson, R. (1999). *Public Private Interaction and the Productivity of Pharmaceutical Research*. NBER Working Paper 6018. Cambridge, MA: National Bureau of Economic Research.

Cohen, S., and DeLong, B. (2005). Shaken and Stirred. *Atlantic Monthly*, 295, 112–117.

Cohen, W., and Klepper, S. (1992a). The Anatomy of Industry R&D Intensity Distributions. *American Economic Review*, 82, 773–799.

Cohen, W., and Klepper, S. (1992b). The Tradeoff between Firm Size and Diversity in the Pursuit of Technological Progress. *Small Business Economics*, 4, 1–14.

Cohen, W., and Levinthal, D. (1989). Innovation and Learning. *Economic Journal*, 99, 569–596.

Cohen, W., and Levinthal, D. (1990). Absorptive Capacity: A New Perspective on Learning and Innovation. *Administrative Science Quarterly*, 35, 128–152.

Coleman, J. (1988a). The Creation and Destruction of Social Capital: Implications for the Law. *Notre Dame Journal of Law, Ethics and Public Policy*, 3, 375–404.

Coleman, J. (1988b). Social Capital in the Creation of Human Capital. *American Journal of Sociology*, 94, 95–121.

Colombo, M., and Delmastro, M. (2001). Technology-Based Entrepreneurs: Does Internet Make a Difference? *Small Business Economics*, 16, 177–190.

Cringley, R. (1993). *Accidental Empires: How the Boys of Silicon Valley Make Their Millions, Battle Foreign Competition and Still Can't Get a Date*. London: Viking.

Cumming, D., and MacIntosh, J. (2003). A Cross Country Comparison of Full and Partial Venture Capital Exits. *Journal of Banking and Finance*, 27, 511–548.

Davis, S., Haltiwanger, J., and Schuh, S. (1996a). *Job Creation and Destruction*. Cambridge: MIT Press.

Davis, S., Haltiwanger, J., and Schuh, S. (1996b). Small Business and Job Creation: Dissecting the Myth and Reassessing the Facts. *Small Business Economics*, 8, 297–315.

Deeg, R. (1998). What Makes German Banks Different. *Small Business Economics*, 10, 93–101.

Degryse, H., and Van Cayseele, P. (2000). Relationship Lending within a Bank-based System: Evidence from European Small Business Data. *Journal of Financial Intermediation*, 9, 90–109.

Der Spiegel. (1994). Es kann jeden treffen. 5, 82–83.

Der Spiegel. (2000). Handys Hightech und Reformen—Guten Morgen, Europe! Wie der alte Kontinent die Wirtschaftsmacht USA attackiert. 22, 110.

Dertouzos, M., Lester, R., and Solow, R. (1989). *Made in America: Regaining the Productive Edge*. Cambridge: MIT Press.

DeWit, G., and van Winden, F. (1989). An Empirical Analysis of Self-Employment in the Netherlands. *Small Business Economics*, 1, 263–272.

Diamond, D. (1984). Financial Intermediation and Delegated Monitoring. *Review of Economic Studies*, 51, 393–414.

Diamond, D. (1989). Reputation Acquisition in Debt Markets. *Journal of Political Economy*, 97, 828–862.

Die Zeit. (1996). *Wenn der Profit zur Pleite führt: Mehr Gewinne und mehr Arbeitslose: Wo bleibt die soziale Verantwortung der Unternehmer?* (When Profits Lead to Ruin: More Profits and More Unemployment: Where Is the Social Responsibility of the Firms?). 2 February.

Dittmann, I., Maug, E., and Kemper, J. (2004). How Fundamental Are Fundamental Values? Valuation Methods and Their Impact on the Performance of German Venture Capitalists. *European Financial Management*, 10, 609–638.

Dosi, G. (1982). Technical Paradigms and Technological Trajectories: A Suggested Interpretation of the Determinants of Technical Change. *Research Policy*, 2, 147–162.

Dosi, G. (1988). Sources, Procedures, and Microeconomic Effects of Innovation. *Journal of Economic Literature*, 26, 1120–1171.

Dunne, T., Roberts, M., and Samuelson, L. (1989). The Growth and Failure of U.S. Manufacturing Plants. *Quarterly Journal of Economics*, 104, 671–698.

Dybwig, P., and Wang, Y. (2002). *Debt and Equity* (Working paper). Saint Louis: Washington University in Saint Louis.

Economist, The. (1995a). A Survey of Telecommunications: The Death of Distance. 30 September.

Economist, The. (1995b). Those German Banks and their Industrial Treasures. 21 January.

Economist, The. (2002). Innovation's Golden Goose. 12 December.

EIM. (2002a). The European Observatory for SMEs, 2002. (Report submitted to the European Commission, Enterprise Directorate-General). Duesseldorf: KPMG Special Services and EIM Business School and Policy Research.

EIM. (2002b). SMEs in Europe. The European Observatory for SMEs, Volume 2, 2002. (Report submitted to the European Commission, Enterprise Directorate-General). Duesseldorf: KPMG Special Services and EIM Business School and Policy Research.

Ellison, G., and Glaeser, E. (1997). Geographic Concentration in U.S. Manufacturing Industries: A Dartboard Approach. *Journal of Political Economy*, 105, 889–927.

Elston, J., and Audretch, D. (2004). Can Institutional Change Impact High Technology Firm Growth? Evidence from Germany's Neuer Markt. *Discussion Papers on Entrepreneurship, Growth and Public Policy*. Jena, Germany: Max Plank Institute of Economics (#25-2004).

Ergas, H. (1987). Does Technology Policy Matter? In B. R. Guile and H. Brooks (eds.), *Technology and Global Industry: Companies and Nations in the World Economy* (pp. 191–245).Washington, DC: National Academy Press.

Ericson, R., and Pakes, A. (1995). Markov-Perfect Industry Dynamics: A Framework for Empirical Work. *Review of Economic Studies*, 62, 53–82.

European Commission. (1995). *Green Paper on Innovation*. Brussels: European Commission.

Evans, D., and Jovanovic, B. (1989a). An Estimated Model of Entrepreneurial Choice under Liquidity Constraints. *Journal of Political Economy*, 97, 808–827.

Evans, D., and Jovanovic, B. (1989b). Small Business Formation by Unemployed and Employed Workers. *Small Business Economics*, 2, 319–330.

Evans, D., and Leighton, L. (1989a). The Determinants of Changes in U.S. Self-Employment. *Small Business Economics*, 1, 11–120.

Evans, D., and Leighton, L. (1989b). Some Empirical Aspects of Entrepreneurship. *American Economic Review*, 79, 519–535.

Evans, D., and Leighton, L. (1990). Small Business Formation by Unemployed and Employed Workers. *Small Business Economics*, 2, 319–330.

Fabel, O. (2004). Spinoffs of Entrepreneurial Firms: An O-Ring Approach. *Journal of Institutional and Theoretical Economics*, 160, 760(3), 416–438.

Fabel, O., Lehmann, E., and Warning S. (2002). Der relative Vorteil deutscher wirtschaftswissenschaftlicher Fachbereiche im Wettbewerb um studentischen Zuspruch. *Zeitschrift für betriebswirtschaftliche Forschung*, 54, 509–526.

Fama, E., and Jensen, M. (1983). Separation of Ownership and Control. *Journal of Law and Economics*, 26, 301–325.

Fazzari, S., Hubbard, G., and Petersen, B. (1988). Financing Constraints and Corporate Investment. *Brookings Papers on Economic Activity*, 1, 141–195.

Feldman, M. (2000). Location and Innovation: The New Economic Geography of Innovation. In G. Clark, M. Feldman, and M. Gertler (eds.), *Oxford Handbook of Economic Geography* (pp. 373–394). Oxford: Oxford University Press.

Feldman, M., and Audretsch, D. (1999). Innovations in Cities: Science-Based Diversity, Specialization and Localized Monopoly. *European Economic Review*, 43, 409–429.

Feldman, M., and Desrochers, P. (2003). Research Universities and Local Economic Development: Lessons from the History of the Johns Hopkins University. *Innovation and Industry*, 10, 5–24.

Feldman, M., and Desrochers, P. (2004). Truth for Its Own Sake: Academic Culture and Technology Transfer at Johns Hopkins University. *Minerva*, 42, 105–126.

Feldman, M., Feller, I., Bercovitz, J., and Burton, R. (2002). University Technology Transfer and the System of Innovation. In M. Feldman and N. Massard (eds.), *Institutions and Systems in the Geography of Innovation* (pp. 55–78). Boston: Kluwer.

Feller, I. (1997). Federal and State Government Roles in Science and Technology. *Economic Development Quarterly*, 11, 283–296.

Ferguson, C. H. (1988). From the People Who Brought You Voodoo Economics. *Harvard Business Review*, 66, 55–62.

Fitzenberger, B. (1999). *Wages and Employment across Skill Groups*. Heidelberg: Physica.

Fitzenberger, B., Koenker, R., and Machado, J. A. (2002). Economic Applications of Quantile Regressions. *Studies in Empirical Economics*. Heidelberg: Physica.

Florida, R. (2002). *The Rise of the Creative Class*. New York: Basic Books.

Florida, R., and Cohen, W. (1999). Engine or Infrastructure? The University Role in Economic Development. In L. Branscomb, F. Kodama, and R. Florida (eds.), *Industrializing Knowledge, University-Industry Linkages in Japan and the United States* (pp. 589–610). Cambridge: MIT Press.

Foelster, S. (2000). Do Entrepreneurs Create Jobs? *Small Business Economics*, 14, 137–148.

Fortune. (1993). *The Best Cities for Knowledge Workers*. 15 November, 44.

Foti, A., and Vivarelli, M. (1994). An Econometric Test of the Self-Employment Model: The Case of Italy. *Small Business Economics*, 6, 81–94.

Fotopoulos, G., and Louri, H. (2000). Location and Survival of New Entry. *Small Business Economics*, 14, 311–321.

Franzke, S. (2001). *Underpricing of Venture-Backed and Non Venture-Backed IPOs: Germany's Neuer Markt* (Working paper). Center of Financial Studies No. 2001/01.

Frick, B., and Lehmann E. (2005). Corporate Governance in Germany: Problems and Prospects. In H. Gospel and A. Pendleton (eds.), *Corporate Governance and Labour Management* (pp. 122–147). Oxford: Oxford University Press.

Fritsch, M. (1997). New Firms and Regional Employment Change. *Small Business Economics*, 9, 437–448.

Fujita, M., Krugman, P., and Venables, A. (1999). *The Spatial Economy: Cities, Regions and International Trade*. Cambridge: MIT Press.

Galbraith, J. (1956). *American Capitalism*. Boston: Houghton Mifflin.

Galbraith, J. (1962). *Economic Development in Perspective*. Cambridge: Harvard University Press.

Gallagher, C., and Stewart, H. (1986). Jobs and the Business Life-cycle in the U.K. *Applied Economics*, 18, 875–900.

Gartner, W., and Carter, N. (2003). Entrepreneurial Behaviour and Firm Organizing Processes. In Z. Acs and D. Audretsch (eds.), *Handbook of Entrepreneurship Research* (pp. 195–221). Dordrecht: Kluwer.

Geroski, P. (1995). What Do We Know about Entry. *International Journal of Industrial Organization*, 13, 421–440.

Gertler, M. (2003). Tacit Knowledge and the Economic Geography of Context, or The Undefinable Tacitness of Being (There). *Journal of Economic Geography*, 3, 75–99.

Gilder, G. (1989). *Microcosm*. New York: Touchstone.

Glaeser, E., Kallal H., Scheinkman J., and Shleifer, A. (1992). Growth in Cities. *Journal of Political Economy*, 100, 1126–1152.

Gomes-Casseres, B. (1997). Alliance Strategies of Small Firms. *Small Business Economics*, 9, 33–44.

Gompers, P. (1995). Optimal Investments, Monitoring, and the Staging of Venture Capital. *Journal of Finance*, 50, 1461–1489.

Gompers, P. (1996). Grandstanding in the Venture Capital Industry. *Journal of Financial Economics*, 42, 133–156.

Gompers, P., and Lerner, J. (2001). The Venture Capital Revolution. *Journal of Economic Perspectives*, 15, 145–168.

Gorman, M., and Sahlman, W. (1989). What Do Venture Capitalists Do? *Journal of Business Venturing*, 4, 231–248.

Greene, W. (2000). *Simulated Likelihood Estimation of the Normal-Gamma Stochastic Frontier Function* (Working paper). New York: New York University.

Greene, W. (2003). *Econometric Analysis*. Upper Saddle River, NJ: Prentice Hall.

Griliches, Z. (1979). Issues in Assessing the Contribution of Research and Development to Productivity Growth. *Bell Journal of Economics*, 10, 92–116.

Griliches, Z. (1984). *R&D, Patents and Productivity*. Chicago: University of Chicago Press.

Griliches, Z. (1990). Patent Statistics as Economic Indicators: A Survey. *Journal of Economic Literature*, 28, 1661–1707.

Griliches, Z. (1992). The Search for R&D Spillovers. *Scandinavian Journal of Economics*, 94, 29–47.

Grossman, G., and Helpman, E. (1991). *Innovation and Growth in the Global Economy*. Cambridge: MIT Press.

Gruber, W., Mehta, D., and Vernon, R. (1967). The R&D Factor in International Trade and Investment of the Untied States. *Journal of Political Economy*, 75, 20–37.

Grupp, H., Jungwittag, A., Schmoch, U., and Legler, H (2000). *Hochtechnologie 2000 — Neudefinition der Hochtechnologie für die Berichterstattung zur technologischen Leistungsfähigkeit Deutschlands*. Karlsruhe/Hannover: Fraunhofer ISI/NIW.

Hall, B. (1987). The Relationship between Firm Size and Firm Growth in the U.S. Manufacturing Sector. *Journal of Industrial Economics*, 35, 583–605.

Hall, B., Link, A., and Scott, J. (2001). Barriers Inhibiting Industry from Partnering with Universities: Evidence from Advanced Technology Program. *Journal of Technology Transfer*, 26, 87–98.

Hall, B., Link, A., and Scott, J. (2003). Universities as Research Partners. *Review of Economics and Statistics*, 85, 485–491.

Hamilton, R. (1989). Unemployment and Business Formation Rates: Reconciling Time Series and Cross Section Evidence. *Environment and Planning*, 21, 249–255.

Hannan, M., and Freeman, J. (1989). *Organizational Ecology*. Cambridge: Harvard University Press.

Harhoff, D. (2000). R&D Spillovers, Technological Proximity, and Productivity Growth — Evidence from German Panel Data. *Schmalenbach Business Review*, 52, 238–260.

Harhoff, D., and Körting, T. (1998). Lending Relationships in Germany. Empirical Evidence from Survey Data. *Journal of Banking and Finance*, 22, 1317–1353.

Harhoff, D., and Stahl, K. (1995). Unternehmens- und Beschäftigungsdynamik in Westdeutschland: Zum Einfluss von Haftungsregeln und Eigentümerstruktur. *ifo-Studien: Zeitschrift für empirische Wirtschaftsforschung*, 41, 17–50.

Harhoff, D., Stahl, K., and Woywode, M. (1998). Legal Form, Growth and Exit of West-German Firms: Empirical Results for Manufacturing, Construction, Trade and Service Industries. *Journal of Industrial Organization, 46,* 453–488.

Harhoff, D., and Steil, F. (1997). Die ZEW-Gründungspanels: Konzeptionelle Überlegungen und Analysepotential. In D. Harhoff (ed.), *Unternehmensgründungen — Empirische Analysen für die alten und neuen Bundesländer* (pp. 11–28). Baden-Baden: Nomos.

Harris, R. (2001). The Knowledge-Based Economy: Intellectual Origins and New Economic Perspectives. *International Journal of Management Review, 3,* 21–41.

Hart, M., and Hanvey, E. (1995). Job Generation and New Small Firms: Some Evidence from the Late 1980s. *Small Business Economics, 7,* 97–109.

Hart, O. (2001). Financial Contracting. *Journal of Economic Literature, 39,* 1079–1100.

Hart, O., and Moore, J. (1998). Default and Renegotiation: A Dynamic Model of Debt. *Quarterly Journal of Economics, 113,* 1–41.

Hébert, R., and Link, A. (1989). In Search of the Meaning of Entrepreneurship. *Small Business Economics, 1,* 39–49.

Hellmann, T., and Puri, M. (2000). The Interaction between Product Market and Financing Strategy: The Role of Venture Capital. *Review of Financial Studies, 13,* 959–984.

Henderson, J., Kuncoro, A., and Turner, M. (1995). Industrial Development and Cities. *Journal of Political Economy, 103,* 1067–1081.

Henderson, R., and Cockburn, I. (1994). Measuring Competence? Exploring Firm Effects in Pharmaceutical Research. *Strategic Management Journal, 15,* 63–84.

Henderson, R., Jaffe, A., and Trajtenberg, M. (1998). Universities as a Source of Commercial Technology: A Detailed Analysis of University Patenting 1965–1988. *Review of Economics and Statistics, 65,* 119–127.

Henderson, V. (1997). Externalities and Industrial Development. *Journal of Urban Economics, 24,* 449–470.

Hermalin, B., and Weisbach, M. (1998). Endogenously Chosen Boards of Directors and Their Monitoring. *American Economic Review, 88,* 96–118.

Hermalin, B., and Weisbach, M. (2003). Boards of Directors as an Endogenously Determined Institution, Federal Reserve Bank of New York. *Economic Policy Review,* April, 7–26.

Heshmati, A. (2001). On the Growth of Micro and Small Firms: Evidence from Sweden. *Small Business Economics, 17,* 213–228.

Highfield, R., and Smiley, R. (1987). New Business Starts and Economic Activity: An Empirical Investigation. *International Journal of Industrial Organization, 5,* 51–66.

Hirschman, A. (1970). *Exit, Voice, and Loyalty.* Cambridge: Harvard University Press.

Hoang, H., and Antoncic, B. (2003). Network-Based Research in Entrepreneurship: A Critical Review. *Journal of Business Venturing, 18,* 165–187.

Hofstede, G., Noorderhaven, N., Thurik, A., Wennekers, A., Uhlaner, L., and Wildeman, R. (2002). Culture's role in Entrepreneurship: Self-Employment Out of Dissatisfaction. In T. E. Brown and J. Ulijn (eds.), *Innovation, Entrepreneurship and Culture: The Interaction between Technology, Progress and Economic Growth* (pp. 162–203). Brookfield, UK: Edward Elgar.

Hohti, S. (2000). Job Flows and Job Quality by Establishment Size in the Finnish Manufacturing Sector, 1980–1994. *Small Business Economics, 15,* 265–281.

Holmes, T., and Schmitz, J. Jr. (1990). A Theory of Entrepreneurship and Its Application to the Study of Business Transfers. *Journal of Political Economy, 98,* 265–294.

Holtz-Eakin, D., and Kao, C. (2003). *Entrepreneurship and Economic Growth: The Proof Is in the Productivity.* Syracuse: Center for Policy Research, Syracuse University.

Hopenhayn, H. (1992). Entry, Exit and Firm Dynamics in Long Run Equilibrium. *Econometrica*, 60, 1127–1150.

Horst, T. (1972). Firm and Industry Determinants of the Decision to Invest Abroad: An Empirical Study. *Review of Economic Statistics*, 54, 258–266.

Intriligator, M. (1992). Productivity and the Embodiment of Technical Progress. *Scandinavian Journal of Economics*, 94, 75–87.

Intriligator, M., Bodkin, R., and Hsiao, C. (1996). *Econometric Models, Techniques and Applications*. Upper Saddle River: Simon and Schuster, Prentice Hall.

Jacobs, J. (1969). *The Economy of Cities*. New York: Vintage Books.

Jaffe, A. (1989). The Real Effects of Academic Research. *American Economic Review*, 79, 957–970.

Jaffe, A. (2002). Building Program Evaluation into the Design of Public Research-Support Programs. *Oxford Review of Economic Policy*, 18, 22–34.

Jaffe, A., Trajtenberg, M., and Henderson, R. (1993). Geographic Localization of Knowledge Spillovers as Evidenced by Patent Citations. *Quarterly Journal of Economics*, 63, 577–598.

Jensen, M. (1993). The Modern Industrial Revolution, Exit, and the Failure of the Internal Control Systems. *Journal of Finance*, 47, 831–881.

Jensen, M., and Meckling, W. (1976). Theory of the Firm: Managerial Behavior, Agency Costs, and Ownership Structure. *Journal of Financial Economics*, 3, 305–360.

Jorde, M., and Teece, D. (1990). Innovation and Cooperation: Implications for Competition and Antitrust. *Journal of Economic Perspectives*, 4, 75–96.

Jorgenson, W., and Nishimizu, M. (1978). U.S. and Japanese Economic Growth, 1952–1974. *Economic Journal*, 88, 707–726.

Jovanovic, B. (1982). Selection and the Evolution of Industry. *Economica*, 50, 649–70.

Jovanovic, B. (1994). Entrepreneurial Choice when People Differ in Their Management and Labor Skills. *Small Business Economics*, 6, 185–192.

Kaplan, S., and Strömberg, P. (2003). Financial Contracting Theory Meets the Real World: An Empirical Analysis of Venture Capital Contracts. *Review of Economic Studies*, 70, 281–318.

Kaplan, S., and Strömberg, P. (2004). Characteristics, Contracts, and Actions: Evidence from Venture Capitalist Analysis. *Journal of Finance*, 2177–2210.

Keesing, D. (1966). Labor Skills and Comparative Advantage. *American Economic Review*, 56, 249–258.

Keesing, D. (1967). The Impact of Research and Development on United States Trade. *Journal of Political Economy*, 75, 38–48.

Keilbach, M. (2000). *Spatial Knowledge Spillovers and the Dynamics of Agglomeration and Regional Growth*. Heidelberg: Physica.

Kendrick, J. (1956). Productivity Trends: Capital and Labor. *Review of Economic Statistics*, 38, 248–257.

Kihlstrom, R., and Laffont, J. (1979). A General Equilibrium Entrepreneurial Theory of Firm Formation Based on Risk Aversion. *Journal of Political Economy*, 87, 719–748.

Kim, P., Aldrich, H., and Keister, L. (2003). *If I Were Rich? The Impact of Financial and Human Capital on Becoming a Nascent Entrepreneur*. Chapel Hill: University of North Carolina and Ohio State University.

Kindleberger, C., and Audretsch, D. (1983). *The Multinational Corporation in the 1980s*. London: MIT Press.

Klandt, H. (1984). *Aktivität und Erfolg des Unternehmungsgründers. Eine empirische Analyse unter Einbeziehung des mikrosozialen Umfeldes*. Bergisch Gladbach.

Klandt, H. (1996). Gründerpersönlichkeit und Unternehmenserfolg. (Entrepreneurial Personality and Firm Success). In *Chancen und Risiken der Existenzgründung*,

(Chances and Risks for New Firm Startups) (pp. 18–22). Bonn: BMWi-Dokumentation Nr. 392.

Klepper, S. (1996). Entry, Exit, Growth, and Innovation over the Product Life Cycle. *American Economic Review, 86,* 562–583.

Klepper, S., and Sleeper, S. (2000). *Entry by Spinoffs* (Working paper). Pittsburg: Carnegie Mellon University.

Klette, T., and Mathiassen, A. (1996) Job Creation, Job Destruction and Plant Turnover in Norwegian Manufacturing. *Annales d'Economie et de Statistique, 41/42,* 97–125.

Klofsten, M., and Jones-Evans, D. (2000). Comparing Academic Entrepreneurship in Europe—The Case of Sweden and Ireland. *Small Business Economics, 14,* 299–309.

Knight, F. (1921). *Risk, Uncertainty and Profit.* Boston: Houghton Mifflin.

Koenker, R., and Hallock, K. (2001). Quantile Regression. *Journal of Economic Perspectives, 15,* 143–156.

Kogut, B., and Zander, U. (1992). Knowledge of the Firm, Combinative Capabilities, and the Replication of Technology. *Organizational Science, 3,* 383–397.

Konings, J. (1995). Gross Job Flows and the Evolution of Size in U.K. Establishments. *Small Business Economics, 7,* 213–220.

Kortum, J., and Lerner, S. (1997). Stronger Protection or Technological Revolution: What Is Behind the Recent Surge in Patenting? NBER Working Papers 6204. Cambridge, MA: National Bureau of Economic Research.

Kortum, S., and Lerner, J. (2000). Assessing the Contribution of Venture Capital to Innovation. *Rand Journal of Economics, 31,* 674–692.

Krueger, N. (2003). The Cognitive Psychology of Entrepreneurship. In *Handbook of Entrepreneurship Research.* Dordrecht: Kluwer Academic Publishers, 105–140.

Krugman, P. (1991a). *Geography and Trade.* Cambridge: MIT Press.

Krugman, P. (1991b). Increasing Returns and Economic Geography. *Journal of Political Economy, 99,* 483–99.

Krugman, P. (1998). Space: The Final Frontier. *Journal of Economic Perspectives, 12,* 161–174.

Kulicke, M. (1987). *Technologieorientierte Unternehmen in der Bundesrepublik Deutschland: Eine empirische Untersuchung der Strukturbildungs- und Wachstumsphase von Neugründungen.* Frankfurt.

Lambson, V. (1991). Industry Evolution with Sunk Costs and Uncertain Market Conditions. *International Journal of Industrial Organization, 9,* 171–196.

Lazear (2002). *Entrepreneurship.* NBER Working Paper 9109. Cambridge, MA: National Bureau of Economic Research.

Lehmann, E. (2006). Does Venture Capital Syndication Spur Employment Growth and Shareholder Value? *Small Business Economics* (forthcoming).

Lehmann, E., and Lüders, E. (2005). Is IAS Really as Bad? Unpublished manuscript. Max Planck Institute, Jena, and University Lavalle.

Lehmann, E., and Neuberger, D. (2001). Do Lending Relationships Matter? Evidence from Bank Survey Data in Germany. *Journal of Economic Behavior and Organization, 45,* 339–359.

Lehmann, E., Neuberger, D., and Raethke, S. (2004). Lending to Small and Medium Sized Firms: Is There an East-West Gap in Germany? *Small Business Economics, 23,* 23–39.

Lehmann, E., and Warning, S. (2004). *Teaching and Research: What Affects the Efficiency of Universities?* (Working paper). University of Konstanz.

Lehmann, E., and Weigand, J. (2000). Does the Governed Corporation Perform Better? Governance Structures and Corporate Performance in Germany. *European Finance Review, 4,* 157–195.

Lel, U., and Udell, G. (2002). *Financial Constraints, Start-up Firms, and Personal Commitments* (Working paper). Bloomington: Indiana University.

Lerner, J. (1994). Venture Capitalists and the Decision to Go Public. *Journal of Financial Economics,* 35, 293–316.

Lerner, J. (1995). Venture Capitalists and the Oversight of Private Firms. *Journal of Finance,* 50, 301–318.

Lerner, J. (1999). The Government as Venture Capitalist: The Long-Run Effects of the SBIR Program. *Journal of Business,* 72, 285–318.

Liebeskind, J., Amalya, O., Zucker, L., and Brewer, M. (1996). Social Networks, Learning, and Flexibility: Sourcing Scientific Knowledge in New Biotechnology Firms. *Organizational Science,* 7, 428–443.

Link, A. (1995). The Use of Literature-Based Innovation Output Indicators for Research Evaluation. *Small Business Economics,* 7, 451–455.

Link, A., and Rees, J. (1990). Firm Size, University-based Research and the Returns to R&D. *Small Business Economics,* 2, 25–31.

Link, A., and Scott, J. (2003). U.S. Science Parks: The Diffusion of an Innovation and Its Effects on the Academic Mission of Universities. *International Journal of Industrial Organization,* 21, 1323–1356.

Loveman, G., and Sengenberger, W. (1991). The Re-emergence of Small-Scale Production: An International Perspective. *Small Business Economics,* 3, 1–38.

Lucas, R. (1978). On the Size Distribution of Business Firms. *Bell Journal of Economics,* 9, 508–523.

Lucas, R. (1988). On the Mechanics of Economic Development. *Journal of Monetary Economics,* 22, 3–42.

Lucas, R. (1993). Making a Miracle. *Econometrica,* 61, 251–272.

Lugar, M. (2001). The Research Triangle Experience. In C. Wessner (ed.), *Industry-Laboratory Partnerships: A Review of the Sandia Science and Technology Park Initiative* (pp. 35–38). Washington: National Academy Press.

Lugar, M., and Goldstein, H. (1991). *Technology in the Garden: Research Parks and Regional Economic Development.* Chapel Hill: University of North Carolina Press.

Lundström, A., and Stevenson, L. (2001). *Entrepreneurship Policy for the Future.* Stockholm: Swedish Foundation for Small Business Research.

Lundström, A., and Stevenson, L. (2002). *On the Road to Entrepreneurship Policy.* Stockholm: Swedish Foundation for Small Business Research.

Lundström, A., and Stevenson, L. (2005). *Entrepreneurship Policy. Theory and Practice.* International Studies in Entrepreneurship Series. Vol. 9. New York: Springer.

Machauer, A., and Weber, M. (1998). Bank Behavior Based on Internal Credit Ratings of Borrowers. *Journal of Banking and Finance,* 22, 1355–1383.

MacPherson, A. (1998). Academic-Industry Linkages and Small Firm Innovation: Evidence from the Scientific Instruments Sector. *Entrepreneurship and Regional Development,* 10, 261–276.

Mankiw, N., Romer, D., and Weil, D. (1992). A Contribution to the Empirics of Economic Growth. *Quarterly Journal of Economics,* 107, 407–437.

Mansfield, E. (1962). Entry, Gibrat's Law, Innovation, and the Growth of Firms. *American Economic Review,* 52, 1023–1051.

Mansfield, E. (1988). The Speed and Cost of Industrial Innovation in Japan and the United States: External versus Internal Technology. *Management Science,* 34, 1157–1168.

Mansfield, E. (1995). Academic Research underlying Industrial Innovations: Sources, Characteristics and Financing. *Review of Economics and Statistics,* 77, 55–65.

Mansfield, E. (1998). Academic Research and Industrial Innovation: An Update of Empirical Findings. *Research Policy, 26*, 773–776.

Manski, C. (2000). Economic Analysis of Social Interactions. *Journal of Economic Perspectives, 14*, 115–136.

Marshall, A. (1920). *Principles of Economics*. 8th ed. London: Macmillan. Reprint, 1994.

Martinelli, C. (1997). Small Firms, Borrowing Constraints, and Reputation. *Journal of Economic Behavior and Organization, 33*, 91–105.

Mata, J. (1994). Firm Growth during Infancy." *Small Business Economics, 6*(1), 27–40.

Mata, J., Portugal, P., and Guimaraes, P. (1995). The Survival of New Plants: Start-up Conditions and Post-entry Evolution. *International Journal of Industrial Organization, 13*, 459–481.

McClelland, D. (1961). *The Achieving Society*. Princeton: Van Nostrand.

McWilliams, A., and Siegel, D. (2000). Corporate Social Responsibility and Financial Performance: Correlation or Misspecification? *Strategic Management Journal, 21*, 603–609.

Mills, D., and Schumann, L. (1985). Industry Structure with Fluctuating Demand. *American Economic Review, 75*, 758–767.

Modigliani, F., and Miller, M. (1958). The Cost of Capital, Corporate Finance, and the Theory of Investment. *American Economic Review, 48*, 261–297.

Moore, G., and Davis, K. (2004). Learning the Silicon Valley Way. In T. Bresnahan and A. Gambardella (eds.), *Building High-Tech Clusters. Silicon Valley and Beyond* (pp. 7–39). Cambridge: Cambridge University Press.

Mowery, D. (2005). *The Bayh-Dole Act and High-Technology Entrepreneurship in U.S. Universities: Chick, Egg, or Something Else?* Paper presented at the Eller Centre Conference on Entrepreneurship Education and Technology Transfer, University of Arizona, 21–22 January.

Mowery, D., and Shane, S. (2002). Introduction to the Special Issue on University Entrepreneurship and Technology Transfer. *Management Science, 48*, v–ix.

Mowery, D., and Ziedonis, A. (2001). *The Geographic Reach of Market and Non-Market Channels of Technology Transfer: Comparing Citations and Licenses of University Patents*. NBER Working Paper No. 8568. Cambridge, MA: National Bureau of Economic Research.

Myers, S. (2001). Capital Structure. *Journal of Economic Perspectives, 15*, 81–102.

Myers, S., and Maljuf, N. (1984). Corporate Financing and Investment Decisions when Firms Have Information Investors Do Not Have. *Journal of Financial Economics, 13*, 187–221.

Nadiri, I. (1997). *Innovations and Technological Spillovers*. NBER Working Paper 4423. Cambridge, MA: National Bureau of Economic Research.

Nature. (2003). Making the Switch from Science to Business. October 30, 988–989.

Nelson, R. (1981). Research on Productivity Growth and Differences: Dead Ends and New Departures. *Journal of Economic Literature, 19*, 1029–1064.

Nelson, R. (1990). Capitalism as an Engine of Progress. *Research Policy, 19*, 193–214.

Nelson, R. (1992). National Innovation Systems: A Retrospective on a Study. *Industrial and Corporate Change, 2*, 347–374.

Nelson, R. (1995). Recent Evolutionary Theorizing about Economic Change. *Journal of Economic Literature, 33*, 48–90.

Nelson, R., and Winter, S. (1982). *An Evolutionary Theory of Economic Change*. Cambridge: Belkap Press.

Neuberger, D. (1998). Industrial Organization of Banking: A Review. *International Journal of the Economics of Business, 5*, 97–118.

New York Times. (1985). Making Mergers Even Easier. 18 November.

New York Times. (1998). Schroeder Tries for Consensus in Fight to Cut Jobless Rate. 8 December.

Nickerson, J., and Zenger, T. (2004). A Knowledge-Based Theory of the Firm—The Problem-Solving Perspective. *Organization Science*, 15, 617–632.

Organization for Economic Cooperation and Development (OECD). (1998). *Fostering Entrepreneurship*. Paris: OECD.

Oxenfeldt, A. (1943). *New Firms and Free Enterprise*. Washington, D.C.: American Council on Public Affairs.

Parker, S. (2004). *The Economics of Self-Employment and Entrepreneurship*. Cambridge: Cambridge University Press.

Parker, S. (2005). The Economics of Entrepreneurship. *Foundations and Trends in Entrepreneurship*, 1(1), 1–54.

Parker, S., Belghitar, Y., and Barmby, T. (2005). Wage Uncertainty and the Labor Supply of Self-Employed Workers. *Economic Journal*, 115, 190–207.

Peters, T., and Waterman, R. (1984). *In Search of Excellence*. New York: Harper and Row.

Petersen, M., and Rajan, R. (1994). The Benefits of Lending Relationships: Evidence from Small Business Data. *Journal of Finance*, 49, 3–37.

Piore, M., and Sabel, C. (1984). *The Second Industrial Divide: Possibilities for Prosperity*. New York: Basic Books.

Porter, M. (1990). *The Comparative Advantage of Nations*. New York: Free Press.

Porter, M., and Stern, S. (2001). Innovation: Location Matters. *MIT Sloan Management Review*, Summer, 28–36.

Posner, R. (1976). *Antitrust Law: An Economic Perspective*. Chicago: University of Chicago Press.

Powell, W., Koput, K., and Smith-Doerr, L. (1996). Interorganizational Collaboration and the Locus of Innovation: Networks of Learning in Biotechnology. *Administrative Science Quarterly*, 41, 116–145.

Powers, M. (2005). Forecasts from Biased Experts: A "Meta-Credibility" Problem. *Journal of Risk Finance*, 6, 47–59.

Pratten, C. (1971). *Economies of Scale in Manufacturing Industry*. Cambridge: Cambridge University Press.

Prevenzer, M. (1997). The Dynamics of Industrial Clustering in Biotechnology. *Small Business Economics*, 9, 255–271.

Prodi, R. (2002). *For a New European Entrepreneurship*. (Public Speech). Instituto de Empresa in Madrid.

Putnam, R. (1993). *Making Democracy Work. Civic Traditions in Modern Italy*. Princeton: Princeton University Press.

Putnam, R. (2000). *Bowling Alone: The Collapse and Revival of American Community*. New York: Simon and Schuster.

Rajan, R., and Zingales, L. (2000). The Governance of the New Enterprise. In X. Vives (ed.), *Corporate Governance* (pp. 201–207). Cambridge: Cambridge University Press.

Reynolds, P. (1999). Creative Destruction: Source or Symptom of Economic Growth? In Z. J. Acs, B. Carlsson, and C. Karlsson (eds.), *Entrepreneurship, Small and Medium-sized Enterprises and the Macroeconomy* (pp. 97–136). Cambridge: Cambridge University Press.

Reynolds, P., Hay, M., Bygrave, B., Camp, M., and Autio, E. (2000). *Global Entrepreneurship Monitor: 2000 Executive Report*. Wellesley: Babson College.

Reynolds, P., Miller, B., and Maki, W. (1995). Explaining Regional Variation in Business Births and Deaths: U.S. 1976–1988. *Small Business Economics*, 7, 389–407.

Reynolds, P., Storey, D., and Westhead, P. (1994). Regional Variations in New Firm Formation—Special Issue. *Regional Studies*, 28, 343–456.

Riesman, D., Denney, R., and Glazer, N. (1950). *The Lonely Crowd: A Study of Changing American Character.* New Haven: Yale University Press.

Ritsila, J., and Tervo, H. (2002). Effects of Unemployment on New Firm Formation: Micro-Level Panel Data Evidence from Finland. *Small Business Economics,* 19, 31–40.

Ritter, J. (1991). The Long-Run Performance of Initial Public Offerings. *Journal of Finance,* 42, 365–394.

Romer, D. (1984). The Theory of Social Custom: A Modification and Some Extensions. *Quarterly Journal of Economics,* 99, 717–727.

Romer, P. (1986). Increasing Returns and Long-Run Growth. *Journal of Political Economy,* 94, 1002–1037.

Romer, P. (1990). Endogenous Technological Change. *Journal of Political Economy,* 98, 71–102.

Romer, P. (1994). The Origins of Endogenous Growth Theory. *Journal of Economic Perspectives,* 8, 3–22.

Rosenthal, S., and Stange, W. (2003). Geography, Industrial Organization and Agglomeration. *Review of Economics & Statistics,* 85, 377–393.

Rostow, W. W. (1987). Here Comes a New Political Chapter in America. *International Herald Tribune,* January 2.

Sahlman, W., and Stevenson, H. (1991). *The Entrepreneurial Venture.* Boston: McGraw Hill.

Sarasvathy, S., Dew, N., Velamuri, R., and Venkataraman, S. (2003). Three Views of Entrepreneurial Opportunity. In Z. Acs and D. Audretsch (eds.), *The International Handbook of Entrepreneurship* (pp. 141–160). Dordrecht: Kluwer.

Saxenian, A. (1990). Regional Networks and the Resurgence of Silicon Valley. *California Management Review,* 33, 89–111.

Saxenian, A. (1994). *Regional Advantage: Culture and Competition in Silicon Valley and RTE.* Cambridge: Harvard University Press.

Scarpetta, S., Hemmings, P., Tressel, T., and Woo J. (2002). *The Role of Policy and Institutions for Productivity and Firm Dynamics: Evidence from Micro and Industry Data.* OECD Working Paper 329.

Schartinger, D., Schibany, A., and Gassler, H. (2001). Interactive Relations between Universities and Firms: Empirical Evidence for Austria. *Journal of Technology Transfer,* 26, 255–268.

Schefczyk, M., and Gerpott, T. (2001). Qualifications and Turnover of Managers and Venture Capital-Financed Firm Performance: An Empirical Study of German Venture Capital-Investment. *Journal of Business Venturing,* 16(2), 145–163.

Scherer, F. (1970). *Industrial Market Structure and Economic Performance.* Chicago: Rand McNally.

Scherer, F. (1977). *The Economic Effects of Compulsory Patent Licensing.* New York: New York University Press.

Scherer, F. (1991). Changing Perspectives on the Firm Size Problem. In Z. Acs and D. Audretsch (eds.), *Innovation and Technological Change: An International Comparison* (pp. 24–38). Ann Arbor: University of Michigan Press.

Schmookler, J. (1952). The Changing Efficiency of the American Economy. *Review of Economic Statistics,* 34, 214–231.

Schultz, T. (1953). *The Economic Organization of Agriculture.* New York: McGraw Hill.

Schumpeter, J. (1911). *Theorie der wirtschaftlichen Entwicklung. Eine Untersuchung über Unternehmergewinn, Kapital, Kredit, Zins und den Konjunkturzyklus.* Berlin: Duncker und Humblot. (English translation, 1934, *The Theory of Economic Development,* trans. Redvers Opie, Cambridge: Harvard University Press.)

Schumpeter, J. (1942). *Capitalism, Socialism and Democracy.* New York: Harper and Brothers.

Servan-Schreiber, J. J. (1968). *The American Challenge.* London: Hamish Hamilton.

Shane, S. (2000). Prior Knowledge and the Discovery of Entrepreneurial Opportunities. *Organization Science*, 11, 448–469.

Shane, S. (2001a). Technological Opportunities and New Firm Creation. *Management Science*, 47, 205–220.

Shane, S. (2001b). Technology Regimes and New Firm Formation. *Management Science*, 47, 1173–1190.

Shane, S., and Eckhardt, J. (2003). The Individual-Opportunity Nexus. In Z. Acs and D. Audretsch (eds.), *Handbook of Entrepreneurship Research* (pp. 161–191). Dordrecht: Kluwer.

Shane, S., and Venkataraman, S. (2001). Entrepreneurship as a Field of Research: A Response to Zahra and Dess, Singh, and Erickson. *Academy of Management Review*, 26, 13–17.

Simmie, J. (2003). Innovation and Urban Regions as National and International Nodes for the Transfer and Sharing of Knowledge. *Regional Studies*, 37, 607–620.

Smith, R. (2003). *Entrepreneurial Finance*. New York: Wiley.

Solow, R. (1956). A Contribution to Theory of Economic Growth. *Quarterly Journal of Economics*, 70, 65–94.

Solow, R. (1957). Technical Change and the Aggregate Production Function. *Review of Economics and Statistics*, 39, 312–320.

Solow, R. (1991). Growth Theory. In D. Greenaway, M. Bleaney, and I. Stewart (eds.), *Companion to Contemporary Economic Thought* (pp. 393–412). London: Routledge.

Sorge, A. (1991). Strategic Fit and the Societal Effect: Interpreting Cross-national Comparisons of Technology, Organization and Human Resources. *Organization Studies*, 12, 161–190.

Spence, M. (1984). Cost Reduction, Competition, and Industry Performance. *Econometrica*, 52, 101–121.

Stephan, P. (1996). The Economics of Science. *Journal of Economic Literature*, 34, 1199–1235.

Stephan, P., Sumell, A., Black, G., and Adams, J. (2002). *Public Knowledge, Private Placements: New Ph.D.s as a Source of Knowledge Spillovers* (Working paper). Georgia State University.

Stern. (1997). *Deutschland vor dem Absturz?* 13 February.

Sternberg, R. (1990). The Impact of Innovation Centers on Small Technology-Based Firms: The Example of the Federal Republic of Germany. *Small Business Economics*, 2, 105–118.

Sternberg, R. (1996). Technology Policies and the Growth of Regions: Evidence from Four Countries. *Small Business Economics*, 8, 75–86.

Sternberg, R., and Litzenberger, T. (2003). Regional Clusters—Operationalisation and Consequences for Entrepreneurship (Working paper). University of Cologne.

Stevenson, H., and Jarillo, J. (1990). A Paradigm of Entrepreneurship: Entrepreneurial Management. *Strategic Management Journal*, 11, 17–27.

Stiglitz, J., and Weiss, A. (1981). Credit Rationing in Markets with Imperfect Information. *American Economic Review*, 71, 393–410.

Storey, D. (1991). The Birth of New Firms—Does Unemployment Matter? A Review of the Evidence. *Small Business Economics*, 3, 167–178.

Storey, D., and Johnson, S. (1987). *Job Generation and Labour Market Change*. London: Macmillan.

Streeck, W. (1991). On the Institutional Conditions of Diversified Quality Production. In E. Matzner and W. Streeck (eds.), *Beyond Keynesianism: The Socio-economics of Production and Full Employment* (pp. 21–61). Aldershot: Elgar.

Sutton, J. (1997). Gibrat's Legacy. *Journal of Economic Literature*, 35, 40–59.

Teece, D. (1976). *The Multinational Corporation and the Resource Cost of International Technology Transfer.* Cambridge: Ballinger.

Teece, D. (1981). The Market for Know-how and the Efficient International Transfer of Technology. *Annals of the Academy of Political and Social Sciences, 458,* 81–196.

Teece, D. (2005). Technology and Technology Transfer: Mansfieldian Inspirations and Subsequent Developments. *Journal of Technology Transfer, 30,* 17–33.

Teece, D., Pisano, G., and Shuen, A. (1997). Dynamic Capabilities and Strategic Management. *Strategic Management Journal, 18,* 509–533.

Thornton, P., and Flynn, K. (2003). Entrepreneurship, Networks and Geographies. In Z. Acs and D. Audretsch (eds.), *Handbook of Entrepreneurship Research* (pp. 401–433). Dordrecht: Kluwer.

Thurow, L. (1985). Healing with a Thousand Bandages. *Challenge, 28* (November–December), 29–31.

Thurow, L. (2002). *Fortune Favors the Bold.* Cambridge: MIT Press.

Thursby, J. (2000). What Do We Say about Ourselves and What Does it Mean? Yet Another Look at Economics Department Research. *Journal of Economic Literature, 38,* 383–404.

Tveteras, R., and Eide, G. (2000). Survival of New Plants in Different Industry Environments in Norwegian Manufacturing: A Semi-Proportional Cox Model Approach. *Small Business Economics, 14,* 65–82.

Tykvová, T. (2003). *Is the Behavior of German Venture Capitalists Different? Evidence from the Neuer Markt.* CFS Working Paper No. 2003/24.

Tykvová, T., and Walz, U. (2003). *Are IPOs of Different Venture Capitalists Different?* (Working paper). University of Frankfurt.

Ueda, M. (2004). Bank versus Venture Capital: Project Evaluation, Screening and Expropriation. *Journal of Finance, 59,* 601–621.

Varga, A. (2000). Local Academic Knowledge Transfers and the Concentration of Economic Activity. *Journal of Regional Science, 40,* 289–309.

Venkataraman, S. (1997). The Distinctive Domain of Entrepreneurship Research. In J. A. Katz (ed.), *Advances in Entrepreneurship, Firm Emergence and Growth* (pp. 119–138). Greenwich: JAI Press.

Vernon, R. (1966). International Investment and International Trade in the Product Cycle. *Quarterly Journal of Economics, 80,* 190–207.

Vernon, R. (1970). Organization as a Scale Factor in the Growth of Firms. In J. Markham and G. Papanek (eds.), *Industrial Organization and Economic Development* (pp. 47–66). Boston: Houghton Mifflin.

Vitols, S. (1998). Are German Banks Different? *Small Business Economics, 10,* 79–91.

Wagner, J. (1992). Firm Size, Firm Growth, and Persistence of Chance: Testing Gibrat's Law with Establishment Data from Lower Saxony, 1978–1989. *Small Business Economics, 4,* 125–131.

Wagner, J. (1994). Small Firm Entry in Manufacturing Industries: Lower Saxony, 1979–1989. *Small Business Economics, 6,* 211–224.

Wagner, J. (1995). Exports, Firm Size, and Firm Dynamics. *Small Business Economics, 7,* 29–40.

Wagner, J. (2001). A Note on the Firm Size-Export Relationship. *Small Business Economics, 17,* 229–237.

Wallsten, S. J. (2004). The Role of Government in Regional Technology Development: The Effects of Public Venture Capital and Science Parks. In T. Bresnahan and A. Gambardella (eds.), *Building High-Tech Clusters: Silicon Valley and Beyond* (pp. 229–279). Cambridge: Cambridge University Press.

Warning, S. (2004). Performance Differences in the German Higher Education System: Empirical Analysis of Strategic Groups. *Review of Industrial Organization, 24*, 393–408.

Weiss, L. (1976). Optimal Plant Scale and the Extent of Suboptimal Capacity. In R. T. Masson and P. D. Qualls (eds.), *Essays on Industrial Organization in Honor of Joe S. Bain* (pp. 126–134). Cambridge: Ballinger.

Wernerfelt, B. (1984). A Resource-Based View of the Firm. *Strategic Management Journal, 12*, 75–94.

Wessner, C. (2000). *The Small Business Innovation Research Program (SBIR)*. Washington, D.C.: National Academy Press.

Westhead, P., and Birley, S. (1995). Employment Growth in New Independent Owner-Managed Firms in Great Britain. *International Small Business Journal, 13*, 11–34.

Whyte, W. (1960). *The Organization Man*. Hammondsworth, Middlesex, England: Penguin.

Williamson, O. (1968). Economies as an Antitrust Defense: The Welfare Tradeoffs. *American Economic Review*, March.

Williamson, O. (1975). *Markets and Hierarchies: Analysis and Antitrust Implications*. New York: Free Press.

Winston, G. (1999). Subsidies, Hierarchy and Peers: The Awkward Economics of Higher Education. *Journal of Economic Perspectives, 13*, 13–36.

Winter, S. (1984). Schumpeterian Competition in Alternative Technological Regimes. *Journal of Economic Behavior and Organization, 5*, 287–320.

Yamawaki, H. (1990). The Effects of Business Conditions on Net Entry: Evidence from Japan. In P. A. Geroski and J. Schwalbach (eds.), *Entry and Market Contestability: An International Comparison* (pp. 168–186). Oxford: Basil Blackwell.

Zucker, L., Darby, M., and Armstrong, J. (1998). Intellectual Human Capital and the Birth of U.S. Biotechnology Enterprises. *American Economic Review, 88*, 290–306.

Index